D0953537

PRAISE FOR
WALKING WITH GIANTS

Dr. Elmer Towns is a giant among men. His influence on tens of thousands of students, laity, and ministers places him at the forefront of educators. His heart for the Church and prayer has had ripple effects across denominational lines. He is a hero for many, and his life and ministry are a blessing!

MICHAEL CATT

Senior Pastor, Sherwood Baptist Church
Executive Producer, Sherwood Pictures

Elmer Towns is my friend. We met first in 1978, and he has been an encouragement to the Lord's work here in Korea. *Walking with Giants* tells of his friendship with many of the pastors of the world's largest churches and many nations of the world. He has a love for all the believers in all the denominations and has been a friend of pastors in all of these groups. Elmer Towns is a Baptist, and he has great love for those who love Jesus Christ. My church is Pentecostal, and he preached here, and was used of God. I recommend this book to all who want to walk with giants and learn from them.

DAVID YONGGI CHO

Pastor, Yoido Full Gospel Church, Seoul, South Korea (World's Largest Church)

On July 4, 1971, when I was four years old, my family was having a picnic with Elmer and Ruth Towns, and we walked up to the top of Sharp Top, the highest mountain in Virginia. It was hot, and I was tired and wouldn't go on. So Elmer lifted me onto his shoulders and took me to the top. I thank God for the many different ways Elmer has carried me over the years. Now, it is my privilege to be his pastor and to "carry" him and the work of Thomas Road Baptist Church forward. One of the things I like about this book is that Elmer honors my father, noting it was Jerry Falwell, Sr., who had a vision to start Liberty University and had great faith to make it happen. This book talks about what God has accomplished at Liberty and how Dr. Towns was involved. Read this book and praise God for what He has done.

JONATHAN FALWELL

Senior Pastor, Thomas Road Baptist Church, Lynchburg, Virginia

Elmer Towns is a gifted Bible teacher and faithful preacher of the Word of God. His life's story will warm your heart as he shares the deepest hurts of a young boy who overcame the struggles and turmoil of a difficult childhood by meeting the Savior. His commitment to Jesus Christ has led him into pulpits and classrooms, and many young men and women have learned the great truths of Scripture under the careful teaching of my friend, Elmer Towns.

Franklin Graham
President and CEO, Billy Graham Evangelistic Association
President and CEO, Samaritan's Purse

Walking with Giants is a moving account of how God used a man who was committed to service, righteousness and humility before the Lord. As a graduate of Liberty University, I walked behind the giants mentioned in this book, and God used them to influence my life in profound ways. I would not have had the family, the husband or the life I'm living if they had not served the Lord so well. Those who are unfamiliar with the circumstances of Elmer Towns's life will read this book with wonder . . . and those who have been blessed to know him will read it with gratitude.

Dr. Angela Hunt
Christy Award Winner and Bestselling Author

Walking with Giants takes us on an insightful journey through the last 70 years of evangelicalism from the perspective of one of its key movers and shakers. During the trip, you will laugh out loud as the 19-year-old preacher, Elmer Towns, motivates the recently regenerated town drunk to help paint their dilapidated church. Six decades later, you will weep as he relates the loss of Jerry Falwell, his dear life-long teammate. *Walking with Giants* is a great read.

Dr. Bill Jones
President, Columbia International University

Elmer Towns has been my mentor for more than 40 years. He first touched my life through his books and then through his life. He has spent his life challenging pastors and church leaders around the world to enlarge their vision and passion for the cause of Christ. His life has touched mine and now will touch yours as you read this book. To Elmer, my great friend and mentor, I say, "Well done! You have lived well!"

John C. Maxwell
New York Times Bestselling Author

Dr. Towns is one of the most influential Christian leaders of the twentieth century. As co-founder of Liberty, the Lord worked through Dr. Towns to truly change the course of history. All of Liberty's now-innumerable graduates carry within them the influence of Dr. Elmer Towns—myself included. This giant of the faith has shaped my life as a minister. Dr. Towns has been my Sunday School teacher, professor, ministry colleague and friend. I am confident that his amazing story will continue to point lives toward Christ for decades to come.

Alex McFarland

Apologetics Director, North Greenville University

Walking with Giants gives helpful insight into the life of Elmer Towns, one of the greatest giants of our day. This great man has served as my teacher, mentor and friend. He has influenced me to be a better husband, father, pastor and author. Now, in this revealing book, you too will have the incredible opportunity to learn and gain from his many years of experience. This book will inspire you to love God and do great things for God.

Steve Reynolds

Lead Pastor, Capital Baptist Church, Annandale, Virginia, and Author, *Bod4God*

I remember joking about my friend Dr. Towns in front of thousands of Liberty University students at convocation. I said, "Dr. Towns has no unpublished thought," to the roaring laughter of those who know and love him. It seems to be true—my shelf is filled with his wisdom, just as that convocation arena was filled with those influenced and touched by his life. Read this memoir of a man who changed the world.

Ed Stetzer

President, LifeWay Research

I first met Dr. Towns when I was a college student working on staff with John C. Maxwell in Lancaster, Ohio. From 1972 until this day, he has been a friend and mentor to me. I've had the opportunity to co-author books and share speaking events with him. What you see is what you get! Elmer Towns is a good and godly man whose walk matches his talk. *Walking with Giants* is a reflection of a life well lived by one of my heroes of the faith.

Dr. Stan Toler

Bestselling Author, Oklahoma City, Oklahoma

Jesus' teaching on humility would preclude any establishment of a Christian Leaders Hall of Fame. However, if there were one, Elmer Towns would surely be inducted as our "Number One Number Two Leader." His obedience to God's call to enable Jerry Falwell to skyrocket to a legendary Number One did not detract in the least from his own destiny to emerge as a top-ranking history-maker in American Evangelicalism. The chronicle of Elmer Towns is like no other, and I speak for multitudes when I express deep gratitude that his story will now be perpetuated through this superb memoir.

C. Peter Wagner

Vice president and Apostolic Ambassador, Global Spheres, Inc

Elmer Towns is my friend, my mentor, my golfing companion and, most importantly, my prayer partner! *Walking with Giants* is the story of a life well lived. You will be inspired, encouraged and motivated to make yourself available to the power of God. These memoirs are proof of what God can do through one individual who fully surrenders himself to God. After reading this book, I am reminded of the words of missionary C. T. Studd: "Oh, let us not rust out—let us not glide through the world and then slip quietly out, without having even blown the trumpet loud and long for our Blessed Redeemer. At the very least let us see to it that the devil holds a thanksgiving service in hell, when he gets news of our departure from the field of battle."

Dr. Steve Wingfield

Evangelist, Steve Wingfield Evangelistic Association

D. L. Moody once said that when a believer is fully dedicated to the Lord, it is amazing to see what God can do through that person's life. This is certainly true of Elmer Towns. As you read this book, you will marvel at how God has used Dr. Towns in numerous ways around the globe for His glory. Elmer and I were students together at Dallas Seminary in the fifties. He and his wife, Ruth, and I and my wife, Dottie, were good friends. His dedication to the Lord was obvious even then. May you glorify the Lord as you read how He has worked in Dr. Towns's life and ministry. To quote his favorite Bible verse, "Faithful is He who calls you, and He also will bring it to pass" (1 Thess. 5:24, *NASB*).

Dr. Roy B. Zuck

Senior Professor Emeritus of Bible Exposition, Dallas Theological Seminary
Editor, *Bibliotheca Sacra*

WALKING *with* GIANTS

The *Extraordinary* Life of an *Ordinary* Man

a memoir

ELMER L. TOWNS

For more information and
special offers from Regal Books, email us at
subscribe@regalbooks.com

Published by Regal
From Gospel Light
Ventura, California, U.S.A.
www.regalbooks.com
Printed in the U.S.A.

Library of Congress Cataloging-in-Publication Data
Towns, Elmer L.
Walking with giants : the extraordinary life of an ordinary man / Elmer Towns.
p. cm.
Includes bibliographical references and index.
ISBN 978-0-8307-6382-5 (hardcover : alk. paper)
1. Towns, Elmer L. 2. Baptists—United States—Clergy—Biography. I. Title.
BX6495.T597A3 2012
286'.1092—dc23
[B]
2012007937

Rights for publishing this book outside the U.S.A. or in non-English languages are administered by Gospel Light Worldwide, an international not-for-profit ministry. For additional information, please visit www.glww.org, email info@glww.org, or write to Gospel Light Worldwide, 1957 Eastman Avenue, Ventura, CA 93003, U.S.A.

To order copies of this book and other Regal products in bulk quantities, please contact us at 1-800-446-7735.

To Ruth Jean Towns

She gets all the credit for anything I've ever accomplished. God has used her to mold my character when I didn't know it was being done, to influence my decision-making when I felt I was an independent thinker, and to direct me into the will of God when I was making autonomous decisions.

Ruth, who has never raised her voice to me in anger, was praying when Jerry Falwell and I were planning Liberty University, and was mother to our three children.

Ruth has forgiven my weaknesses, believed in me when I felt no one else did, and is the perfect wife. She is the Proverbs 31 woman.

With love,
Elmer Towns

Contents

Foreword by Jerry Falwell, Jr. 11

Preface: What Really "Makes" a Person? 13

1. The Early Years: Birth Through Elementary School (1932–1943) 23
2. Junior High and High School Years (1943–1950) 49
3. The Columbia Bible College Years (1950–1953) 63
4. The Northwestern Years: The Long, Cold, Dark Winter's Night (1953–1954) 87
5. The Dallas Theological Seminary Years (1954–1958) 95
6. The Midwest Bible College Years (1958–1961) 115
7. The Canadian Years (1961–1965) 127
8. The Trinity Evangelical Divinity School Years (1965–1971) 147
9. The Early Liberty University Years (1971–1973) 165
10. A Desert Experience in the Interim Years (1973–1977) 185
11. Great Ministry at Liberty (1977–1999) 197
12. A New Century (2000–2012) 237

Epilogue 249

Liberty University's 40 Years 251

Endnotes 253

Curriculum Vitae for Dr. Elmer Leon Towns 257

List of Resources by Elmer L. Towns 269

FOREWORD

Jerry Falwell, Jr.

Dear Readers:

One thing I like about this book is that it shows the strong role my father—Jerry Falwell, Sr.—had in starting Liberty University. This university was founded on his strong faith, because he believed that God wanted him to build Liberty. It was also founded on his vision. From the beginning, my father said Liberty would be a university for the evangelicals, just as Notre Dame was a university for the Catholics and Brigham Young was a university for the Mormons. He also said from the beginning that Liberty would play Notre Dame in football and beat them.

Elmer Towns was the co-founder of Liberty, and he understood his role in making the school great. In their first conversation, my father asked Dr. Towns to be the president, but Towns said no, because he had been a college president. My father's vision was to build one of the greatest colleges, and Towns knew my father had to be its president to make it happen. He told my father, "Great leaders build great colleges, average leaders build average colleges, and poor leaders hurt colleges." Dr. Towns believed in the greatness of my father because he had built one of the 10 largest churches in America and had expanded its television outreach to more than 200 metropolitan areas in the United States.

My father wanted to begin a Bible college, because that was his Baptist Bible Fellowship heritage, and he had graduated from Baptist Bible College in Springfield, Missouri. But Towns told him, "Jerry, I know your heart and I know what you want to do with this college. You'll want to start a Christian liberal arts college if you want to accomplish all that's in your heart." My father replied, "No . . . not liberal." His commitment to the fundamentals meant he opposed anything to do with liberalism.

Dr. Towns explained that the word "liberal" meant a broad curricula. Then Towns said, "Jerry, I know your heart. You want to train school teachers, business people, and engineers." They even talked about starting a law school in their first planning discussions. Finally, my father said, "I'll raise the money, recruit the students, and construct the buildings. You write the catalogue, hire the faculty, and plan the classes. Together, we'll build one of the greatest colleges in the world." My father's vision was correct. Liberty has become one of the greatest colleges in the world.

Walking with Giants tells the story of building Liberty from Dr. Towns' perspective. (My father gave his perspective in *Strength for the Journey*, and my mother told her perspective in *Jerry Falwell: His Life and Legacy*.) Read this book, because it tells the early spiritual struggles of Liberty and how God continually answered prayer to make Liberty what it is today.

Sincerely yours in Christ,

Jerry Falwell, Jr.
Chancellor and President, Liberty University

WHAT REALLY "MAKES" A PERSON?

What really "makes" a person? I say it's the epoch events in our lives that make us . . . break us . . . challenge us . . . and give us dreams. As you read the story of my life, look for those events that transformed me . . . re-directed me . . . and filled me with determination.

How could a cursing teen—one who couldn't quit cursing no matter how hard he tried—suddenly never curse again?

How can a seventh grader who had never once read a whole book all the way through read an entire book in one night—and then read a complete book each day for the next two weeks?

How can a boy who only made honor roll once in 12 grades become a college president—and do it at the unheard-of age of 27 years old?

Each successful epoch encouraged me to reach higher, work harder and endure more to achieve goals that I had once thought unattainable.

Don't miss my wife's observations about what God was doing in her life and mine. My memoirs are not complete without hers.

Perhaps the best way to begin to tell "who I am" is to describe how I answered a radio announcer who interviewed me recently. He was probing to understand "the real Elmer Towns." I thought it was a good interview, so I've written out my answers to introduce *Walking with Giants*.

Radio Question One: What Event Irrevocably Changed Your Life?

Many people thought I was a Christian because I joined the Church when I was 12 years old.

On Easter Sunday 1944, my pastor, Reverend Lawrence Williams, sat about 14 of us in a circle in his office. He asked each one a theological question—then looked to the rest of us to ask, "Do you agree?"

"Yes," we dutifully answered.

When my turn came, he asked, "Do you believe in the virgin birth?"

I knew what the answer had to be. "Yes."

"Do the rest of you agree?"

Then Reverend Williams asked Frank Perry the last question: "Do you believe Jesus could return at any time to take us to heaven?"

"Yes," I answered when Williams asked the rest if we agreed. But I knew in my heart I was not ready to meet Jesus. I knew I was not a Christian. I knew the Scriptures about two people working in the field: One was taken, and the other was left behind. I had picked cotton on my grandfather's farm, and I knew I'd be left behind when the others were taken. I also knew the Scriptures about two people sleeping in the bed: One was taken, but the other was left behind. I slept with my little brother Richard, and I'd be left behind when he was taken.

The thought of being left behind plagued me throughout my high school years. I'd be riding my bicycle, delivering newspapers, and cry out, "Lord, save me." I must have prayed that prayer 50 times in the next five years. But I didn't feel saved, nor did I think God had answered.

I even prayed the right words—"Jesus come into my heart"—but nothing happened. I was as empty as before.

After graduating from high school, I was converted at a revival meeting at a country church about seven miles away from my home—Bona Bella Presbyterian Church. The little church was experiencing a true Holy Spirit revival.

The revival began during the last week of July 1950; four or five people walked forward for salvation every night. The most startling conversions were Mr. and Mrs. Ernest Miller. (Of their six children, Alyce, the oldest, was already saved. The remaining five were soon to follow their parents.) He was Jewish, and she was Catholic. About the second night of the revival, she stood up in the small congregation to testify, "I now know the real Jehovah is Jesus who came into my heart." Then she pointed to her Jewish husband, who was too bashful to speak publicly.

"You know my husband, Ernest, is Jewish. Last night he believed in Jesus Christ as the true Jewish Messiah."

The roof was lifted with shouts of *"AMEN!"* A ripple of excitement went through the neighborhood and surrounding Presbyterian churches in Greater Savannah. The revival grew in size and enthusiasm for a week and a half. But then a crisis happened.

No one came forward to be saved on Thursday, July 25, during the second week of meetings. Bill Harding, a junior at Columbia Bible College, was a summer pastor of the church. He stepped down from the pulpit and stood next to the communion table to announce, "Someone here is breaking the revival." I had been deeply convicted of my sin and felt the urge to go forward—each evening—but had always refused. Bill said, "You're hanging on to the back of that pew so hard, your knuckles are white."

I looked down to see my knuckles clenched around the pew, and instantly jerked my hands away.

"Here's what I want you to do," Bill explained. "Go kneel by your bed, look into heaven and pray, 'Lord, I've never done it before. Come into my heart and save me.'"

That sounded easy, so I determined to do exactly as he instructed. *Maybe this time it will work.*

After church I went out to eat with some friends, so I did not go to bed until around 11:15 P.M. I crashed into bed. When I thought about my sinful condition, I remembered what Bill Harding had instructed. I knelt, looked out the window into heaven, and began talking to God as sincerely as I could—but I couldn't pray what Bill Harding had instructed. I argued with myself: *I've prayed it before—many times—but it didn't work.* So I decided to pray something different—the Lord's Prayer:

> Our Father, which art in heaven, Hallowed be thy name.Thy kingdom come, Thy will be done in earth, as it is in heaven. Give us this day our daily bread (Matt. 6:9-11, *KJV*).

Then I prayed as sincerely as I could, "Forgive us our debts, as we forgive our debtors" (v. 12).

I crawled into bed, still convicted of my sin. I tossed and turned, but couldn't go to sleep. I didn't realize it, but that hot July night, God and Satan were wrestling for my soul. Was it possible Satan could win? When I couldn't shake off the conviction, I again knelt by my bed, looked into heaven, and was about to pray, "Lord, I have never done it before." Again I stopped. *It doesn't work, and neither does the Lord's Prayer work.*

Then I remembered what my mother had taught me, so I prayed:

Now I lay me down to sleep,
I pray the Lord my soul to keep.
If I should die before I wake,
I pray the Lord my soul to take.

I prayed that last phrase several times . . . very sincerely. I wanted God to take my soul to heaven. Then I climbed again into bed.

The Holy Spirit wouldn't give up. I was more miserable than ever before. So a third time I got on my knees, looked out the window into heaven, and approached God as sincerely as possible. I put all those other times out of my mind and prayed, "Lord, I've never done it before . . ."

Instantly, the horrors of hell gripped me, as though I were already in flames. Quickly I begged, "Jesus, come into my heart and save me."

That was it. That's all I prayed—and a miracle happened. I immediately knew I was saved. I jumped to my feet and fist-pumped in the dark room, shouting inwardly, *AMEN and HALLELUJAH!*

How do I know I was saved? How does a blind man know when he can see? How does a man know he is wet when thrown into a river? Later I would say, "I know . . . that I know . . . that I know." That means first, I knew in my heart (thinking); second, I knew by experience; and third, I knew innately—just as you know that up is up, and fire is hot.

As I stood in that dark room, I began to sing, "Amazing grace, how sweet the sound, that saved a wretch like me. I once was lost, but now am found, was blind but now I see."

That last phrase explained what happened that evening. I had been spiritually blind, but instantly I had spiritual insight.

My salvation involved a new relationship with Jesus Christ. I had previously believed He walked the paths of Galilee and died for sins. But His physical life was not enough to save me. Now Christ lived in my heart, and I pledged myself to follow Him. Christ's indwelling began a transformation! I had new desires and a divine reason to live. "For to me, to live is Christ" (Phil. 1:21).

Inner transformation led to outer changes. I determined I would obey every command in Scripture. I would not drink alcohol, I would not dance to worldly music, and I would not drink any soft drinks. (I kept this last pledge for one year, and then broke it. I had squandered so much money on soft drinks that I was ashamed of my waste. When I later realized the issue was biblical stewardship of my finances, I again drank soft drinks—in moderation.)

Spiritual transformation is God's gift of grace when we renounce sin (called repentance) and adopt a lifestyle—spiritual rule—that becomes more pure and inwardly motivated, so that total submission to Jesus Christ occurs over and over again.

I had cursed steadily since the fourth grade and tried several times to stop. Many times I had struggled to quit cursing, and each time I had failed. But after I was saved—transformed by Christ—I didn't have to struggle. I just quit cursing.

Every Saturday, I received a bundle of newspapers to deliver to my customers. I had always turned quickly to the movie ads for the coming week. I'd plan my week by the movie I wanted to see each evening. After salvation, I quit going to movies—because Bill Harding said they were sinful. So instead, I immediately turned to the Saturday church page. I would plan my week by revival meetings in different churches—Baptist, Pentecostal, Christian Missionary Alliance and Presbyterian. The denomination did not make any difference. I wanted to go where people were being saved, the Word was preached, and Christian music was sung. I could not get enough of Jesus.

Because I thought I was completely yielded to God, I did not think there was much growth left for me. How wrong I was! There would be pressures, assaults by the enemy, and defeats down the road. But in July 1950 I was as happy as a new believer could be. Jesus Christ had transformed me.

Radio Question Two: What Is Your Greatest Achievement?

One's greatest achievement in life is not measured by the greatness of the event. It's measured by how far you had to climb, and what little support and resources you had to reach the achievement. My greatest achievement was very small in the eyes of most, but to me it was greater than expected. At the beginning of my ministry, I rallied more than 70 people to paint a large, old, white-frame church building in one day. I am still amazed!

I was a 19-year-old sophomore at Columbia Bible College—150 miles away—when I began a weekend student pastorate at Westminster Presbyterian Church in Savannah, Georgia. I thought of myself as the weakest leader of all the guys in college. I was young, inexperienced in leadership skills, had never taken a college class in pastoral ministry, and did not understand how to motivate people.

The Westminster Presbyterian Church was a beautiful, old, colonial church, with a tall steeple and bell tower, located in a neighborhood that had once been the home of wealthy middle-class residents of Savannah. It stood approximately two miles from downtown—a short ride by carriage in the days of horse and buggy, or later on a trolley car that ran down Old Augusta Road. When I started at the church, the neighborhood had deteriorated to the point of being considered inner-city.

The people of West Savannah had built a colonial church sanctuary that reflected their dignified lifestyle. The building boasted four tall pillars reaching two stories from the front porch to hold up the roof, over which a towering steeple pointed toward heaven.

When I was visiting a neighbor one Saturday afternoon, trying to present Christ to her, the woman told me, "Your church doesn't need revival. Your church needs a coat of paint."

I was embarrassed. The building hadn't been painted in years, so the white paint was cracked, puckered and chalky. I could see raw wood between the gaping cracks in the paint. I noticed crumbling window frames, broken molding, and loose deck boards on the front porch.

The next day, when I announced to the small congregation of 20 or 30 people that we needed to paint the church, I was greeted with silent resistance. The body language of their folded arms told me, "No!" Maybe they thought a 19-year-old preacher couldn't do anything about getting their church painted. Maybe they thought it would cost too much and the church was broke.

I fussed at them. Since my mother had fussed at me to get things done, I fussed at them. Then I tried embarrassing them about their "ugly" church. Still no response.

During the offering, I discovered a short piece of blue chalk in my coat pocket. It gave me an idea, and as soon as the offertory was over, I jumped into action.

"See this piece of blue chalk," I announced eagerly from behind the pulpit. "I'm going to paint the church this Saturday with this piece of chalk." I held the blue chalk up high as I explained that blue chalk could make a difference.

I told the congregation that on Saturday morning I was going to start at the front porch and walk around the building, drawing a blue line every 10 feet. I dramatically pretended to draw a blue line from high in the sky down to the floor of the platform. Then I announced, "I am going to write your name on your 10 feet."

I explained that their names would be written in blue chalk on the bottom of their sections. Everyone would have to start scraping off old paint and applying new paint from under the eaves all the way down to the lowest board, finally painting over their names. Right on the spot, a slogan came to me: "We can paint the whole church in a whole day."

"Mr. Miller, will you paint 10 feet this Saturday?" I pointed to a man sitting in the second row.

"Sure," he enthusiastically responded.

Mr. Miller had been the biggest drunk in the neighborhood. I'm talking fall-down-in-the-street-coming-home-from-work drunk. Miller was saved following the second sermon I preached to the little congregation. He repented from liquor and was willing to do anything for God, including painting 10 feet of his church building. I kept calling on people I knew well enough to know they'd agree.

Like a sky filled with lightning during a summer storm, the small audience bristled with electricity. For the next two or three minutes,

I continued to explain the project, but no one listened. People began whispering to one another. At the time, I was not sure whether they were rebelling or supporting my idea.

Mr. Seckinger put his hands up, which was the custom in this small church at announcement time. "I got a two-story extension ladder." He told the group that we'd need a lot of extension ladders if everyone was going to paint at the same time. He volunteered to scout for more ladders.

"We need to get the ladies organized for a picnic dinner," the Mrs. Smith in charge of Ladies Auxiliary spoke up. (There were three Mrs. Smiths in the church.)

"Who's going to get the paint?" Mr. Strickland asked. He was a plumbing contractor and understood what it meant to get supplies for workers. I hadn't thought about paint, or where it was coming from. Then Strickland volunteered, "I'll get the paint . . . and the brushes . . . and the thinner."

I learned that morning that dreams are a powerful tool for leaders to move a congregation. As a matter of fact, the vision of painting "the whole church in a whole day" was much greater than the sermon I preached that day. I don't remember what I preached.

On Saturday morning, I rode up to the church on my bicycle at about 10 minutes to 7:00; the place was a beehive of active people everywhere. Already, cars, pickup trucks and baby strollers surrounded the church.

There were at least a dozen long ladders leaning up against the cracking paint of the building. On the front porch were dozens of gallons of white Dutch Boy paint; Mr. Strickland had gotten a donation from a local distributor. Out on the lawn, blankets were spread everywhere, occupied by babies, diaper bags, and teenage girls alternately playing and changing diapers.

I sent a couple of the junior boys scurrying through the church to gather everyone to the front porch for prayer. There were people there I had never seen in my life. Family members and neighbors were captivated by the idea: "Painting the whole church in a whole day."

"Start the marking," someone yelled. "We're burning sunlight"—a Southern expression that means "get on with it."

Holding the blue chalk in my hand, I began marking the name "MILLER" in caps, indicating the section that the Miller family would paint. After 10 steps, I wrote the name "HAIR," for Silla Hair, who had been instrumental in getting me to the church.

Almost immediately after I drew the blue line, a ladder was thrown up against the building. Scraping began, with powdered paint puffing out into the morning breeze.

Scrrr . . . scrrr . . . scrrr . . .

By noon, the white building glistened in the midday sun. When you got close to the boards, you could see that the church needed a second coat of paint. But the original coat had been so weather-beaten and faded—while in comparison the new white coat sparkled—that no one seemed to care.

That day, a 19-year-old-kid preacher became that congregation's pastor. Because I loved the old church building that the neighborhood loved, they accepted me. They got me to baptize their babies, visit their sick relatives in the hospital, marry their young and bury their aged. I didn't set the world on fire, but I began with five ladies and ended with a congregation of 60 to 70 adults. Size was not the greatest achievement, though. I learned that there was power in vision. When the people bought into my vision of painting the whole church in a whole day, they bought into my leadership.

Keep Reading

I have told these stories to whet your appetite. Keep reading to learn about some other great victories, as well as some disastrous defeats and difficulties. There seem to be as many failures as successes—in publishing terminology, as many duds as bestsellers. Over the years, I've had as many "dumb" ideas as innovative plans that worked. I guarantee you'll laugh at my failures, and be intrigued by some of the ways God intervened in my life.

I don't have great faith, but I have a great God who has been faithful in both dark nights and sunlit days. God has been faithful to punish me when I sin and correct me when I stray, and He's also been faithful to bless me when I obey and follow His leading.

I want you to read my stories, learn from my lessons, and then do something tremendous for God. If transforming your life were as easy as reading a book, it would be wonderful! Unfortunately, in this world of temptation, sin and corrupt thinking, you will have to go through many of the same mistakes and heartaches as I have. But remember one thing from these memoirs—God is faithful!

My Life's Verse

Faithful is he that calleth you, who also will do it.

1 THESSALONIANS 5:24, *KJV*

1

The Early Years: Birth Through Elementary School

(1932–1943)

My father named me Elmer Leon Towns Jr. after him, and yet, it's a name I never really liked. It's quite possible that the name "Elmer" is what gave me an inferiority complex. When I was very small, there was a radio program about "Elmer Burp," a bumbling door-to-door salesman who basically was dumb. Listeners didn't laugh at his jokes; they laughed at him. I remember thinking people laughed at me because of my name.

Do you know of any famous people named Elmer? Is there a respected statesman, or a revered movie star, or even a respectable business entrepreneur? People hated the liquor-drinking evangelist named Elmer Gantry, and they laughed at Elmer Fudd. There's Elmer's glue and Elmer the Safety Elephant. Not much respect there.

But perhaps the deepest reason that I rejected the name Elmer was because I didn't want to be like my father. The problem was alcohol. His drunkenness was always the cause of fighting at home. We lived in poverty because he drank up most of the money. Today, people would call my father "alcohol dependent" or "drug addicted," but growing up I had to bear the shame of people telling me that my dad was a "drunk."

I started dating Elmer when he was a fun guy with a funny name. The name didn't bother me until he said, "I think I'm falling in love with you."

I thought, How can I ever marry a man named Elmer, and how can I ever be Mrs. Elmer Towns?

As I prayed, God made me look beyond his name to his heart. God asked me, "Is he the type of man you could be happy with the rest of your life?"

I told God, "Yes," and then I said "yes" to Elmer the person, and "yes" to Elmer the name. —Ruth Towns

Drinking Whiskey Never at All

When I was seven years old, my father came home on the bus one day, late as usual because he was totally soused. About 100 feet from our house, he stumbled in the street and fell in the dirt. Try as he might, he could not get up. There he was, flailing away on the ground, trying to stand up.

In those days, people sat on their front porches to get away from the heat of their homes. I remember the people on different porches, laughing at the man who couldn't stand up in the street.

"Take your wagon and go get your father!" my mother commanded. She was referring to the brand-new Radio-Flyer wagon I had gotten the previous Christmas.

Obviously, I could not pick my father up and put him in the wagon, but he could use the wagon to steady himself and get up.

"Look at that kid trying to help his father stand up!" I heard someone laugh behind a porch screen.

I was bone-deep embarrassed. But finally, Daddy was able to use the wagon to stand, and he got into the house without falling again. As a seven-year-old kid, I made a life-changing vow as I followed my father into the house.

I'll not be a drunk. I'll never take my first drink.

This was not a casual vow—the depths of my humiliation and embarrassment had driven me to take it.

One night, Daddy beat me with a belt in the kitchen. He was drunk and driven by rage. Mother screamed at him to stop, and finally pounded him with her fists.

I went to the backyard to cry and stop hurting. There were red welts all over my leg, but the physical pain was not the issue that evening.

Mother screamed at my father, "You'll never beat my boy again when you're drunk!" When Mother was mad, her sin of anger was as destructive as Dad's sin of drunkenness. Her acid words could peel paint off of the wall. So, think about what her withering criticism would do to a timid child. It could peel the skin off of a tender conscience.

I heard my father surrender to my mother that night: "All right, from now on, he's your boy. From now on, you correct him, and you spank him . . . I'm through with him."

Mother swore, "You'll never touch him again—when you're drunk, or sober either."

Both Daddy and Mother kept the promises they made that night.

That contractual surrender lasted for a lifetime. Daddy never spanked me again. As a matter of fact, he didn't do much in the way of correction or instruction, nor did he show much affection. So what did my Daddy do instead? He got drunk.

The Mother of a Preacher

My mother, Erin Azalea McFaddin, came from a farming family in Sardinia, South Carolina, about 150 miles from Savannah, Georgia. She was the tenth of 11 children in the family of Robert E. Lee McFaddin Jr. After graduating from high school in the eleventh grade, she took a summer school course in secretarial and accounting skills at Winthrop College in Rock Hill, South Carolina. Since Sardinia was only a crossroads with two stores, there were no jobs for her there. My mother moved to Savannah, Georgia, to live with her older sister Ina, who also had secretarial and accounting skills. My mother lived in one of the bedrooms in Ina's two-and-a-half story home at the corner of Thirty-fourth and Paulson Streets.

Mother became the accountant for Annette Dairy, famous for their horses pulling wagons through the streets of Savannah to deliver fresh milk every morning.

Mother was a party girl, forgetting her training at the little Presbyterian church in Sardinia. She epitomized the flapper of the 1920s; she loved to dance, and even later in life, when she was more than 80 years old, she could still entertain us with the Charleston.

Very early on, she learned to like highballs and occasionally consumed a bottle of beer. My mother was cute, skinny, and the life of the party. So it was only natural that my father first met my mother at a party at 17 Mastick Street. Daddy had brought another girl that evening, but Mother caught his attention immediately as she made her grand entrance into the living room. Then she and some other girls flew upstairs to deposit their coats and check their make-up.

"I told my friends that night, 'I'm going to marry that girl,'" my daddy later bragged to me. He explained that it was love at first sight, and he wanted to marry the prettiest girl in Savannah.

Their wedding took place at the Sardinia Presbyterian Church, and the young couple moved into a fashionable riverside home out on Montgomery River, in the county outside Savannah. Daddy drove a Ford Roadster with a rumble seat. My parents were "hip"; a young couple who seemingly had it all.

Daddy worked at White Hardware Company (where he remained for 42 years) and was invaluable to the owners for his ability to remember accounting numbers on most every item in the store. Daddy was a walking computer who would notice that the stock of a certain screw—or nail, or any other type of supply—was low and then, returning to the desk, fill out the order blank without looking up the product's number. He kept the storage bins of White Hardware filled at all times. I got my ability to remember numbers, names and events from my daddy.

Today, Paula Deen has her famous restaurant, The Lady and Sons, in the old White Hardware building where my father worked for so long.

I was born two and a half years after Mom and Dad married, at the Central of Georgia Hospital, close to their edge of town. Later, people would tell me that my father was drunk at home when I was born, but he told some friends, "This boy will be the president of the United States, or a great Baptist preacher."

He gave me the name Elmer Leon Towns Jr., but my mother accidentally gave me a different one. She was still groggy from the anesthesia and birth process, and when an African-American nurse came into the room to ask the name for the birth certificate, what she heard was, "Alma Leon Towns Jr."

Whether it was my mother's Southern drawl, or the young girl's hearing ability, the nurse wrote down "Alma"—and that is what was registered in the Chatham County office.

When my mother got the birth certificate in the mail, she noticed the spelling mistake, took an eraser, made a correction, and thought, *That's it.* The trouble is she never changed the registration downtown, so in 1961, when I emigrated to Canada to become president of Winnipeg Bible College, I discovered that my birth certificate was different from the name I had been using all my life. I had to have a legal office prepare a document to correct the birth certificate. Can you imagine that? I'm really Alma, not Elmer. I guess I struggled with that name for nothing.

Because they were the fashionable young couple, Mom and Dad went to all the nightclubs in Chatham County. These were the days of prohibition, and revenuers were always looking for illegal whiskey. My mother carried a bottle in her purse, because revenuers never searched the ladies.

Their favorite restaurant was Johnny Harris, characterized by its large round dance floor and a number of booths around the edge of the circle, each outfitted with a curtain so customers could drink and break the law in privacy. As Daddy's drinking got worse, Mother's acid tongue accelerated to meet the challenge. The more he drank, the more loudly she criticized. By the time I was ready to go to school, they had stopped going out to fashionable places. Daddy just got drunk after work, and then came home and drank some more. Gradually, the once socially active couple withdrew behind the walls of their rented house in town.

I had heard about the drinking habits of Elmer's father. The first time I saw him, I threw my arms around his neck and said, "I love you."

He then looked at Elmer and said, "Marry this one."

Later, Elmer told me, "That's the first time I ever saw anyone hug my daddy." Isn't it true we all want love in life? —Ruth Towns

First, we lived on Adair Street. Then we moved out to Goebel Avenue, across from the Savannah Golf Club. There I saw doctors, lawyers and dentists in their white shirts and ties playing golf. Maybe that is where I picked up a subconscious desire to be sophisticated. I thought if you want to be someone in the world, you should play golf, wear white shirts, and hang around the rich people.

Introduction to Sunday School

We didn't live there long. Before I started the first grade, we moved to 107 Wagner Street, and we were still living there when I graduated from high school.

My life changed in the summer of 1938, when I was five years old. I walked into our living room to see a door-to-door salesman down on his knees, spreading various coffee products on the floor. He was trying to sell my mother Jewel Tea coffee.

Jimmy Breland (his real name was Earnest Wendell) was about six feet tall, skinny, and had a big Adam's apple poking over the collar of the white shirt he wore. He also was a hairy man—there was black hair surrounding the Adam's apple. He only had an eighth-grade education, and the only job he could find in Depression days was selling Jewel Tea coffee door to door. He turned to me to ask, "Where do you go to Sunday School?"

"What's Sunday School?" I inquired.

"It's a place where we sing songs, color books, tell Bible stories, and we have a sand table . . ."

"Whoa," I interrupted, "what's a sand table?"

Jimmy explained that it was a table with sand on the top to show Bible-land geography.

"Doesn't the sand fall off the table?" I asked.

"No, it's got boards on the edges to keep the sand in." Jimmy saw that he had a live fish on the line and began to reel me in slowly.

"If you come to my Sunday School, I'll make a mountain in the sand and show you how Jesus walked across the mountains." I had never heard the name Jesus until that time. Then Jimmy made his two fingers pretend to walk, showing me how Jesus walked.

"Mom, can I go to Sunday School?" I quickly begged.

Mother turned to Jimmy Breland to ask, "What kind of Sunday School are you talking about?" She was afraid that his enthusiasm might be generated by a cult or some off-brand religion.

"Presbyterian," Jimmy reassured her. "I go to Eastern Heights Presbyterian Church, on the corner of Thirty-seventh and Ott Streets."

Because Mother had been reared Presbyterian as a child, she was glad to hear that Jimmy came from the same background. Later, she would tell me that I had been baptized as a baby in a Presbyterian church.

But Mother still had an objection to Jimmy's invitation. She didn't want to mix church with her already complicated life. So she came up with a reason that I couldn't go to Sunday School.

"That church is more than three miles away. He's a little kid, and he'll get lost walking that far."

Jimmy turned and pointed through the screen door toward a big, black, shiny Jewel Tea truck. Then he asked, "Wanna ride my truck to Sunday School?"

What little boy doesn't like to ride in a truck? When I was outside, I had peered through the back windows to see what was in the truck. It was full of packages and boxes of coffee and tea.

"Yeah! I wanna ride your truck to Sunday School."

"Wait a minute," Mother said. She still didn't want to get involved in a church. "That church is located in the neighborhood where all those houses went into bankruptcy. Those houses are half finished, and there are dangerous ditches and boards lying around. He'll run over there to play and get hurt."

Jimmy turned to me and said, "When you get ready to go to the first grade, I'll come take you to Sunday School."

"Okay."

As a result of that life-changing conversation, I've been wrapped up in Sunday School ever since I began attending the first grade.

On the Sunday after Labor Day in 1938, misty morning rain clouded Wagner Street. I was dressed in white short pants with a sharp crease, a shirt, and some type of fancy little tie attached to an elastic band. I was waiting on the edge of the front steps when I saw Jimmy Breland's Jewel Tea truck splashing through the dirt mud puddles of Wagner Street. I ran down the steps. But Mother yelled, "Get back up here on the porch! You'll get wet. Wait 'til he gets here."

Waiting for Jimmy, I had wondered where I would sit among all the boxes and packages I had once seen in the back of his truck. But when he arrived, it was empty. Every Saturday night, Jimmy took all of the coffee products and put them in the living room of his house so that he could drive children to Sunday School.

Jimmy drove one block over to Henrietta Street to pick up the four Aimar boys, and then drove over to Adair Street to pick up the Drigger children. When we arrived at the church, I attended Mrs. Pittman's beginner class.

When I got home, Mother said, "You're never going to miss Sunday School; they give a gold pin to everyone who has perfect attendance throughout the year. Fifty-two Sundays without missing."

"Yes, Ma'am."

"All those children who go to that church come from the rich section of town, and you're going to be just like those rich children."

"Yes, Ma'am."

"When I send you to Sunday School, don't you go play in those half-built houses. If you miss Sunday School and don't get that gold pin, I'll beat you good."

"Yes, Ma'am."

I never missed Sunday School for the next 14 years. Perfect attendance!

We spent our summers on my grandfather's farm in Sardinia, South Carolina. Both Grandpa and Uncle Paul had died intestate, and the 11 children fought over the farm and house. The only one the family trusted was Mother, so she was appointed executrix of the estate, and every summer she and my brother and sister moved to Sardinia to manage the farm.

So, at the end of each summer, I brought a note back from the Sardinia Presbyterian Church attesting that I had not missed any Sunday School classes.

Sometimes I would catch a cold and complain, "Mother, I can't go to Sunday School. I am sick."

"You're not sick. You're just sickening," she would bark. "Get dressed and go to Sunday School."

So off I went, sniffles and all. One time, I came home from Sunday School sick—not with a cough, but a fever. I didn't know I had the mumps, and they began to swell on Sunday afternoon. As you may know, mumps are most infectious when you are catching them, not when they're going away. The next Sunday, I still had swollen jaws. Mother drove me to church, and we sat outside and waited until opening exercises were over. Everyone sang hymns and read the International Uniform Bible lesson in unison, and then each class was dismissed—from the youngest to oldest—singing "Onward Christian Soldiers" as they marched to class.

Mother and I waited until the music was over and all the children were in their classrooms. She had arranged with Mrs. Pittman for me to have a chair near the door, away from the other children. Then Mother said to me, "Be quiet, sneak in, and if anybody looks at you–*suck in*."

Later in life, people criticized my mother about the "suck in" statement. But she always sarcastically answered, "You like the way he turned out, don't you?" Meaning I was a good, obedient boy because I went to Sunday School.

One of the first qualities I liked about Elmer was his dependability. He did what he was supposed to do, the way it was supposed to be done—all the time.
—Ruth Towns

My public school days were not memorable. For grades one through six, I attended Waters Avenue Elementary School, which was approximately a mile and a half from home. I walked each day, unless it was bad weather. Then Mother would pick me up in the car, which meant she also had to take Dad to work and bring him home at night.

I don't remember ever cutting a class all the way through high school. But while I was not a truant problem, I also was not a good student. I daydreamed a lot in class–my visions were filled with pirates and cowboys, and I was always the hero. Whether I won a war, rescued a damsel in distress, or saved a city from pillaging, I dreamed about being victorious and having people cheer for me.

Perhaps my life in public school is best summed up by an incident that happened on the fiftieth anniversary of my high school graduation. Peggy Storey had been a cute, petite, vivacious girl that I always liked to hang around. I tried to talk to her several times throughout our school years, and I think I even took her on one date in high school.

When we met again at our 50-year class reunion, Peggy was in her sixties and pudgy–no longer the girl that I remembered. I asked her a dumb question: "Do you remember me? I'm Elmer Towns."

"No." She went into deep thought and said again, "No, I don't remember you!"

I was crushed. Here was one of the cutest girls I knew, and my name didn't even sound familiar to her. The next day, Peggy came back to say, "I've been thinking about it, and I talked to a couple of the other girls, and yes, we do remember you. You were the guy who always came to school. You were quiet and didn't say much, and then you went home." Ouch!

Talk about not making an impact on the girls! I was the guy who did nothing. As a result, I seldom dated until I went to college.

But Sunday School was an entirely different story. There I mattered—especially to Jimmy Breland. Every year, our church held an Easter sunrise service at the nearby Hillcrest Cemetery. I remember Jimmy quietly walking up to our front porch around dawn, scratching on the screen next to my bed. "Elmer, get up. We've got to go to Sunrise service."

I would get dressed in my new Easter clothes, sit in the front seat of Jimmy's truck, and drink a Coca-Cola he had waiting for me. I remember very little about what happened at the sunrise services, except that I was usually cold, and we went to Sunday School after it was over.

One day, while I was walking home from school, I got into a fight with one of the boys from the Garden Homes Housing Project. I lived in Wagner Heights, a neighborhood of single-family homes, where most of the residents were homeowners—except the Towns family, who rented a two-bedroom house at $25 a month. The boys in Wagner Heights looked down on the "delinquents" in the housing projects. There were lots of fights between the guys from Wagner Heights and those from Garden Homes.

This guy was bigger than I was, and I knew he would win the fight. But my ego wouldn't let me back down. I wasn't going to let anyone call me a sissy. I'd rather go home crying from being beaten up than crying from having been teased. The boy (I can't remember now which boy it was) and I stood on the edge of Henry Street, cursing each other with every swear word we could think of. I dropped my books, curled my fists, and was egged on by my buddies from Wagner Heights.

Suddenly, the front fender of a black truck edged into the crowd of boys, stopping the fight. The window of the truck rolled down and I heard, "Elmer, get in here." It was Jimmy Breland.

I wiped my eyes, picked up my books, and climbed in beside him—thinking, *I sure hope he didn't hear the words I said.*

Jimmy didn't say a word about fighting, or cursing, or anything that had happened. He talked to me as though it were a normal day—like we might have been driving to Sunday School or to an Easter sunrise service. What was important was that Jimmy accepted me and liked me. As a matter of fact, in my subconscious, Jimmy Breland was my idol. I wanted to be like him, not like my father.

When I was nine years old, and promoted to the fourth grade in public school, I was also promoted to the junior Sunday School class, where Jimmy Breland became my teacher. That first day in class was electrifying. He said, "I'm going to teach you the *whole* Bible."

Wow. I quietly sucked in my breath. *I want to learn the whole Bible.* The Bible had been a black book that just sat on a pile of magazines on an end table in the living room. In our house, we didn't throw away magazines. We just piled them on the end table, and the stack was usually at least a foot tall. But we never put a magazine on top of the Bible, because that was disrespectful to God.

"Always put the Bible on top," Mother would demand.

Now, in Jimmy Breland's class, I had the opportunity to "learn the *whole* Bible." Jimmy's Sunday School class met in the church kitchen on the second floor. On three sides of the kitchen, food preparation counters stood against the wall, with cabinets hanging over them. A large table in the middle of the room was covered with stainless steel. This was probably the best institutional kitchen of its day—but Eastern Heights Presbyterian Church had never finished constructing the dining room. The rest of the second floor was open, with studs and wiring exposed. The kitchen had a long, low, flat window ledge, designed to pass food out into a dining room that was never used.

The Greatest Teacher in the World

The Bible came to life in that kitchen. We all sat on large, wooden folding chairs—the kind where the feet of small children never reach the ground. There were seven or eight girls on one side of the stainless steel table, and seven or eight boys on the other side. I sat with Albert Freundt, Bobby Myers, L.J. McEwen, Frank Perry, and (later on) Art Winn.

Whereas I never paid attention in public school, I don't remember my mind ever drifting while Jimmy Breland lectured on the greatness of Scripture. This was a Presbyterian church, and their Reformed theology usually began everything with God's covenant with Abraham. So, Jimmy Breland started his class by saying, "Abraham, who began it all . . ." That was a phrase he used quite often: "Abraham began the whole plan of God."

Jimmy Breland told us, "Listen to me with your eyes." Isn't it interesting that he didn't say listen with your ears? He knew that when our eyes paid attention, he had our hearts. So he announced, "If anyone is not looking at me when I ask a question, you'll have to stand on your chair and whistle the 'Battle Hymn of the Republic.' " That was anathema to a little Southern boy. We wouldn't have minded whistling "Dixie," but not the "Battle Hymn of the Republic"—the theme song of the Yankees.

Hanging high over the stainless steel table were two rows of large hooks, and suspended from the hooks were pots, pans, knives, sharpeners, and every other utensil needed for cooking a church dinner.

I remember Jimmy reaching up, taking a large, old water pitcher, and holding it high while he announced, "This water pitcher is Abraham, who began it all." He went on to say, "If I ask you who the water pitcher is, you have to say . . . what . . . ?"

We answered, "Abraham, who began it all."

During that first lesson, Jimmy walked over to a large, dirty, smelly galvanized sink in the open end of the kitchen. He explained, as the water trickled into the pitcher, "Just as this pitcher is slowly being filled with water, God slowly filled the life of Abraham with His love and grace."

Then, just as dramatically, Jimmy poured out the clean liquid, announcing, "So God used Abraham to pour His grace into his family and the world, and ultimately to us."

Jimmy Breland had my eyes and heart in rapt attention. I was ready for him to ask, "Elmer Towns, who is the water pitcher?"

I was ready to yell out, "Abraham, who began it all."

The next week, Jimmy reached to the middle of the stainless steel tabletop to pick up a sugar bowl, then held it high and announced, "This sugar bowl is Isaac, the son of Abraham." Then he told us how Isaac committed the same sins as his father, Abraham. Jimmy warned us about generational sins: "You were born with the same weakness as your parents, and you will commit the same sins as they."

"Not me," I whispered to myself, "I'll never drink, even though my father is a drunk. I'll be different."

Each week, Jimmy Breland began Sunday School by saying, "Let's review . . ." He'd hold the water pitcher high above his head and ask who it was. We would scream out the answer: "Abraham, who began it all."

When he held the sugar bowl up high, we would scream: "Isaac."

Next came Isaac's sons: Jacob and Esau. So Jimmy reached for two things that naturally went together: salt and pepper shakers.

The following Sunday we learned the names of the 12 sons of Jacob. Jimmy reached into a kitchen drawer and pulled out 12 ordinary, dull table knives—the kind used in church dinners. He dramatically dropped each knife onto the stainless steel table with a loud *CLANG*. We had to call out the name of each son of Jacob: "Rueben . . . Simeon . . . Levi . . . Judah . . ." and so we memorized all 12 names.

Whereas I never raised my hand or answered questions in public school, preferring to travel incognito through each class, I was always one of the first to yell out the answer for Jimmy Breland. Why? Because I loved to answer what I knew. My fear at school was of being embarrassed by being called on for something I didn't know.

On the surface of the stainless steel table, Jimmy would line up the kitchen implements that stood for the people of the Old Testament—the water pitcher, sugar bowl, salt and pepper shakers, and the 12 dull table knives that stood for the sons of Jacob. A butcher knife represented the 400 years in Egypt, because that divided Genesis from Exodus. Each Sunday, something new would appear on the table, and each Sunday a new name was memorized. I memorized my way through the Old Testament, and then one fateful Sunday, Jimmy held up a Coca-Cola cup and asked, "Who's the Coca-Cola cup?"

"We don't know."

Then he said, "It's Job," pronouncing the man's name correctly.

To me, the name looked like job—as in employment or "I have a job to do." So I chimed in, "It's job," mispronouncing the word.

When Jimmy corrected my pronunciation, I smiled back and said, "If that's what you want, that's what it'll be."

Then Jimmy asked, "Where does Job go?"

"We don't know."

He held the Coca-Cola cup dramatically over all the utensils spread out over the stainless steel table. "Does Job go here?" he asked, starting to place Job next to one of the kings of Judah.

"We don't know."

"Does the Coca-Cola cup go in the judges?"

"We don't know."

Then he emphatically placed the Coca-Cola cup next to the water pitcher and said, "If Job and Abraham were little guys, they might have lived in the same neighborhood and played together." That was how I learned that Job and Abraham might have been contemporaries. Jimmy made learning memorable, and I never forgot the chronology of the Old Testament.

As a matter of fact, years later I wrote a book called *History Makers of the Old Testament.* I interpreted history through the theory of "great men"—believing that great men produced great events throughout history. Common men only endured history. Somehow, I wanted to be one of those great men who influenced history; I never wanted to be common and only endure the events that were going on around me.

When it came to Old Testament kings, Jimmy Breland told us we would have to memorize all 22 kings in the southern kingdom of Judah, because many of them were godly and we might see them in the streets of heaven. "You may want to say good morning to King Hezekiah," he told us. "Or you may want to say, 'Hello, King Josiah.' " That made sense to me.

Then Jimmy told us that we didn't have to memorize the kings of the northern kingdom of Israel (again, there were 22 of them). He maintained, "Not one of those kings were saved; they were all lost and went to hell." Yes, he actually used the word "hell." So I never memorized their names. To this day, when I write about or teach the chronology of the Old Testament, I still maintain that none of the northern kings were born again—not even King Jehu, who did many righteous things, but personally did not know God.

Learning to Love Work

Like most other kids, I rebelled at any hard work I had to do around the house. Mother had a vegetable garden, and I hated digging the weeds and shoveling up the dirt for planting. Also, I had to cut the grass. I think I most hated mowing the lawn with the old-fashioned push mower.

I usually divided our yard up into seven small plots of grass. There were three sections in the front yard, a long strip of grass down the driveway between the two concrete strips for the tires, and three plots of grass along the side of the house. A flower garden, a pear tree and a fence separated these last three. Don't little boys love to put off doing their jobs for as long as they can? I would cut one of the seven plots of grass, and then relax on the front porch to drink some iced tea. I could stretch grass cutting out to a whole afternoon, up to three hours, with my frequent tea breaks.

Then a life-changing day arrived. I had put Mother off for two or three days, and so she informed me: "Tomorrow you'll cut the grass before you do anything else."

"Yes, ma'am," I meekly answered.

As I got ready to cut the grass, all the boys from the neighborhood came to play football in the field next to our house. Sergeant Sullivan had plowed up his summer crop, and the field just invited boys to come and play on the soft sod. We would run at one another—though not very fast—through that plowed field. We tackled and threw one another to the ground, but never got hurt on the soft sod.

Do you get the picture? The boys laughed, played and yelled about football all afternoon, while I silently cursed under my breath and cut the seven small plots of grass, one after another.

About the time I got finished, the guys came over, looking like dust-covered zombies. They had dirt embedded in their hair, on their clothes, under their fingernails and plastered around their eyes.

With a big garden hose, we squirted one another–me included–and washed away any remnants of dirt. As we lay drying in the warm autumn sun on the neatly mowed grass, some of the guys complained about aching muscles, sore feet, and how tired they were.

Me, too, I thought–but unlike the others, I hadn't enjoyed getting my sore muscles. Lying there in the sun, I had a revelation. I realized I was as sore as they were, but they'd had fun and I was miserable. They got dirty and I got dirty. They hurt and I hurt. But now they were enjoying pleasant recollections of their game, while I was miserable because I hated cutting the grass. Then it came to me: *If I made work fun, I'd never hate cutting the grass again.*

That was a profoundly life-changing moment. I turned over to let the warm sun heal my aching back, and I decided that from that moment on, work would be different.

About a week or so later, I came home from school, and my mother reminded me, "Don't forget, you have to cut the grass today."

Rather than procrastinate, I eagerly got out the tools and attacked the yards with vigor. I tore into the seven patches of grass, and I didn't take a single break for iced tea.

When I finished mowing, I went into the house to get Mother's scissors–we didn't have trimming shears–and I trimmed around the water meter cover and some bricks that lined the sidewalk. Then I lay flat against the grass to check to see if there was a single blade sticking above the rest; I wanted to do a perfect job.

After hosing off and lying in the sun, I felt good all over–inside and out. I had done a good job, it hadn't taken long, and I was happy. I concluded that work can be fun. Work defines our lives and gives us dignity. When you feel good about your work, and you know that your work contributes to others–but most of all, when you realize your work is pleasing to God and advances the kingdom of God–then your work can give you great enjoyment, because you've fulfilled God's purpose for your life.

Learning to Cuss

Reginald McDuffy taught me to curse in the fourth grade. I really can't blame him, though. The sinful heart is rebellious against God—so if I hadn't learned from Reginald, I'm sure I would have learned some other way.

Although Jimmy Breland had warned us against taking the name of the Lord God in vain, I still developed an appetite for cursing. I was as addicted to cursing as my father was to alcohol.

It started when Reggie, who sat in the desk in front of me at school, turned around to show me a curse word he had written on a sheet of paper. He sneered and chuckled softly as he whispered its pronunciation, so the teacher couldn't hear. Then he pronounced the word again, urging me, "Go ahead; say it."

I don't remember the exact word, but I do recall pronouncing it inwardly, mouthing the word slowly. Suddenly I sat taller in my seat. Since the "big men" I knew cursed, I suddenly became bigger in my own perception.

I began to repeat some of the other curse words I'd heard from various uncles. My fist got bigger: *Now I can beat up my enemies.* I whispered a few more words, and my legs reached farther under the chair: *Good, I'll stand taller*. Cursing made me feel nine feet tall, when actually I was four feet, six inches small.

During recess, we were playing our version of "cops and robbers." Some guy hit me as he ran by; I chased him down, smashed him back, and cursed him using the d-word. *Yea!* Muscles bulged, my voice deepened; I was now someone to fear.

There was another guy who really tormented me; I chased him down and condemned him to h—.

I marched off the playground that day feeling as victorious as if I had won a championship football game.

Struggling with Cursing

Most of the young people in Jimmy Breland's Sunday School class came back on Sunday nights for PYF, which stands for Presbyterian Youth

Fellowship. One evening, we sat in a large semi-circle in one of the unfinished rooms on the second floor of the church building. In front of us stood a small table holding a lit candle and a large mixing bowl from the church kitchen.

What's that for? I wondered.

Each of us read a short devotional out of a magazine that was called a quarterly. I read my paragraph and passed the quarterly on to the person next to me.

Next, small pieces of paper were handed out, and with them church pencils (a church pencil is one that's almost too short to write with). We were told, "Each one of you is going to write your sins on that sheet of paper, then we'll crumple them up in a bowl, and burn them with a candle. God will purge our sins in flames."

I knew that my worst "sin" was cursing, so I simply wrote "CUSS" on my paper. I was experiencing something called conviction—but it wasn't the conviction of sorrow for sin; it was the conviction of fear. *Would God send me to hell for cursing?*

Then came the moment when we prayed, the candle touched our "sins," and smoke filled the room.

There it goes, I said to myself, thinking that my cursing would now go away. But it didn't. Before long, I got mad on the school playground, and I cursed again.

Stop it! I rebuked myself when my cursing exploded during "cops and robbers." But the next time a guy bumped me, I cursed again and enjoyed feeling bigger.

Maybe six or nine months later, we once again arrived at PYF to find a candle burning on a table at the front of the room. I did the same thing as last time, except this time I began to write out all my curse words: d—, h—, and so on. I was never a good speller, so I was not sure that I had spelled some of the words properly.

This time I mean it, I pledged with all of my heart, determined to keep my word.

But again, on the playground, I slid back into the old habit. I was learning that I couldn't make myself do all the good things that I knew I ought to do. I experienced a growing conflict in my young heart.

I promised to obey God, but when the chips were down, I disobeyed. I also felt rebellious toward Mother when she told me things I had to do—although I wouldn't speak back to her for fear of a spanking. When she fussed at me, I rebelled inwardly. "Get up and go get a bucket of water," she'd tell me at Grandpa's farm. Outwardly I would obey, but on the inside, I harbored a resentful attitude. I tortured myself with the question: *Can I ever make myself do what I'm supposed to do?*

At the end of my junior year in high school, I went to the Presbyterian youth camp at Laura S. Walker State Park in Waycross, Georgia. We always ended camp with a bonfire and a time of commitment and rededication. On that particular night, there was a big bonfire. The young people took turns going forward to throw small chips of wood onto the fire, then pledge to love God, or serve God, or do better with their lives!

As the wood chips landed on the fire, the flames consumed them. When there was a break in the stream of testimonies, I boldly picked up a big wood chip—one that had black mud splattered on its smooth white surface. Then, moralizing, I said, "This piece of wood is just like my tongue." I held it high for all to see. "It's splattered with black mud, just like my tongue is coated with cursing." With a deep vow, I promised to stop cursing and told them that God would be my helper.

For three or four weeks, I kept my pledge, and I felt strong in my commitment. But I broke my vow one rainy afternoon. I was wrapping my newspapers on the porch of Morningside Baptist Church for protection from the weather. The newspapers came in bundles of 100, strapped together by wire. Many of the paperboys carried wire cutters, but I just bent the wire back and forth until it broke. As I began to jerk the wire back and forth, it prematurely broke, and the ragged metal slashed my knuckle. Blood spurted out—and so did a curse word.

Art Winn, my good buddy, said, "I thought you weren't gonna curse anymore . . ." I used the d-word on him. He warned me, "Here comes the preacher. You don't want him hearing you cursing."

I used the d-word on the preacher. I was mad at my carelessness . . . mad at my bleeding finger . . . mad at the wire . . . but mostly I was angry because I couldn't keep my promise not to curse. That day I decided it's impossible to break a cursing habit, and I never again vowed to stop cursing—until I was saved.

Art and I ran around together, and for the most part we didn't have filthy mouths. On a couple of occasions, I heard Art curse, and he could say the same about me. I cursed around the guys at school, where I needed to feel big. But I was always very careful not to curse around women, little children, or any relative. If an uncle heard me curse, he might have told my mother, and she would have spanked me.

It wasn't until July 25, 1950—when I accepted Christ as my Savior—that this part of my life was transformed. That evening, I didn't confess cursing, nor did I ask God to forgive all the curse words I had said. I didn't even ask God to help me stop cursing. I was convicted of my sin, and I knew that before God I was condemned and heading for hell. When I asked God to forgive my sin, I knew that included cursing and a lot of other sins. When I received Jesus Christ, I received His power to transform my life. I never cursed again. I didn't have to try—there was simply never again an urge to curse. "I can do all things through Christ who strengthens me" (Phil. 4:13).

Swift punishment for dangerous sins makes you unlikely to repeat them. Case in point: I was standing in front of the refrigerator in the kitchen. Mother said no to something I asked—the particular issue is unimportant—and for the first time in my life, I whispered a curse word I had heard. "RUTH JEAN!!!" my mother yelled in anger. I had never heard her shout that loud. Her voice probably would have been enough to clean out my mouth, but she grabbed me by the ear to march me to the washtub. Pointing a bar of Fels Naptha laundry soap toward my mouth, she demanded, "Bite . . ." Obediently I bit off a huge chunk. Then she demanded, "Chew . . ." I chewed till soap suds seeped out of my mouth, and tears trickled down my cheeks. I never cursed again. —Ruth Towns

Farm Working

Each summer, Mother managed the McFaddin family farm. So right after Memorial Day, we left Daddy working in Savannah and rode a Greyhound

Bus to South Carolina. I did menial work around the place—and I enjoyed it, because I had learned to make work fun.

My favorite job was harvesting tobacco (the locals call it "cropping tobacco"). The hired workers wouldn't let me pick the tobacco leaves, because I was not mature enough to tell the difference between a ripe leaf and a green one. Instead, they had me drive the sleigh that carried the tobacco from the field to the barn. Then the women would tie the leaves to sticks and hang them in the barn, where they would be cooked until they became golden yellow.

There were five sharecropping families on the farm, and one of the men instructed me to use Lightning, the oldest mule on the place, to pull my sleigh. I was guaranteed he would never run away on me. I asked, "Why do you call him 'Lightning' since he's so slow?"

"He's like lightning," I was told, "because we don't know when he'll come."

Early each morning, Uncle Gene and I would stretch a seine-net over the farm's creek. We always had a fish fry when work was over and tobacco was in the barn. About noon, I'd be sent to clean out the seine and put the large fish (or "shiners") in a bucket of water. About 5:00 P.M., I'd gather a second bucket of shiners from the creek.

While the farm hands hung the tobacco, and then started a fire to cook the tobacco, the women filleted the fish. There'd be 50 or 60 small fillets, each big enough for a half-sandwich. They'd be breaded in cornbread crumbs—and they were the best tasting fish in the world.

At an old Southern fish fry, sandwiches consisted of a small fresh fish fillet on a half slice of bread. As a kid, I could eat half a dozen of those. Then I'd find a comfortable place to lie down and listen to the elderly workers talk . . . and tell stories . . . and laugh. A couple of hours would slip by, and then the evening locusts would begin to chirp. I'd watch the evening stars come out, and then count fireflies. Time didn't move, and neither did I—no clock . . . no schedules . . . nothing to do but wait for tomorrow's work.

That life was entirely different from my adult life, where I packed too much into each day. After I was saved, I wanted to do as much for God as possible, so I tried to stuff two days' worth of work into each 24 hours.

God's First Call

Immediately after the tobacco was harvested, we began picking cotton. I was picking cotton with the sharecroppers when I first thought God might be calling me into ministry. I had been working my way down a row of cotton along with several children and their parents. Bobby Johnson, a middle-aged African-American sharecropper on my grandpa's farm, finished his row, and then helped pick my row so I wouldn't get behind. Bobby could pick more than 200 pounds a day—twice what a child could do.

At the end of the row, we all sat on a mound of plowed dirt, our aching legs stretched out for relief. I could see a church building for the African Americans on the other side of the creek, at the east end of my grandpa's property. I asked Bobby why we (meaning white folks) did not go to their church, and they didn't come to ours. (Children are colorblind at birth; they have to be taught distinctions.)

"You folks is Presbyterians," Bobby philosophized, "and we's Baptist." The sun glowed down on us like a red ember in a fireplace.

The other black men cautioned, "Careful, Bobby . . . he's Cap'n's boy." They called Grandpa "Captain," and they did not want Bobby to be in trouble with my grandpa. Then Bobby called me by the name they used for Grandpa. "Cap'n," he said, "you gonna be a preacher." Although that was not the first time I had thought about serving the Lord, Bobby was the first to tell me I was going to be a preacher. Today I know I have a call of God—not just because of Bobby, and not just because I surrendered to preach. From my earliest memory, though, I have always thought about preaching, and I always saw myself as a preacher.

"Cap'n . . . yo' heart's tender to God . . . you gonna be a reveren'," Bobby told me that day.

"I want to come hear you preach," I told Bobby. I never did visit that little country black Baptist church on the other side of the creek, and I never did hear Bobby preach. Yet that church influenced me through its members and their ministry as they worked the fields of my grandpa's place.

I never forgot that first time someone told me I was going to be a preacher. It was good news, and the message made me happy. I stretched out on the dirt of that cotton row on Grandpa's farm and thought about how the message "fit." I wanted to be a preacher.

Trying to Impress Girls

Like most teenage boys, I showed off to get attention. During my senior year in high school, at a picnic for our church's youth group, a bunch of us were floating with inner tubes at high tide on the Wilmington River at Thunderbolt, Georgia. There were no strong currents in that part of the otherwise dangerous river. I bragged about diving from the top of a drawbridge (the steel rose about four stories high). Betty Farthing quickly squealed, "Elmer, don't do it!" Doesn't that challenge a guy's ego? Now I had to do it. But when I climbed to the top of the bridge, I had second thoughts.

When I was five years old, my mother asked me what I wanted to be when I grew up. I answered, "A wife like you."

Then Mother said, "You'd better start praying for a husband so you'll get the right one."

So from five years old, I prayed:

"Now I lay me down to sleep,
I pray the Lord my soul to keep.
If I should die before I wake,
I pray the Lord my soul to take.

"God bless Mommy, Daddy and David . . . and the man I'm going to marry. Make him cute and protect him. Amen." I had no idea how many ways God would protect Elmer. —Ruth Towns

I'll die, I thought, gasping at the height. Then I pondered my predicament more specifically: *I'll surely be killed if I dive head first.* So I decided to jump feet first—at least that was better than a coward's climb down the steel works.

"Don't do it!" Betty kept screaming. But that just egged me on.

I'll die, was the refrain running through my mind. My consolation was the thought: *A dead hero is better than an emasculated coward climbing down to the laughter of his friends.*

I screamed as I jumped feet first. My scream was like a Confederate soldier's rebel yell as he charged into rifle fire, facing a quick hero's death. My scream hid my fear.

I hit the water—toes pointed down—and immediately pointed them out so I wouldn't go too deep and hit the bottom. (This was stupid; I had no idea how deep the water was.) As I plunged deeper, I thought, *I'm not dead—if I ever get out of here, I'll never do something this idiotic again.*

I wasn't hurt, but climbing back onto my tube, I realized that even the cheers of women didn't make being reckless worth it. Later that night, Betty forgot all about me risking my life to get her attention. She talked to Charles Lomel for the rest of the evening.

Focusing on Being Exceptional

In 1945, Mother volunteered to clean up the family cemetery right outside Sardinia. We did it on Memorial Day. I was 13 years old and could swing a weed sling fairly well, so I had to slice away all the weeds on the inside of the picket fence that surrounded the cemetery. Mother and my younger sister, Martha, used small hand trowels to dig up the weeds from my grandparents' gravesite.

Right in the middle of the cemetery stands a large, 10-foot-tall granite stone on which is inscribed the history of the McFaddin family who pioneered that section of South Carolina. John McFaddin arrived from Scotland in 1732 (the same year that Savannah, Georgia, was founded) and was the American titular head of the McFaddin clan. The McFaddin family tree was chiseled into that stone, right down to my grandfather, Robert E. Lee McFaddin Jr. (named for the famous Southern general of the Civil War).

Mother stood Martha and me in front of the huge granite stone and challenged us: "Remember, you are McFaddins. You've got our blood flowing in your veins, so I expect you to live better than other children." Then Mother turned to point out the cleared fields surrounding the cemetery on the edge of the Black River. We could see three or four farmhouses within view. She said, "Our forefathers cleared this wilderness for farms and built homes for their families. I want you to do something great with your lives, like they did." I've never forgotten her last words: "You are McFaddins; you can do anything you set your minds to do."

As I looked up at that tall granite stone, I was overwhelmed by the weight of its legacy upon my shoulders. Mother's words interrupted my thoughts: "Remember, you've got McFaddin blood in your veins. You can do anything you want to do."

That moment became a turning point in my life. Mother gave that speech only once, but I revisited the McFaddin stone many times in my mind. Her faith in me made me believe that I could do anything I set my mind to do. It was probably not the legendary stone itself that became a motivational tool. Perhaps it was the Spirit of God preparing me to attempt to live an exceptional life.

There was something about Elmer Towns that was different from all the other boys at Columbia Bible College. The other guys wanted to serve God, but Elmer had an aura of destiny about him that said, I'm going to do something exceptional for God. He didn't say it in so many words, but it came out when he prayed, and when he told me what he was learning from the Bible, and when he told me what he wanted to do for God. —Ruth Towns

2

Junior High and High School Years

(1943–1950)

Let me tell you about the best year I ever had in public school. I left my childhood at Waters Avenue Elementary School behind me when I finished the sixth grade. I had conquered the five blocks of Wagner Heights and the nine-block walk to the schoolhouse. My next conquest was to ride an old streetcar into downtown Savannah, where Chatham Junior High School was located in an old restored school building. As I moved into adolescence, I felt ready to conquer downtown Savannah. I walked into Room 107 and thought, *This is the same address as our house on Wagner Street.* There I met the teacher who would change my life—Ms. Margaret Logan.

"Elmer Towns, I've heard about you," she greeted me as I entered the room.

"Oh no! This is going to be another terrible year," I complained under my breath. "She's already got it in for me."

Because Ms. Logan assigned seats alphabetically, and my last name begins with *T*, I sat near the back of the room. It was a comfortable place because I was out of her sightline. I wouldn't bother her if she didn't bother me. I could daydream, scribble, or whisper to some of the other guys. I could hibernate in my own private world in the back of the room.

Learning to Read a Book

Ms. Logan rattled my world when she announced, "Let's go to the library; we're going to learn how to read a book."

I already know how to read, I thought sarcastically.

There were 50 students in that class, because the Second World War was still raging, and the schools where flooded with children whose parents had come to work in Savannah's shipyards. With both parents working, many of those children were undisciplined and unruly, just like me.

Nevertheless, all 50 of us sat obediently on the library floor, underneath a giant skylight. Margaret Logan sat on a low stool; her big, round, full skirt reached the floor on all sides. She had a stack of books at her right hand; she'd read a page or two out loud, and then ask, "Who wants to take this book home to read it?" I was intrigued by all the hands that flew up into the air to get each book. I didn't dare move a hand.

After several books were distributed, I became intrigued as she began reading a fiction story about baseball. I thought to myself, *She'll never see my hand; I'm at the back of the class. I'd better do it now if I want the book.* I lifted my hand and interrupted her reading. "Ms. Logan, I want to read that book."

"Sure, Elmer." She smiled and passed it back.

That night I went home and read the entire book from beginning to end. I didn't go out to play with my buddies, and I didn't listen to my favorite radio programs ("Fibber McGee and Molly," "The Bob Hope Program" and "The Red Skelton Comedy Hour," among others). The next morning I proudly stood before Ms. Logan's desk to announce, "I read the *whole* book."

"That's nice," she said.

Because I thought she didn't fully understand, I repeated, "I read the *WHOLE* book." She still didn't seem to realize how significant that was. What I should have said was that I had never before, in my entire life, read a whole book. I had never begun at the first page and read right through to the last. Ms. Logan taught me to read books.

During recess, I marched into the library and checked out a second book. The following morning I was again able to report, "I read a *whole* book." Each day for the next two or three weeks, I would make the same announcement, and I'm sure she got tired of hearing me say, "I read the *whole* book."

Conquering Journalism

In the fall of 1944, Ms. Logan once again sat us on the library floor underneath the large skylight. This time she announced, "Today I'm going to teach you how to write a term paper." I had heard that something fearful like a term paper was coming. The idea of writing a term paper terrified me, like a German *Blitzkrieg* bombing or a surprise attack by the Japanese. I had never written more than one page about anything. Ms. Logan rattled my world when she said, "You have to write a seven-page term paper."

"Aagggah . . ." I rolled over on the floor, pretending to choke. Two or three other scallywags writhed on the floor with me.

"I'll help you," Ms. Logan promised with a smile. "It'll be easy if you do what I tell you."

She passed out 3x5 cards, and instructed us to take notes on these small cards. Then she said, "Bring your cards and let's go find help."

We walked over to the left-hand side of the library, where huge, dark, ominous books were shelved. They were dusty and fearful, and I was not sure if they had ever been opened.

"I've already written out a topic for each of you," Ms. Logan said, waving a handful of small pieces of paper about three times the size of Chinese fortune cookie slips. As she began to hand out the pieces of paper, each student obediently took one. When she came to me, I didn't want to touch them; they were like poison that would instantly kill me. I felt as if I were reaching for a snake. But I pulled one from her fingers and read it slowly, almost like a condemned man reading his death sentence. All the paper said was, "The Panama Canal."

When she finished handing out the papers, Ms. Logan turned to a girl and asked, "What's your topic?"

As our teacher's delicate fingers cracked open a formidable book, she announced that it was an encyclopedia, and that inside it we would find a world of knowledge—everything we wanted to know.

Ms. Logan asked three or four more people what their topics were, and each time she opened an encyclopedia volume and began reading some information about the assigned topic.

I raised my hand to call out, "The Panama Canal." She took the book marked *P* and began reading about the Panama Canal. She explained that we would copy information from the encyclopedia onto our 3x5 cards, and on the back of these cards we would write the bibliographic information.

"Follow me," Ms. Logan instructed, smiling at us again. All 50 students trekked across the library to a very large wooden box standing on four legs. I had never seen anything like it. Ms. Logan called it a card catalog. As she opened the small drawers, we saw hundreds of small cards, and she explained that every book in the library was filed under the Dewey decimal classification system. Then she asked, "Who has a topic?"

I quickly yelled out, "The Panama Canal," and she went to the small drawer marked *P* and began to read the names of books about the Panama Canal. There were five books in the library, and before that day was over, I was dragging all five home with me.

I began making notes on the Panama Canal, and then I started writing—including footnotes, quotations and dates. When I had finished writing the seven pages, an idea hit me. One of the large books I had used for research contained an architectural drawing of the Panama Canal from the Atlantic to the Pacific Ocean. Being creative, I took some onionskin paper and traced that sectional view, creating an eighth page of my term paper.

The drawing must have caught Ms. Logan's attention, because as I was leaving for recess, she asked, "Elmer, would you give your report on the Panama Canal after lunch?"

"Yes, Ma'am."

When Ms. Logan and the students left for lunch, I hung back and closed the classroom door. Then, using a yardstick, I drew to scale the side sectional view of the Panama Canal on two large sections of the chalkboard. Just about the time I was finishing, the bell rang, and the students and Ms. Logan returned to the room. (Never before in my life had I given up play for anything academic.)

"What's this?" Ms. Logan asked, pointing to the drawing.

"That's the Panama Canal," I replied proudly.

Then I gave the first public speech of my life. For the next 12 to 15 minutes, I stood before the chalkboard and explained how the Panama Canal was built, how many people died in various hospitals from malaria, and how many thousands of dollars were spent to dig through mountains. I even described the pipes used for transferring water from one lock to another. As I talked, I made eye contact—looking at the students, looking at the blackboard, and finally looking at Ms. Logan. I could see in her eyes that she was captivated by my report. When I sat down, I heard, "Elmer, that's wonderful."

I had never had a teacher tell me, "That's wonderful." As a matter of fact, I couldn't remember any other adult ever telling me I had done something wonderful. Then Ms. Logan said, "I've learned more about the Panama Canal from you than from any other person on earth."

Aw, shucks, I said to myself, scraping my feet on the floor. But I enjoyed her praise. As a matter of fact, I was like a hungry man gulping down a meal; I savored each word in my mind, especially rolling over the phrase, "That's wonderful." I must have repeated it a million times during that day and that night as I tried to go to sleep. *Maybe—just maybe—I could somehow do something wonderful with my life.*

The next day, I went straight to the library, taking my 3x5 cards to write another term paper—this time on the Suez Canal. I was disappointed to find that the Suez Canal didn't have locks. In another disappointing turn, I couldn't find an architectural sectional view to trace onto onionskin paper. Still, without an assignment, I wrote an eight-page term paper on the Suez Canal.

When I handed it in to Ms. Logan she said, "That's nice." I waited for her praise—"That's wonderful!"—but it never came. I waited for her to ask me to give a report to the class, but that never came either. However, I was not discouraged—in fact, I was motivated to work even harder.

During that fall and winter, I became extremely interested in school. At the beginning of every day, Ms. Logan would sit at her desk to read the morning newspaper and tell us what was happening in the world. Personal example is a powerful teaching tool. To this day I am an avid newspaper reader, thanks to the influence of Ms. Logan.

She responded in kind to my response. Towards the middle of the year, she moved me to the front of the room—not to the very front, but much closer than I had been before.

Writing Audaciously

During the spring semester of 1945, Ms. Logan once more walked us up to the library. "Last semester you wrote a term paper on geography," she reminded us. "This semester you're going to write a term paper on social studies."

What's social studies? I wondered to myself. Then sarcastically I thought, *Do we study socials . . . ?*

Ms. Logan explained that we were going to study how people related to one another in the various nations of the world.

Then she began to hand out those small sheets of paper about three times the size of Chinese fortune cookies. I hurried to be first in line to get my assignment. Quickly I opened the paper to find: "The History of the Wars Between China and Japan." I knew the exercise. First look in the encyclopedias, next go to the card catalog, and then write all your footnotes, quotations and information on 3x5 cards.

I'm going to write a bigger paper, maybe twice as long, maybe even 15 pages, I decided.

The two bedrooms in our rented house didn't have any place for me to study. Sometimes I would push away the junk on the dining room table and write there, but other times I studied on the kitchen table—which meant I had to pack away all my books during mealtimes.

There was an old, termite-infested, single-car garage behind our house that should have fallen down, but was propped up by a fig tree. Men had changed the oil in their cars and let oil spill on the dirt floor of that smelly old garage. I built a table out of scrap wood in the middle of the garage. Then I added some old linoleum so I would have a smooth top for writing term papers. I nailed a wooden apple box to the garage wall for a bookshelf. I brought home several books on the history of Japan and China from the library, and I stashed them in my homemade bookshelf. I was beginning to look academic.

After dinner, I went out to the garage to write my term paper. *Oh no!* There had been light in the afternoon, when I built my "study," but in February the sun went down early—so now the garage was pitch black.

What am I gonna do? I went to the supermarket about three blocks away, bought several extension cords for a nickel apiece, and ran a line from the outlet on the back porch—down the fence, through the fig tree, and into the garage, where I hung a light bulb directly over my makeshift desk. Every night, I went out to the privacy of my own study, writing page after page.

Someone once said, "Every man must have his own cave to get strength," and that garage was my cave during the winter and spring of 1945. I gave up all my evening radio programs, and when I had used all the paper I had, I went to the store and bought two or three more packs of three-holed Blue Horse paper. When I finished my term paper, it was 99 pages long, replete with footnotes on "The History of the Wars Between China and Japan."

Ms. Logan didn't say, "That's wonderful." Nor did she ask me to stand in front of the room to give a report. As a matter of fact, I don't remember anyone telling me that my extraordinarily long paper was wonderful.

But even as a seventh grader, I knew that one's great achievement becomes its own reward. I had done something no seventh-grade student had ever done. I didn't need the applause of men, nor did I need to hear Ms. Logan say, "That's wonderful!" The excellence of the project was its own prize. No one had to tell me I'd achieved the unachievable; I knew it. Just the sheer size of the term paper was its own "Red Badge of Courage."

Many times later in life, the accomplishment of a predetermined goal has been its own reward. When I wrote a book, I didn't do it for money or fame, nor did anyone have to tell me it was great. While I am ego-driven and love praise, there have been times when I've retreated from the compliments of others. Just knowing I had completed a challenging task—perhaps a book that others didn't write—and scaled the unscalable was all the recognition I needed.

My mother kept that 99-page paper for years. When we moved her out of her home into a nursing home, many of her keepsakes were lost. That term paper was probably lost then, but I will never forget the important lesson I learned in writing it.

Getting Through School

Attending junior high school changed my life, and ultimately it changed me. I no longer played in the afternoons with the gang from Wagner Heights that I called the "cat patrol." I began delivering newspapers for spending money—something I did for the next five years.

My eighth-grade teacher, Mrs. Grady, was as bad as Ms. Logan was good—as negative in motivation as Ms. Logan was positive. Mrs. Grady "grated" on me. The first day in her class, she thought I was marking my desk with a pencil, even though I was only doodling as I listened. "Stop that!" she yelled at me—and sent me to the last row. Three cute girls sitting in the other front seats laughed at me. I never forgot that, and I sat in the back seat until I was in the twelfth grade. Neither Mrs. Grady nor any of my other teachers was ever able to motivate me to study the way Ms. Logan did.

In high school, I became a close friend of Art Winn. We were inseparable. Somehow, we both stumbled across racing bicycles. His was from England, and mine was a Troxel, made in Germany, with wooden racing rims. Cars liberate today's young people, but those bicycles gave us freedom, and the city of Savannah became our adventure ground. We went everywhere, quickly and easily. When we wanted to go to Savannah Beach to swim or fish, it was only a 20-mile bike ride away.

When the Presbyterian youth held a big rally in Waycross, Georgia—100 miles away—Art and I decided to ride our bicycles there. We attempted to do what we thought no high schooler had ever done. We left about 4:00 A.M. We could cover about 15 to 20 miles an hour, and at the end of each hour, we rested.

We arrived at the church about five minutes after 11:00—the time when their meeting began. We changed into long trousers and then triumphantly walked down the center aisle of the church to sit on the front row. Why such a grand entrance? We just wanted to let all the kids know that we had done the impossible by riding 100 miles that day. Later, Art and I rode to Sardinia, South Carolina—150 miles—and then we turned around and rode back home through Statesboro, Georgia—a 200-mile return trip.

In the summer of 1949, we decided to visit Art's grandmother in Washington, DC. We pushed our bicycles down the train tracks past all the passenger cars to the freight car, and checked them as freight. The next morning in Washington, we again walked to the rear of the train to the freight cars, got our bicycles, and for the next two weeks made Washington, DC, our playground. We visited just about every site, locking our bikes at the entrances, and saw more of Washington, DC, than just about any other tourist. As I looked down on the U.S. Senate chambers, not even in my wildest imagination did I dream that one day I'd show my press pass and gain entrance to the Senate lounge, where I would ask a page to summon Senator Charles Grassley for an interview.

On June 8, 1950, both Art and I graduated from high school. There were approximately 500 graduates, and I was right about in the middle—number 258 in academic rank. Art was around number 450 in academic rank. But we didn't care; we were like prisoners paroled to freedom and ready to get on with life.

On graduation night, Art got his father's car—and like most high school graduates, we planned to stay up all night. We went to two or three of the drive-ins to eat, then drove out to Savannah Beach for a swim, and then we came back to see a double feature at the drive-in movie theater. After driving around got boring, we went to Al Remler's nightclub for breakfast. There were no girls along; we didn't even think about dating. About four in the morning, we got bored and went home to sleep. So much for our wild night on the town!

My high school years were filled with weekly Youth for Christ meetings, and services every Sunday morning and evening at Hope Congregational Church in St. Louis, Missouri. During the summers, I worked the registration desk at Gideon conventions, because both of my parents were active in Bible placement. When Mother asked me what I wanted to do with my life, I told her, "Marry a preacher." She told me I'd have to go to college—"where they make them"—so I could find one. We visited Wheaton College, Bob Jones University and Columbia Bible College. I chose Columbia because the faculty and staff lived simple, dedicated lives. They had a walk with God that was bigger than anything I had experienced thus far. —Ruth Towns

A couple of days after graduation, we heard about a revival going on out in the county at Bona Bella Presbyterian Church. People said things were happening just like in the book of Acts. Two brothers, Bill and Burt Harding, from Columbia Bible College were pastoring that little church, and God was showing up in "unusual" ways.

My First and Only Date with Betty

Betty Farthing phoned me, saying she wanted "to chat." This was an absolutely astounding event. I had asked that girl for a date several times, but her mother told her not to go out with me, as I wouldn't amount to anything. *Why is she phoning me?* I wondered.

Eventually Betty got around to the reason for her call. She wanted me to ask Art to borrow his father's car so we could go on a double date—to a prayer meeting at Bona Bella Presbyterian Church. Betty and me on a date—I jumped at the opportunity, even though I knew I was being used. She wanted to check out the two cute Harding brothers.

Only about 17 people attended this small prayer meeting, so we gathered behind the pulpit in a large circle. Burt Harding taught with his back to the pulpit, using a chalkboard as he preached. I had never seen anyone outline a sermon as he taught the Bible. *This is refreshing and innovative,* I thought.

When the message was over, Burt erased the board, and prayer requests were listed on the chalkboard: sick people . . . unsaved people . . . missionaries. I had never heard that kind of prayer request. *Does he really expect God to intervene?* I asked myself.

We all knelt down, and Burt expected everyone to pray. I don't remember ever kneeling in public before, and I was a little stiff and embarrassed. When my turn came, I prayed as I always had: "Dear Lord, bless the church, bless our parents, bless the children, bless . . . bless . . . bless . . ." It was a meaningless prayer, especially since I was not talking to God, but making a speech to the 17 people who were there.

The Presbyterians of Bona Bella had just built a new concrete block building. The old building could only seat 30 or 40 people; this one would hold more than 200 people. But the grand new building was still very much a work in progress. The walls were not painted, and the floor smelled of raw acidic concrete. They had installed aluminum-frame windows, but there were no screens.

When the prayer meeting began, there was sunlight outside, but during our prayer time, darkness fell and mosquitoes invaded the church. If the windows were closed, it was stifling hot. When the windows were opened to let the night air in, mosquitoes swarmed into the room. As we ended prayer, swatting mosquitoes, Burt said, "Let's pray for screens for the windows."

No, I objected silently. *You pray for spiritual things, but no one asks God for screens.* I rebelled at the idea of praying for specific material things like screens. Someone ran to count: There were 27 windows in the new church. Burt erased the chalkboard and wrote, "27 screens."

"Let's kneel again and ask God for 27 screens," Burt instructed.

I wouldn't pray. I didn't like the idea of making prayer into a shopping list.

But God heard and answered those prayers, and when He did, it transformed my thinking about prayer and about God Himself.

The following Sunday, Burt Harding was making announcements in Sunday School assembly, and he asked, "Are there any other announcements?"

Bo Burroughs owned the general store in Bona Bella—the only store in Bona Bella—and he stood up to say, "If we're going to have a revival meeting, we've gotta have screens on these windows." He explained that the screens would cost about $4.70 each, and offered to donate four screens. When Bo sat down, Mrs. Alcorn stood to ask him, "Can I buy screens for $4.70?"

"Yes, Woman, that's what I meant," the cranky storeowner replied.

"I'll buy four," Mrs. Alcorn told the church.

Quickly, Burt Harding pulled the chalkboard to the front of the auditorium. Everyone saw the phrase "27 screens." He began writing names as people volunteered. When we got close to the goal, I put up my hand and said, "I'll buy two." That's the first time I remember giving money directly to God. Previously I had just dropped a dollar into the collection plate without thinking about where it was going. But this time, I was giving to God as He answered the prayers of those who had knelt to ask Him for screens.

Going home that day, I thought, *These people can pray and get answers; they must be real Christians.* At the same time, I also thought the reverse: *I can't get answers to prayer, so I must not be a Christian.*

Later I learned that Bill and Burt Harding were praying for my salvation. They announced to the church that they would pray individually or in small groups from 5:00 to 8:00 every morning for revival. Wow . . . that long!

Bill and Burt were staying in an apartment over a garage in back of Mrs. Alcorn's home on LaRoach Avenue. Men and women on their way to work would quietly pull their cars into the large sandy backyard, and then make their way up narrow steps to a screened porch that hung out over the doors to the garage. On that porch were an old army cot and a metal glider. Bill and Burt would take turns meeting the people, in half-hour shifts. They provided a dog-eared paper listing names of young people to guide people's prayers. Each morning, they would pray for the salvation of around 60 young people: "Save Elmer Towns . . . save Art Winn . . . save Anne Perry . . . save L. J. McEwen." They prayed for several weeks for young people to be converted in that revival.

Bona Bella was on a rural mail delivery route. On about the fourth night of the revival, the mailman went forward for salvation. Afterward, he stood in front of the pulpit to give testimony: "Everyone here knows me. I'm your mailman, and I know all of you and your box numbers. Each day as I came down LaRoach Avenue towards the church, I felt heat coming from this building. When I passed the building, I felt the heat go away. After two or three days of feeling this heat, I decided to come to the revival and see what was going on."

The mailman continued, "I was raised a Baptist and was baptized by immersion as a young boy. I've been a Baptist Sunday School teacher and deacon . . . but tonight I was born again. I met the Lord, and He's in my life."

The audience erupted in shouts of "AMEN" and "HALLELUJAH!"

What the postman described as "heat," I would later in life describe as "atmospheric revival." What is revival? It is God pouring His presence out on His people. God's Shekinah glory cloud coming upon the people of the Old Testament was revival. The Holy Spirit coming upon the new church at Pentecost—"I will pour out my Spirit on all flesh" (Acts 2:18, *ESV*)—was revival. The "heat" that the postman felt was the presence of God, which is available to those who are open to Him. God was in that Presbyterian church changing lives, and within a week my life would be changed. (See the Preface for details concerning my conversion experience.).

3

The Columbia Bible College Years

(1950–1953)

I was converted on July 25, 1950, and immediately felt God's call into full-time Christian service. Since Bill and Burt Harding were students at Columbia Bible College (CBC), I felt compelled to go there to study for the ministry.

I had previously applied for and won a scholarship, sponsored by the Kiwanis Club, to attend Armstrong Junior College in Savannah, Georgia. The award was announced in the *Savannah Morning News* about two weeks before my conversion. Everyone at work congratulated my father because I had gotten a "full ride" to Armstrong College. He was disappointed when I turned it down to go to Columbia Bible College.

Mother was in South Carolina managing my grandfather's farm, so I didn't have to debate my decision with her. I think it's providential that she was not there when I turned down Armstrong College, because it was almost impossible to win an argument with her. Would she have talked me out of going to Columbia Bible College? I don't know.

I believe love can cover a multitude of sins and mend a broken heart. Elmer had a wounded ego when I first met him. Maybe it was from his mother's constant complaining. Her will dominated Elmer's life. Nothing was ever good enough for her. But at the same time, Elmer had strong self-determination, and maybe that came from his mother's great love and belief that her son could do anything he chose to do. It was my duty and privilege to love and support him, but never once did I fuss at him or lose my temper. Like his mother, I believed he would do incredible things for God. —Ruth Towns

Since the scholarship had been announced in the newspaper, I went to tell the editor—also chairman of the scholarship committee—that I was turning it down and going to Columbia Bible College. He responded, "But I thought you said you didn't have any money to go to college."

"God will take care of me," was all I could say.

That evening, I had to repeat that answer to my father. Two weeks later, when she couldn't do anything about it, I told my mother. I assured her, "God will take care of me."

I had $247 accumulated in my bank account from delivering newspapers. I drew that money out and applied it to my room, board and tuition at Columbia Bible College. The cost was $360 a semester. I laugh today at how cheap college was back then, compared to the enormous price students pay for just one course. But $360 might as well be a million dollars when you don't have anything.

I was assigned to a room with Bob Yount, a young man from Michigan who had his own car. His father was a minister, and Bob helped me understand the expectations of ministry. He told me, "You have to wear a tie," and he taught me to tie a Windsor knot.

One of the best things about CBC was that I had to go to bed every night at 10:30 and get up each morning at 6:05 to spend 30 minutes at my bed or desk, praying and studying the Bible. The floor leader checked on us to make sure we were obedient. That discipline has forever been healthy for my spirituality.

God Supplies Money

My first Sunday afternoon at Columbia, with nothing to do, I sat down to begin writing letters to all of my aunts and uncles. Remember, Mother came from a family of 11, and Dad from a family of 9. I wrote to everyone, telling each person that I had been born again, that God had called me into the ministry, and that I was studying at Columbia Bible College. I ended each letter asking the recipient to accept Christ as Savior. I did not ask for money, and never in my wildest imagination did I ever think that these letters would touch people financially. But relatives soon began sending me letters with cash or a check enclosed. The largest was for $25 from Uncle Herman and Aunt Alice, and three or four sent $5. All that money was immediately applied against my bill at the college.

Mrs. Alcorn at Bona Bella Presbyterian Church led her junior Sunday School class to help provide money as well. Her students caught crabs in the saltwater creeks around Bona Bella, cooked them in the backyard, and then went door to door selling the cooked crabs for five cents each. But they went beyond simple sales: "We're selling crabs to put a preacher through Columbia Bible College. The crab is only five cents, but would you like to give a dollar?"

I read what they did and saw the check: $25. I began to weep, went to my room, locked the door, and spread the letter and check out on the bed. "Oh God, I am so unworthy to receive this gift from these small children. Lord, I dedicate myself to studying as hard as possible and learning everything You are teaching me."

I got a job in the CBC kitchen, waiting tables for 20 cents an hour. The good thing about that job was that I didn't have to wear a white shirt and tie, saving money on laundry. They supplied a white starched serving jacket. Later I worked in the dish pit, working an hour before meals and an hour after meals. More money to apply to my bill.

Then I got a job in a chandelier store for 50 cents an hour. I climbed a tall ladder to polish the chandeliers with ammonia water. Whenever a sale was made, the store owner took me out to the customer's house, where I climbed another tall ladder to install the chandelier.

In high school, I'd had lots of money to spend, because I had a big paper route—and it was easy come, easy go. I went to the movies almost every night, and often paid for my buddies to come along. But I went to CBC to prepare for ministry, so I didn't want to waste money. I was too cheap even to get a haircut; but after I'd let my hair grow for three months, a girl said to me, "Elmer, you look like a shaggy dog; get a haircut." It was then that I discovered that some men in the dorms cut hair for 25 cents.

When Elmer and I first dated, I knew he worked hard for his money and s-t-r-e-t-c-h-e-d every penny. I had money and could have paid, but that would have embarrassed him. A Coke was not as important as his self-esteem, so I thought it would be cute to ask for "two straws." —Ruth Towns

I took Jean Anderson—Ruth Forbes's roommate—out on a date, and she ordered hamburgers, French fries and a milkshake. I got the same. That cost me more than a dollar. I later told Ruth, "Jean Anderson was a gold-digger." So when Ruth and I went out on our first date, Ruth said,

"Let's go to Seasee's Drugstore and get a Coca-Cola with two straws; I'm not very thirsty." She won my heart.

CBC's campus had been built for Columbia Theological Seminary in the early 1800s. Legster Hall, where I roomed, was more than 100 years old. Commodes had been added later, along with one shower that the 16 boys on my floor shared. The shower had been taken from some World War II army barracks; it was old and rusty. I remember some of the college guys complaining about the antiquated shower. But my response was different. When I turned the handles, I got hot, running water. I stood and cried, the hot water washing away my tears. I had never lived in a house with hot, running water before.

"Thank You, God, for hot water . . . thank You, God, I don't have to carry water in a bucket . . . thank You, Lord, I don't have to heat water on a stove." I wanted to make sure I didn't complain about the gifts God had given to me, as some of the guys on the floor were complaining. I determined very early on that *gratitude is the least remembered of all virtues, but is the acid test of character*.

Struggling with Self

I became extremely legalistic while at CBC. Students didn't go to movies, listen to secular music, dance, or participate in any other form of worldliness.

CBC taught me the deeper Christian life, but I didn't always get it right. That first year, I heard a missionary speak on this text: "Knowing this, that our old man is crucified with him, that the body of sin might be destroyed" (Rom. 6:6, *KJV*). Her sermon challenge was: "What have you crucified lately?"

Her question brought deep conviction to me. I decided to crucify my love of Ping-Pong and give it up for a week. Then I crucified my love of touch football and decided not to play with the guys. I kept looking for anything that I could "crucify" in order to get to know God more intimately.

The men's dormitories had one central furnace, with hot water pipes that ran underground to all the dormitory rooms. The furnace was turned off around 8:30 each evening, and throughout the men's campus, you could hear the pipes crack as they cooled down. When we went to bed at 10:30, the rooms were cold.

I had a small rug near my bed, and only slept in underwear. As I was praying one evening, I began to shiver and felt an urge to jump under the warm covers.

Crucify your desire for warmth, I told myself. So I kept praying until I was shivering so hard I couldn't think straight.

"This is foolish," I muttered, getting under the covers. I hunkered down on my elbows and knees, and as I continued praying, my body warmed up. Once I was toasty, guilt set in: *If you're spiritual, you'll crucify your body and not pay attention to the cold.*

So I crawled out from under the "comfy" covers, got on my knees and prayed for 5 or 10 minutes. Soon I was once again shivering so badly I couldn't think straight. So again I crawled back under the covers, hunkering down to pray—and again when I got toasty, guilt set in. Back on my knees on the floor I went.

Two or three times that evening, I jumped in and out of bed, trying to feel spiritual about praying. I think an angel may have been sitting in the corner of that darkened dorm room, laughing at Elmer Towns, who was trying so hard to please God in his flesh.

Praying for a Date

Quite often I heard that CBC was a "marriage factory," and that weddings were born among the students. Thinking I was going to be a preacher, I began to pick out girls I thought would be a good preacher's wife. However, my fleshly nature struggled against my spiritual nature, so I was trying to find the cutest, most petite young ladies in school but also the most spiritual, because that was one of my criteria. My overtures to these girls resulted in a litany of nos. It perplexed me that when I asked a girl for a date, she answered, "I have to wash my hair . . ." or "I have to write a term paper . . ." Who does those things on Friday night—date night? I heard every excuse in the world, but in my heart I knew that I was lacking in their eyes.

Then came January 1951. I had started a prayer notebook and had several pages dedicated to my various prayer requests. I had two or three pages focused on foreign missions, two or three pages dedicated to unsaved relatives, and additional pages given to praying for the salvation of friends. Then there was one page for current needs. Halfway down on the sheet of current requests, I wrote, "Ruth Forbes." I decided to ask her for a date because she was good looking and smart, and her father had money. No one had told me that, but I could tell from her expensive clothes.

God had made light and morning, water, heaven and land, and said, "It is good!"

"But when God created Adam . . ." I say to my Sunday School class of girls, "God said, 'It is not good . . . for man to be alone.'

"Adam was lonely—woman was a companion.

"Adam needed help—woman was created to be a 'help-meet.'

"Adam needed children—God made the female.

"Adam needed a homemaker—God made Eve.

"When God put Elmer and Ruth together, He gave all of that to Elmer and more. He gave everything to both of us that He knew we would ever need to serve, love, honor and obey Him."—Ruth Towns

Since Ruth Forbes was special, I knew I needed a good strategy to get her. She was assigned to my table in the dining room, so one day I told her at the table, "My talk in speech class is on, 'How to Ask a Girl for a Date.' "

"I'm coming to hear it," Ruth said to me.

"No," I said to her, "if you come, I'll ask you for a date."

She came to my speech class anyway. When it was my turn, I gave my motivational speech that included "five steps to ask a girl for a date." My last point was: "Just be bold and do it."

I turned to Ruth. "Would you go out with me on Friday night?"

The class howled; even the teacher thought it was funny. He stood before the class and told Ruth, "Your answer will determine his grade; if you say, 'No,' he flunks."

"Sure, why not!" Ruth said. "Does he get an *A*?"

I went home and wrote in my prayer notebook, "AMEN . . . HALLELUJAH . . . PRAISE THE LORD." I considered this to be one of the biggest answers to prayer that I had experienced to that moment. I had banged on the windows of heaven, and God had opened them.

We talked about our date even before we went out together. I had really wanted to go out with Mary Faith Phillips, who was by far the most brilliant girl in our class. Ruth had wanted to go out with cute Dwayne Black, the red-haired president of our freshman class. So we decided that we would build a strategy to help each of us get a date with our desired one.

On our date, when I opened the door for Ruth, she said, "Thank you, Dwayne."

I responded, "You're welcome, Mary Faith."

When I first met Elmer, I realized how narrow his world was. He had been very few places and seen little of God's work in the world. We always had missionaries in our house, and some of the world's greatest slept in my bed, while I slept on the couch. I determined to help him live in a world much broader than his perception of it had been so far. Yet, Elmer had a vivid grasp of his inner world, and he had a walk with God that I wanted. He never forgot anything God did for him. On our first date, he rattled off every sermon from every chapel held during our first semester at CBC—and I had forgotten everything about all of them. I wanted to learn that inner world where he lived with God. —Ruth Towns

We laughed about it all evening, and we pledged to help each other get the dates we wanted. I think Ruth had one date with Dwayne Black, and I had one date with Mary Faith. For each of us, those dates were strained. We kept coming back to date each other because we were comfortable together. Ruth and I were friends, and we enjoyed each other's company.

During the last week of April, in our first year of college, I felt a new urge in my heart. For the first time, I felt a deep love for someone. I loved Ruth. I didn't know how to properly express it, so on our next date I simply said, "Ruth, I think I'm falling in love with you."

I went back to my room that evening and began to pray, "Lord, I don't like his name—'Elmer.' I don't want to be married to someone with the name 'Elmer.' " Then I yielded myself to God: "Lord, if Elmer is Your will, give me a love for him, and his name." God answered both requests. —Ruth Towns

Columbia Bible College had a rule that freshman dating couples could only have one date a week—they could go out on Friday night, Saturday night or Sunday night. Ruth and I usually went out on Friday night; we wanted to see each other as soon as possible. If a couple was caught talking together for more than two or three minutes during the week, they were given demerits. I want you to know that I got demerits several times, because I just had to talk to Ruth. When we couldn't talk, we wrote notes—I even began writing poetry to her.

As sure as the ivy grows 'round the stump,
  Ruth is my own sweet sugar lump.
Roses are red,
  Violets are blue,
The angels in heaven know,
  I surely love you.

It may sound corny, but the words came from the depths of someone who was starved for love—and who had given his love to Ruth.

Too Young to Be Used Greatly

When I first attended Columbia Bible College, I was part of an evangelistic street meeting every Saturday night. About 10 or 12 young men would gather on the corner of Main and Gervais Streets in downtown Columbia to pray for souls to be saved that evening. Then we would spread out around downtown Columbia, each one inviting three or four people to attend the street meeting with them. That way, approximately 10 young men would create a crowd of more than 30.

Every great love story between a man and a woman is better understood by seeing it in light of an enemy that attempted to keep the couple apart. Sometimes the antagonist is a person, or circumstances, or a war—in our case, it was the rules at Columbia Bible College. What I hated then—rules that kept us apart—I now appreciate, because "forced" separation actually intensified our love for each other. —Ruth Towns

The Army trained new recruits at Fort Jackson on the outskirts of Columbia. These recruits walked the streets aimlessly on Saturday nights; it was always easy to get three or four soldiers to come with you to the street meeting.

A different one of the 10 CBC men preached each Saturday evening, and because I was faithful in attendance, I expected to get a turn to preach. The rotation went around to all the other students, and then it started again. I complained, "Hey, guys, when do I get to preach?"

Because I was extremely young-looking for my age, and probably immature, they passed over me without giving a reason. I continued to ask for my opportunity, and finally I was assigned a Saturday night in February 1951. Another freshman, Gladdie Kreimann, was given the responsibility to lead the singing. The two of us decided to skip lunch for five days and meet in Legster Hall's prayer room to intercede for evangelistic results on the following Saturday night.

"Oh God," I poured my heart out to God, "please save young soldiers on Saturday when I preach."

Saturday night the weather turned bitter; there was a stiff wind and a hint of moisture in the air. Only three CBC guys showed up: Gladdie Kreimann, the organ player and myself. When we got to Main Street, we committed the evening to God in prayer, and then headed out to bring soldiers back. Gladdie led a song with only five or six soldiers, and the singing was pathetically inept. The wind muffled our voices, and there was no group feeling because we couldn't hear one another sing. After two songs, Gladdie turned it over to me to preach.

Shocked by the brevity of the singing, I stumbled into the Scripture reading: "Enter ye in at the strait gate: for wide is the gate, and broad is the way, that leadeth to destruction, and many there be which go in thereat: Because strait is the gate, and narrow is the way, which leadeth unto life, and few there be that find it" (Matt. 7:13-14, *KJV*).

I launched aggressively into my sermon and preached everything I could think of in only three minutes. *Whoa,* I thought to myself, *a sermon has got to be longer than three minutes.* The sermons of other preachers lasted 15 to 20 minutes, so I preached my sermon again—and by then about five minutes had elapsed.

"Let's sing an invitational hymn . . . 'Just as I am without one plea.' "

I gave an invitation for people to come forward and receive Christ. Not one of the five or six soldiers moved from his spot. They didn't even look me in the eye; they stared down as they muttered the words of the hymn. I think we may have sung two verses.

I lifted my hand to offer the benediction—the normal kind of benediction heard from a pastor after a Sunday morning sermon. Right before I said, "Amen," there came a tremendous shout over the crowd: "MAY I SAY A WORD . . ." We looked up to see a towering man—he had to be almost seven feet tall—with shoulders like a football linebacker and greasy, black hair combed straight back. He appeared to me to be a Native American.

"GOD HAS TOLD US ABOUT HEAVEN . . ." The Native American evangelist's voice spread out over the corner, his words piercing the hearts of anyone standing within 40 or 50 feet. "I'M GOING TO TELL YOU HOW TO GO TO HEAVEN."

I watched carefully as he preached standing on his tiptoes. When he got near the six soldiers, he began backing up, pulling them with him up against the building. That way, anyone walking the streets could pass the crowd—but they didn't. Everyone within the sound of this penetrating sermon joined the crowd, which swelled to more than 20 listeners.

Cars going both ways began to stop near the curbs of both Main and Gervais Streets. Within five minutes, the crowd swelled to more than 40. I could feel the presence of God hunkering down over that listening audience—there was power in the Word of God. The Native American quoted entire chapters of Scripture—Isaiah 2, then Isaiah 4, and finally all of Isaiah 11. Later, he quoted most of Revelation 22. He preached for more than 30 minutes, and now more than 60 people were standing around him. Cars were double parked on the curb as their drivers listened spellbound to the sermon.

Then, with a loud shout—almost like an Indian charge during a battle with settlers a hundred years ago—the evangelist pointed his finger to the ground. "KNEEL!" he yelled.

His authoritative demand swept young soldiers to their knees—there must have been eight or nine soldiers who immediately dropped to a kneeling position. I sprang into action, opening my Bible for a soldier to read, then explaining the plan of salvation. They read the Scriptures with me through weeping eyes. First, one prayed to receive Christ, and then another, and then another.

I walked on my knees over to two other young soldiers, and again went through the plan of salvation. After they prayed, I walked—still on my knees—over to three more soldiers. Gladdie Kreimann was doing the same thing, as was the organist.

Then there was silence. There were no more preaching and no more commands to "KNEEL." I heard only the sound of the winter wind. The evangelist was gone, and I hadn't gotten to meet him or shake his hand.

Later, when I shared this story, people tried to tell me that the Native American evangelist was really an angel of God. But I've always resisted that urge, remembering that angels are "ministering spirits . . . for those who will inherit salvation" (Heb. 1:14). They don't preach the gospel to unsaved people; that's our job. If angels did preach, why wouldn't God have used them to evangelize the world by now? But God has a different way to reach the lost. God has given the command for His children to bring the gospel to them.

That cold February evening, my first sermon was both a rousing success and a dismal failure. Twenty to 30 people responded and were saved. But God in heaven didn't use Elmer Towns and Gladdie Kreimann—two young, inexperienced servants—to accomplish that. We were too weak. God heard our incessant banging on the windows of heaven; and when we continually asked for souls to be saved, He determined to answer our prayer. But since my sermon was feeble, and our attempts were weak, God led one of His more experienced servants—the Native-American evangelist—to the street meeting and used him. His spiritual gifts and abilities were equal to the challenge of the evening.

That street meeting gave me a glimpse into future usefulness: The greatness of any of my attempts to serve would be, "Not I, but Christ." For instance, when it came to founding Liberty University, God used the effective leadership of Jerry Falwell, and I just happened to be along to help guide and organize the academic structure of the seminary. Jerry Falwell was the founder and prime mover of Liberty University. I was privileged to become one of Liberty's many teachers, along with Pierre Guillermin, Ed Hindson, Harold Willmington, Glynn Wooldridge, and an army of other qualified instructors.

Summer Away from CBC

After my first year of college, I left CBC on a warm spring day, carrying a large cardboard suitcase. I walked about two miles until I got to Highway 321; from there, I would hitchhike home. Everything I possessed was in that cardboard suitcase, and my heart overflowed with praise to God. I had prayed and trusted God—and through gifts and some part-time work, He had provided more than $800 to pay all my bills. Clearly, God had answered my request. I was crying, but happy. In fact, it had been the happiest year in my life. "Lord, thank You for one year of training."

I looked to the bleak financial future: "And, Lord, if I never get to come back, this has been the most wonderful experience of my life."

Where would I get the money to pay the $360 room and board, tuition and fees for the fall semester? I didn't know!

Finding God's Wonderful Plan

For the first two weeks of summer, I worked at Ben Lippen School, high in the top of the mountains above Asheville, North Carolina. I was paid five dollars a week, plus all my meals. I stayed in a cabin with the young boys who were participating in the school's summer Bible camp. I arrived early to help clean the winter dust from the cabins, and one night I stayed up late, mopping the floors of the large dining hall. I was alone, because the other two guys working with me had gone to bed. But I wouldn't quit until I had finished the entire job. Wearing only blue jeans rolled up to my knees—no shoes or shirt—I had a hose running to mop the floor. As I worked, I came face to face with a small blue sign tacked to a post in the middle of the room. Silver lettering on the sign read:

GOD HAS A WONDERFUL PLAN FOR YOUR LIFE.

I snickered, "Yeah . . . God has a plan for me to wash the floor so my buddies can sack out." Then, resting my chin on the top of the mop, I thought about the meaning of each of the words in that sign.

God . . . yes, the Lord of the heavens has a purpose for my life, I reacted positively. Yes, God purposed for me to mop the floor that night—and I would do the best possible job.

". . . *has* . . ." I realized that if I found God's will and did it today, He would take care of all my tomorrows.

That night I believed that God would take care of me financially, even though $360 seemed like a million dollars. I was no longer afraid of the amount of the money; I trusted God.

When I got back to Savannah, I found a job as a carpenter's helper at Mingledorf's Shipyard, about 15 miles from my home. Mr. Ernest Miller, the Jewish man who was saved at the Bona Bella revival, picked me up around 5:15 every morning in his 1929 Model T Ford. We began work at 6:00 and got off at 3:00 in the afternoon.

I was assigned to a non-Christian carpenter who also led a country and western dance band on the weekends. That put me in constant contact each day with a man who didn't share my core values, but he did not fight Christianity. In fact, I had many opportunities to share Jesus Christ with him. As a result, everyone on the job called me "Preacher."

The foreman was simply called "T," and he liked me, both because I was studying for the ministry and because I was a hard worker. We were working on the aircraft carrier *Hornet*. The landing deck and inside compartments of the ship were being gutted, making room for large bins for grain hauling. As the steel was taken from the *Hornet*, our job was to line the bins with 2x6 planks.

I grew up attending Camp Tadmore in the Ozark Mountains; it was our church camp. I experienced many emotions there growing up as a kid. Christ became real to me in those summer devotionals. When I came home from Columbia Bible College, I became a counselor at the same camp where I had learned my lessons. But this time, Elmer Towns had become my main romantic interest. We were writing letters to each other every day.
—Ruth Towns

One day, "T" came by and told us to slow down, find a nook someplace, and hide. Other carpenters and helpers were being laid off, and later I realized that "T" was trying to save my job so I could get the money I needed to go back to Columbia Bible College. But I was a perfectionistic workaholic who had to be nervously working. I wouldn't hide, though other workers did.

The next day at 6:00 A.M., "T" took me to a large pile of 2x6s on the dock, each one around 12 feet long. "T" instructed me, "I want you to take this entire pile of 2x6s into bin #3." He specifically told me I couldn't take two boards at a time. "Carry only one at a time." I was to walk up six stories of wooden stairs to the deck of the ship. Then I had to climb down crudely constructed stairs six stories into the bottom of bin #3. All day long I worked, transporting one 2x6 at a time. Right before quitting time, "T" approached me with six or seven workmen and feigned displeasure. He brought a crowd of workers with him and, laughing sarcastically, yelled, "TOWNS, WHAT ARE YOU DOING?"

I reacted in horror.

"I told you to put those 2x6s in bin #4. They're all in bin #3."

The crowd of workers began to cackle with laughter. I was in trouble. Then "T" whistled through his teeth to the crane operator, who lowered cables into bin #3. Within two minutes, my entire stack was in bin #4.

I was embarrassed and angry, knowing I had done exactly what "T" told me to do. But as I look back on that day, I see a very conscientious, perfectionistic 18-year-old kid who wanted to work as hard as he could—and I see "T" as a wise old curmudgeon of a man who made work for me in order to save my job, so I could earn money to go back to Columbia Bible College.

God Supplies My Need

Later that summer, I got a phone call from Al Aldridge, owner of a small business out near the shipyard. He asked me to meet him at his place for lunch on Saturday. My German racing bike got me there in quick time, and he took me to a nearby café for lunch. I tried to pay, but he wouldn't hear of it. He inquired, "Exactly how much money have you saved to go back to Columbia Bible College?"

At $1.00 an hour, I had accumulated more than $150—and I still had it all, because I was afraid to spend anything.

Then Al asked, "Can you come to my men's Sunday School class at Independent Presbyterian Church tomorrow?"

I showed up thinking I was just going to teach the class. I was wrong. I gave a testimony about my salvation and the calling of God upon my life to full-time ministry. When I finished, Al said to the other men in the class, "I think we ought to take this young man on as a financial project for the year."

One of the men raised his hand and asked, "How much is room, board and fees per semester?"

"Three hundred sixty dollars." They laughed at how inexpensive the cost was—though to me it still seemed like an insurmountable mountain.

"Our men's Sunday School class will take care of that for you from now on."

I blinked, not knowing how to respond. I should have shouted—or ran up to shake each hand—but I didn't know what to do. I just continued to say, "Thank you . . . thank you . . . thank you."

For the next two years, I received a check for $360 at the beginning of each semester. I had trusted God for the biggest amount of money I had ever needed, and God had supplied it. I was beginning to learn that God had a plan for my life, and He would take care of my financial needs.

Life's Second Biggest Decision

Sunday, September 27, was a warm and beautiful day during my second year at Columbia Bible College. I left the men's dorm and headed for the dining room. This was the biggest day of my life.

An elderly couple sat on their front porch, and I noticed some late-blooming deep red roses in their yard. I approached them: "Good afternoon . . ." They recognized me from CBC. Then I broached the big subject: "I plan to ask a young lady to be my wife today, and I would love to give her one of those red roses from your yard."

Almost as if she had been shot from a gun, the lady sprang into action, bringing scissors and carefully looking at the roses. I chose the biggest and most beautiful flower. The woman tried to give me a dozen roses, but I thought there was a message of simple sincerity in a single red rose.

We ate lunch at one o'clock, and at two o'clock the bell would ring for all the girls to return to their dormitory rooms for the mandatory Sunday afternoon nap. Ruth and I sat in the lobby of the dining room, and I waited for the right moment to give her the rose. Finally, at around five minutes to two, I got on my knee, and she realized that this was the moment all girls dream of.

"I want you to have this rose; it is a symbol of my undying love . . ." I told her. I had written a poem to express my love and to ask her to marry me. I didn't want to say, "Will you marry *me*?" That put too much emphasis on my part of the bargain. So I said, "Will you be my wife?"

"Uh-huh," was all that Ruth could say, she was so overwhelmed with the moment. I danced my way back to the men's dormitory a block away. Ballroom dancing was not allowed at Columbia Bible College, but that day I couldn't keep my feet still. I prayed, *"Lord, this is the greatest day of my life. I've done what You have led me to do; now take care of us as we serve You."*

We had been apart all summer but had written every day. By this time, I was very sure that I was in love with my best friend. Our goals and visions for serving the Lord blended, and our spiritual growth—both as individuals and together—had been constant. We were both eager to return to college in September, knowing that the first priority was not the classroom. The separation had confirmed our love and desire to spend our lives together.

Elmer was a true romantic. One Sunday afternoon, with students milling around us, he suddenly dropped to one knee and pulled a poem from his pocket. With everyone's attention turned toward us, he read the questions in poetic form. Then he explained that if I said "yes," I needed to understand that I would never be number one with him—that he would always put the Lord first in his life, but if we did it together, we would be happy "So, will you be my wife?" he asked.

"Uh-huh," was all I could answer.

A bell signaled time to go—and as I held my poem tightly and started up the stairs to my dorm room, I knew that being second place to God was exactly where I wanted to be. —Ruth Towns

At Christmastime, Ruth and I went to St. Louis to spend the holidays with her parents. That was my first experience of living "up North"—even though it was really the Midwest. While we were in St. Louis, Mr. and Mrs. Forbes negotiated a "deal" for me to buy Ruth an engagement ring. We picked out a quarter solitaire that cost $175, and I put down a few dollars—maybe as much as $15. "Pay us when you can," Mrs. Forbes said.

Over the next two years, I paid in small increments of $5 or $10 each. I had this large, red piggy bank on the mantelpiece in my dormitory room, and when students came in, I would always exhort them to "feed the pig." Then I would explain, "I gotta pay for that ring."

So all the men on my floor got used to "feeding the pig." By my third year of college, I was floor leader over the single men's barracks. There were 24 men in an old renovated army barracks. The men had lots of reasons to come into my room, and I always exhorted them, "Feed the pig." As a result, many of the men at Columbia Bible College can testify that they helped buy Ruth's engagement ring.

But the ring caused a problem. Ruth wore it in St. Louis, but didn't bring it back to campus. There was a rule against announcing engagements during the school year, and you had to have permission from the social committee to announce an engagement even in the summertime. The school watched every part of our lives to make sure we made mature, sensible decisions.

Wearing the ring in St. Louis meant we broke the rule, so I had to pay. I was brought before the social committee and given 10 to 20 hours of punishment work. I sat in the Christian service office and stamped the back of gospel tracts with Columbia Bible College's address. When those were all done, I was sent out to dig up the roots of a tree, using only an axe and shovel. The hole was deep, and the work was hard, but whenever some students walked by, I sang:

I love Ruth,
  A bushel and a peck
A bushel and a peck
  And a hug around the neck.

It was a corny song, but it was my way of laughing as I worked. Remember, I had learned to make work fun, so I didn't mind digging the stump out of the ground.

Called to Pastor a Church

In September 1952, I visited Savannah and led singing at a Youth for Christ rally. I enjoyed the opportunity to motivate people to sing from the bottom of their hearts, so I led choruses with gusto. After the service, a short lady came to the platform and asked, "Would you come and preach at my church tomorrow?"

The Westminster Presbyterian Church was a beautiful, old, colonial structure with a high steeple and bell, four large columns on the front porch that reached two stories into the sky, and 10 beautifully adorned stained-glass windows. But it was located in an area soon to be designated "inner-city."

The presbytery had shut down the church, but Silla Hair had a key, and she thought, *A church ought to have a place to teach children.* So she opened the church, cleaned it, and got four ladies to help gather children every Sunday to teach the Bible. They didn't have a worship service—that's where I came in.

The following morning, I was unprepared, but preached based on my personal devotions from 1 Timothy 2:1-5. I spoke about how God answers prayer. It wasn't a great sermon, but after it was over, Mrs. Hair asked, "Would you stay over and preach for us tonight?" She had already checked to find out that the Seaboard Railway had a train leaving Savannah at approximately 8:00 that night, arriving in Columbia at 10:30.

"I'm supposed to be in my room by 10:30," I answered her.

"Surely," she reasoned, "a Bible college would let you come in late if you had an opportunity to preach."

That afternoon, Mrs. Hair and I, along with some of the other ladies, began canvassing the neighborhood to invite people to the 6:00 evening service.

One of my visits was to the home of the Miller family (not the Miller family of Bona Bella, where I had been converted); the back of their house was kitty-corner to the back of the church. Mr. Miller lay on the living room couch without his shirt, snoring loudly, sleeping off a hangover. He had gotten soused on Saturday, and here he was drunk again on Sunday.

I sat at the dining room table, trying to lead a daughter, Edith Miller, to the Lord. I carefully went through John 3:1-8, emphasizing how Jesus had told Nicodemus, "You must be born again." Edith had a lot of questions, and I tried to answer each one of them from the Word of God. She didn't get saved that evening, even though I tried to convince her to pray to receive Christ.

I stayed much longer than I'd intended—so long that I was still there when Mrs. Miller warmed up some Sunday leftovers for supper.

Walking out of the back of the house toward the church, I prayed, "Oh God, I've got to preach tonight, and I don't know what to say." I confessed to the Lord that my heart was open and promised that if He would speak and fill my heart, I would speak boldly for Him. Then I felt the Lord saying, "*Preach on Nicodemus.*" I decided to tell the church what I had told Edith Miller: "You must be born again."

As I was leading singing, I saw Mr. Miller slip in the back door and sit on the rear seat. He had heard my whole conversation with his daughter and was embarrassed to be drunk in front of the preacher. God used my conversation with Edith to convict him of his sin. He immediately took a bath and came to church.

As I approached the end of the sermon, I remembered how the tall, muscular Native American evangelist had given the invitation. I recalled him bending over, pointing to the ground, and yelling, "KNEEL." I'm a pretty good copycat, so I employed the same theatrics in the front at that little Presbyterian church. I bent at the waist, pointed to the altar, and yelled, "KNEEL." I put my hand out to the 15 or so adults attending the evening church service. "Come and kneel and get born again." Suddenly, Mr. Miller jumped from his seat, hurried down the aisle, and fell on his face at the church altar. Quickly I was beside him, showing him the plan of salvation from God's Word. That night a former drunk prayed to receive Christ, and he would become a sterling testimony for Jesus Christ in the community. He often went with me to knock on doors, and his former reputation gave great credibility to our invitation for people to attend that little church.

On my way to the train station that first evening, I stopped in for a quick visit with Mr. George Kessler, father of Silla Hair. He was dying, so I asked him the question "Have you ever been born again?"

"I like that question," he said to me. "Everybody talks about being a Christian, but many people have joined the Church and have the name of Christian, yet they don't have Jesus Christ."

Then he told me that he had been born again and was ready to meet his Maker. That week he died, and his funeral was planned for 2:00 on Saturday afternoon. I was to be the preacher, but no one told me that.

My First Funeral Was a Failure

Early Saturday morning, I left Columbia Bible College to hitchhike 150 miles back to Savannah. I was amazed at how quickly I caught a ride, and how swiftly I made it home. As I walked into our house at about 1:30 in the afternoon, mother yelled that I had to conduct a funeral at 2:00. Quickly I put on a white shirt and a suit, got on my German racing bicycle, and sped across Savannah (the church was seven miles away), arriving a few minutes before 2:00.

All the way there, I kept praying, *"God help me . . . God help me . . . God help me . . ."* I had never performed a funeral—I didn't even remember ever attending a funeral. I had no idea how to conduct one, and I was scared silly.

As I walked into the church, Reverend Carroll Segall met me and said, "I heard you were going to do your first funeral, so I thought you might need some help."

"Thank God," was all I could say. I told Reverend Segall that I would do everything he told me to do. So, when he told me to pray, I did. When he told me to read the Scriptures, I did. The funeral service went well.

But they were burying Mr. Kessler at a cemetery called Ebenezer—35 miles outside of town, in an old Moravian community—where early settlers were buried. Mr. Segall said, "I don't have time to go up to the cemetery, but you can do it by yourself." Then he told me that when we arrived at the cemetery, I should stand at the back of the hearse, walk in front of the casket to the hole in the ground, and then read a verse, pray, and go over and shake the hands of all the family members sitting under the small tent. After that, I should nod to the funeral director, who would then take over.

Everything went according to Mr. Segall's direction. I waited until the family was seated, and the crowd from the following cars had gathered around the open grave. I quoted from memory John 14:1-4. Then, instead of praying, I remembered a burial scene in a movie where John Wayne had taken some dirt, sprinkled it over the casket, and said, "Ashes to ashes, dust to dust."

That's me, I thought to myself. So I picked up a large glob of red Georgia clay—which, unfortunately, had been baked brick-hard by the blazing Georgia sun. I held it out over the open casket and said dramatically, "Ashes to ashes, dust to dust . . ." I tried to break the rock in my hand, but it wouldn't break. I squeezed so hard my fist shook, but still the sun-baked red clay would not break.

Then, out of the corner of my eye, I saw some people grinning at me.

They're laughing at me, I thought to myself, compounding the problem. I pressed my thumb against the red clay and repeated, "Ashes to ashes, dust to dust." Finally, putting my Bible under one arm, I took two hands to break up the clay. It was still in large pieces, but I dropped them on the top of the casket—which was made from molded tin. To my horror, I heard *clank . . . clank . . . clank . . .* I didn't dare look anyone in the eyes.

I tried to salvage the scene by saying, "Let's pray." By the time I walked over to shake hands with the family, my neck was beet red—not from the hot Georgia sun, but from extreme embarrassment. As quickly as I could, I went to stand beside the hearse, in which I would ride back to the church. The funeral director walked up to me, extended his fist and instructed, "Hold out your hand."

I didn't understand what he wanted, but he motioned again. So I held my hand out, and he opened his fist to reveal a small flower. Then, crushing the petals into my waiting palm, he suggested, "Next time, take a flower and crush it over the casket."

That was easy for him to say—he wasn't the one who had just embarrassed himself. But he prepared the way for my future ministry, saying, "I saw everybody look at you; they were not laughing at you, but rather with you." He continued, trying to calm my fears: "I could see those people loved you and were pulling for you; they will follow you wherever you will go." He concluded, "You will make a great pastor some day."

After the hearse ride back to the church, Mrs. Hair sent a young boy to invite me to her house for the evening meal. It's typical for Southern neighbors to bring a lot of food for the family after a funeral. About 20 of Mr. Kessler's family members sat in a large circle around the perimeter of the dining room. I slinked over to a corner of the room with my plate of food, trying to be as inconspicuous as possible. I didn't want to confront again the embarrassment of hard, red-clay rocks falling on the casket. Finally, Silla Hair interrupted the conversation to say, "Preacher, do you have any words from Scripture for us?"

I was shocked and didn't know what to say. So I read John 3:1-8 and explained it phrase by phrase, concluding with "You must be born again." Then I pointed individually to each person in the room and asked the identical question: "Have you been born again?" I didn't ask if they were Christians, or if they were members of the Presbyterian Church.

Each one answered, "Yes," all the way around the room. Not a single negative.

However, in the next few months, more than half of the people in that room came to hear me preach, walked the aisle, and were born again. On each occasion, they remarked that when I had first asked them that question, they had answered wrongly. Apparently, the question of being born again sunk deep into their hearts.

Silla Hair's second husband was another one of the drunks in the neighborhood who were saved in that little Presbyterian church. As a matter of fact, throughout my ministry at Westminster, several of those with alcohol problems came forward to get saved and went on to live for God. From that evening, I learned the power of putting people on the spot. Don't assume anyone is saved. Ask.

In 1997, I wrote a book called *Stories About My First Church*, which includes a multitude of stories from my Westminster days.[1] Many of the tales are humorous—others are pathetic, because they tell mostly of the failures I had as a 19-year-old pastor at a refined Presbyterian church. I thank God for the people in West Savannah who connected with my preaching and encouraged me in ministry. Because of them, I learned more about serving Christ than I had at any other place up until that time. I learned that God can use a pastor, no matter how old he is and no matter how little he knows. God uses those who are surrendered to His will and diligently seek to glorify His name.

4

The Northwestern Years: The Long, Cold, Dark Winter's Night

(1953–1954)

Why in the world would I leave Columbia Bible College in comfortable South Carolina to transfer to Northwestern College in frigid Minnesota? God was at CBC, and He was speaking to me on a regular basis there. I had lots of friends and a weekend church, and a Sunday School class was paying my college bills. Why change?

Sometimes our lives are defined by our decisions to jump out of the boat like Peter and attempt to walk on water. Leaving CBC was my opportunity to walk on water. But like Peter, I began to sink.

There were all kinds of forces weighing on me as I approached my senior year at CBC. I had gotten married. Could two live as cheaply as one? The ministers of the Savannah Presbytery were telling me I needed a liberal arts education. I was draft age, and the Korean War was lusting for more soldiers. The desire of my heart was to attend Fuller Theological Seminary, but Fuller told me I couldn't be accepted from Columbia Bible College, because it was not accredited.

Dr. Charles Woodbridge had been a pastor in the Savannah Presbytery, ministering at the Independent Presbyterian Church in downtown Savannah—by far the largest and most influential church in our presbytery. Dr. Woodbridge had left the pastorate to join the faculty at Fuller. I knew that was where I wanted to go and felt confident that Dr. Woodbridge could get me in. In reality, Fuller rejected my application on three different occasions.

My father-in-law was wise and godly, and I trusted him. He also liked Fuller and promised to help me financially if I went there. He suggested that I transfer to Northwestern College in Minneapolis. Northwestern was the "hot one" among Christian colleges, because Billy Graham was president (though Graham resigned before I got there). Because Northwestern was so popular, Mr. Forbes thought it was accredited, and I naively never asked if that was really the case. When Ruth and I arrived at Northwestern, we found out that it was *not* accredited. What's more, in academic reputation, it was not as well accepted as Columbia Bible College.

While at Northwestern, I continued to pray for the opportunity to attend Fuller to open up, but it didn't. I banged on that "shut door," claiming the promise: "Ask, and it will be given to you; seek, and you will find; knock, and it will be opened to you" (Matt. 7:7). But the Fuller door didn't budge—at least, not for a very long time. Thirty years later, I completed a Doctor of Ministry degree there, writing my dissertation on "Analysis of the Gift of Faith in Church Growth."

One of the greatest pleasures of a winter snowstorm is creating a big fat snowman. It's fun to choose a hat or a colorful neck scarf or a whole fashion ensemble for him (or her). So you might understand when I say that Elmer's first snowman was one of our greatest pleasures that first winter day in Minnesota. I sat at our window and watched my Southern husband build a snowman for the very first time. He actually played with the snow while he precisely created his masterpiece. This was the first time he'd ever seen snow in his life. Sometimes the simplest things give the most satisfaction.
—Ruth Towns

Becoming a Youth Pastor

Ruth and I ended up renting a place near the intersection of Fifty-third and Central Avenues, about five miles north of Minneapolis. Our first Sunday there, we visited the New Brighton Community Church a few miles away. As I walked into that church of about 300 people, I was asked to become the youth pastor, just because I was a student at Northwestern College. That evening, I began youth meetings with about 30 to 40 high schoolers.

I preached to the youth every week for a year, and many were saved, but in the end, they taught me more about life and ministry than I taught them about Christianity.

I drove a school bus in the area, so I was with the students five days a week, early in the morning and late at night. I lost some of the legalism I had acquired living with "spiritually minded" men in a CBC dorm. In Minneapolis, I learned to deal with problems facing Christian youth in a secular high school. I developed an extensive ministry for young people that found its way into print in my first two books: *Teaching Teens* and *Successful Biblical Youth Work.*[1]

I was more than a youth worker; I was the young people's pastor. Based on that understanding, I later developed the premise: "A youth leader is an extension of the senior church pastor's ministry into the lives of young people. Everything the senior pastor does for his congregation, the youth leader does for his young people."[2]

Because Northwestern was a liberal arts college, I took more philosophy, logic, history, literature and arts courses than I had at Columbia Bible College. But neither Ruth nor I ever lost our vision of preparation for ministry.

We didn't have a television and didn't listen to the radio. So in the evenings Elmer practiced his preaching on me. He stood in front of the fireplace with only an open Bible. When a topic came to mind, I'd throw it out, and he would preach a five-minute extemporaneous sermon—no notes, no preparation. He just did it instantly, with no breaks or stopping. I always told him what was good. The only corrections I made were to his pronunciation. If he was going to preach all over America, he couldn't let his "Southernisms" be a barrier. I never told him his weaknesses or mistakes. I wanted to build him up, not tear him down. —Ruth Towns

Tough Penniless Days

Having very little money, we only spent about $4 for groceries each week. We went through the little A&P grocery store together—and when Ruth picked up a can of soup that was selling for 13 cents, I would check the price, put it back, and then pick up a 9-cent can. Sometimes, I could save almost a dollar a week shopping behind her.

That first year, we ate a lot of macaroni and cheese. It was good back then. Also, there were a lot of tuna fish casseroles, because tuna was only 35 cents a can, and noodles were 5 cents.

My mother always bought Pepsi-Cola by the 24-bottle case. So I insisted we buy 24 bottles of Pepsi; Elmer didn't want to spend that much, but he did it anyway. We left them outside to keep cold, and the following morning all the bottles had burst. I learned my lesson. We lost all of our Pepsi-Cola and did without for the rest of the year. —Ruth Towns

One evening, Ruth put a candle on the dining table and announced that we would fast the next day, because there wasn't enough food in the pantry, and I wouldn't get paid until Friday evening. I remember praying something like this: "Lord, You've always taken care of our needs, and I know You can take care of them now. Thank You for this food. We eat rejoicing in what You've provided and knowing that You will provide more tomorrow."

When we were single, we could eat what we wanted, but when we got married, we couldn't always afford what we wanted. The fact is that we could buy tuna fish for 35 cents a can. I made tuna fish casserole frequently! When we first got married, we both liked tuna, but it wasn't very long before we had both had enough! Now when tuna casserole is served, we eat it politely, but we don't make it at home anymore! —Ruth Towns

Ding-dong. The front doorbell rang, and we looked out the window to see the cleaning truck. We thought he had come to pick up dirty laundry.

"We have no laundry," Ruth greeted him at the door, knowing we couldn't afford to get anything cleaned.

"I didn't come to pick up laundry; I came to give you 20 dollars," the man said.

Three months earlier, during an unusually cold snap, the pipes in the crawl space under the kitchen had frozen, and we had no water, either hot or cold. I borrowed a blowtorch from the school bus garage, and they instructed me how to use it: "Be very careful that you don't melt the solder or burn the house down."

I crawled under the kitchen floor to thaw the pipes. I kept telling God, "I don't have money for a plumber; help me."

God did help me, and I got the pipes unfrozen.

Then, three months later, the owner of the house sent us 20 dollars by the man from the dry cleaners. He had forgotten to pay me for unfreezing the pipes until that moment. I learned that God is always on time, and that when you commit your needs to Him, He will always come through.

Dallas Opens Its Doors

Remember, Fuller Seminary was closed to me. All winter long I was in a dark hole, not knowing what to do after graduation. When spring came, I was invited to a picnic at the home of Dr. Terry Hulbert, a faculty member at Northwestern. There were about six students there that evening, and Dr. Hulbert was going to try to talk us into going to Dallas Theological Seminary (DTS). I wasn't that interested in Dallas. It was unaccredited, just like Northwestern College. I still thought I could pray and change God's mind so that I could get into Fuller.

Dr. Hulbert brought us into his office and pointed to a stack of about 15 books on his desk. He told us, "These books were all written by professors at Dallas Theological Seminary. When you pick out a seminary, go study from the men who write the books; don't go to another seminary where you study from someone else who is only teaching their books."

That sounded brilliant to me, so I filled out an application that evening and was eventually accepted into DTS. At the time, I didn't see the plan of God, but He was going before me to open up doors where I should go—and He was sending me to places where I would have a teaching ministry.

To Become a Teacher

My advisor and Bible teacher, Dr. Edward Simpson, confirmed God's call to a teaching ministry. In the senior exegesis class, we were all assigned a passage from 1 Peter to teach in class. Our presentations were to focus on the use of the Greek language. Today, I don't remember what portion of Scripture I taught, but I do remember that when I got finished, Dr. Simpson said, "Elmer, you ought to be a teacher in a Bible college when you graduate from seminary."

I heard what he said, but raised a question: "Shouldn't I go out and pastor a church for about 20 years, get some good experience, and then go teach in a Bible college?"

Dr. Simpson had the perfect answer: "You don't teach your experience; you teach the Word of God." He went on to explain that the Word of God is powerful, and the message of Scripture can stand on its own legs—I didn't need experience to give it credibility. From that moment on, I planned to be a teacher in a college. I had no idea where I would teach, but I determined to pay whatever price was required to become the best teacher I could be.

Then I did what I previously thought was impossible: I graduated from college, receiving my B.A. on June 4, 1954. The only guests I had that night were Mr. and Mrs. Forbes, my in-laws. I was on my way to Dallas, and Ruth and I were both glad for God's leadership by way of closed doors and open doors.

Learning in the Dark Night

God sends long, cold, dark winter's nights to shut us up to Himself. During my "night" at Northwestern, I learned to squeeze money to get by—and to trust God and Him only for everything. That frightening night taught me to respect closed doors, and to walk through open doors. I learned to live in the midst of trouble, and I realized that there is no such thing as trouble-free living.

Everyone expected me to attend Fuller, and so I begged God continually to open that door. When I finally accepted God's no, He opened the door to Dallas Theological Seminary, and I willingly went there.

In Minneapolis, I learned to live in a northern culture, which was very different from the South, where I felt comfortable. I was exposed to dispensationalism instead of resting in the Covenant theology I had learned as a child in my Presbyterian Sunday School. I was also exposed to aggressive local church evangelism. Whereas Columbia Bible College introduced me to the Keswickian deeper life, in Minneapolis I was exposed to Bible Church Christianity—where I discovered a different tone but the same fundamental faith. My long, cold, dark winter's night prepared me to minister to various communities of the Christian faith, and not be immersed in my familiar Southern Christianity.

5

The Dallas Theological Seminary Years

(1954–1958)

When Ruth and I arrived in Dallas, we went straight to the home of a lady who lived across from Dallas Bible College and had a duplex for rent. We rented 1111 Gordon Street for $50 a month, including utilities, and settled into our new life in Dallas. On our first Sunday in town, we visited the Independent Presbyterian Church. After all, the Presbyterian Church had licensed me (even though I had an ongoing dispute with them because I was not attending a Presbyterian seminary).

Reading the Sunday paper, I noticed that the Dallas Symphony Orchestra was playing at First Baptist Church that evening. I told Ruth we also needed to visit that church—not only because of the concert, but also because the church had a seven-story parking garage in downtown Dallas, plus a gym and weight room on the eighth floor. I'd never heard of a church having something like that; I had to see it.

When we arrived at the parking garage, I drove all the way up to the seventh floor, just to see if it really was that tall. We parked, rode the elevator down, and went to the evening service. I've forgotten everything about that service, but the fact that we attended First Baptist Church changed our lives. In the middle of the night, Ruth woke up with terrible stomach cramps, and I rushed her to the emergency room at Baylor Hospital, a Baptist hospital only three blocks away from our duplex. They took her straight to the operating room to remove a cyst from her ovary. The nurse beckoned for me to follow her to the admissions office to fill out application papers. She asked, "How are you going to pay for this operation?"

"God will take care of us," was my answer.

She smiled, but I knew something she didn't know. My mother-in-law had enough money to pay for the surgery, so I wasn't worried. Yes, I was trusting God, but I also knew Mrs. Elvira Forbes wouldn't leave her daughter in trouble.

"Where is your church membership?" the nurse asked.

"We just moved to town three or four days ago." I told the nurse we didn't have a local church home yet.

"Where did you attend church yesterday?"

I told her about the Presbyterian and Baptist churches. Because we were at the Baptist hospital, she wrote down, "First Baptist Church,

Dallas, Texas." I finished filling out all the papers—more concerned about Ruth's well-being than I was about paying for the operation. When they finally let me into the post-op room, a silver-headed man was standing by the bed, talking to Ruth. I soon found out that this was Dr. Schaffer, the visitation pastor from First Baptist Church. He turned to say, "You kids don't have to worry about paying for this. First Baptist Church will pay for you."

I was shocked. The church didn't know a thing about me, and I was not even a Southern Baptist. I was Presbyterian. Dr. Schaffer went on to explain, "The nurse told me how you trusted God, and that made an impression on her. So I'm going to get the money from the church office and take care of this bill."

I didn't tell him that I was sure my mother-in-law would come and take care of the bill—which she did.

Dr. Schaffer continued, saying, "When you get home tonight, there will be a couple waiting in their car at the curb. The wife will bring in dinner and clean up the house for you." Once again, I was shocked. The pastor added, "The husband will be your Sunday School teacher."

But Dr. Schaffer wasn't done yet. "Tomorrow night another couple from the Sunday School class you will be attending will come. Some couple will be there every night this week. First Baptist Church will take care of you."

Just as Dr. Schaffer had said, there was a couple waiting at the curb when I got home that evening. The wife brought in a casserole and cleaned up the house, and she and her husband promised that another couple would come back every night that week. However, my mother-in-law arrived early the next day, and we told the people from First Baptist that they didn't need to come every night. But I said to Ruth with a smile, "Let's go to that Baptist church, and let's learn how to build a great church, as great as First Baptist . . . but let's not become Baptists." I understood that the greatness of any church was in its concern for the needs of individuals all over its city.

Dr. W. A. Criswell was preaching through the Bible at First Baptist, and Ruth and I started attending when he was preaching in Romans 4. We stayed in the church until he got to 1 Corinthians 1. About three or four weeks after we began to attend, Dr. Criswell announced, "Tonight, I'm going to preach on baptism from Romans chapter 6. The baptism taught in Romans 6 is not water baptism; it's Holy Spirit baptism. There is no water in Romans chapter 6."

This surprised me, because I thought all Baptists taught that Romans 6 was about water baptism. Paul wrote, "We were buried with Him [Jesus Christ] through baptism into death" (Rom. 6:4).

That night, I came early, sat about six rows from the pulpit—right in the middle of the auditorium—and opened my *Nestle's Greek New Testament* to listen through my Presbyterian lens to Dr. Criswell's words on baptism. For more than 30 minutes he kept repeating, "There is no water in Romans chapter 6," and each time I said, "Amen." Then, as he came to the end of the sermon, he proclaimed, "If . . . if . . ." Criswell had my undivided attention. "*If* you died with Jesus, and *if* you have been buried with Jesus, and *if* you have been raised to new life in Jesus . . . why not tell the world in water?"

Instantly the Holy Spirit confirmed the truth of what Dr. Criswell had just said, and I agreed with what I had heard. I slammed my Greek New Testament shut with a silent *AMEN!* I immediately wanted to be baptized in water to complete the picture of my salvation. When Jesus died, I died with Him; when Jesus was buried, I was buried with Him; and when Jesus rose again from the dead, I too received new life in Him. I was ready to tell that story to the world through water baptism.

God's timing is impeccable. About the time this young Presbyterian preacher was becoming Baptist in his thinking, the same thing was happening to Westminster Presbyterian Church (the church I had pastored while at Columbia Bible College) back in Savannah.

When I had left the Savannah church, I turned the ministry over to a deputy sheriff in Chatham County. He was not a great preacher, and attendance had dwindled to about 25 or 30 each Sunday.

Meanwhile, there was a young, dynamic Baptist pastor planning to start a new church in West Savannah, less than a mile from Westminster Presbyterian Church. Cecil Hodges was invited to preach a two-night revival at the Presbyterian church. The first night, about 15 people came forward for salvation. The same thing happened on the second night, and Cecil invited them all to visit his church the following night (Sunday), saying, "I will explain to you the meaning of baptism by water, and if any of you want to be immersed, I will do it at the Bible Baptist Church."

The next morning, the deputy sheriff preached to around 10 people; some of Westminster's remaining members had already trickled over to the Bible Baptist Church. That evening, many of those who had attended the revival meeting, as well as the members of the Presbyterian church, listened to Cecil Hodges lecture for almost an hour on why they should be baptized in water. Then almost every member of the Presbyterian church went forward and was immersed in water. After they were baptized, Cecil announced, "Tonight you joined the Bible Baptist Church; you are no longer Presbyterians."

A few people were shocked and left, never to come back to the Baptist church. But most of them liked the dynamic preaching of Cecil Hodges and stayed.

The following Sunday, Westminster Presbyterian Church had fewer than 10 people. The week after that, they closed down the church.

Every time I went back to Savannah, Georgia, for the next 50 years, I visited Bible Baptist Church and walked among the pews, shaking hands with former parishioners of mine from Westminster Presbyterian Church.

A Compliment Changed My Life

Ruth's and my marriage got off to a rocky start—not because of her, but because of me. Because my mother was a "fusser," I also was a fusser. Mother motivated me by criticism and sarcasm. I can still hear her asking, "Are you bright?"

So when I wanted Ruth to do things, I criticized her or was sarcastic. Boy, did that not work!

When I criticized her, rather than being open to my remarks, Ruth didn't say a word, but her body language spoke volumes. Her jaw was set as she folded her arms. Although Ruth never once raised her voice to me—nor did she stomp her feet—in my heart, I felt her high heels hit the floor with a resounding, "NO!"

We all experience decisive moments when our lives are radically changed. Do you remember the movie *Gone with the Wind*, and the storyline of spoiled, selfish, whiney, rich Scarlett O'Hara? This Southern belle nearly always got her way and never thought of others. But after the Civil War—when her beloved mansion, Tara, was partially burned, and her family had been ravaged—one event changed her life. A servant told her there was no food in the house, so Scarlett went out to the gardens and could only find radishes. She dug one from the red clay of Georgia and lifted it up to heaven with a vow: "I will never be hungry again . . ."

That life-changing moment turned Scarlett O'Hara into a disciplined business woman who owned and ran a successful business to provide for her family. Ruth and I had been married for around three years, and our daughter Debbie was just a babe in arms. I did not understand all the demands a new baby makes on a first-time mom. I fussed at Ruth, but she wouldn't fuss back. I continued to complain and make demands several times a week, but I couldn't seem to motivate her that way.

One day in class, Professor Howard Hendricks got off the topic he was teaching—professors often do this—and spoke the words of the Holy Spirit to my heart. He said, "Gentlemen, if you'd be as nice to your wife as you are to the ladies in your church, maybe your wife would treat you as nice as the ladies in your church do."

Wow . . . I never thought about that.

Professor Hendricks continued, "All you do is fuss, complain and criticize your wife, but you never do that to the women at your church." God continued to speak to me through him: "If you would motivate your wife the way you motivate the women at your church, you would have a much better home life."

I've been dead wrong . . . I analyzed the way I had been trying to motivate Ruth. I vowed on the spot to change—in Scripture, that's called *repentance*.

I'll start tonight . . .

Walking in the front door, I purposely didn't see anything wrong because I was looking for anything to compliment. There were cut flowers in a vase on the mantelpiece, and I immediately picked up the vase to compliment Ruth on the beautiful flowers she had arranged for me. When walking into the dining room, I stopped to look at two pictures I had never noticed on the wall—decorations were never important to me until that moment. "These are beautiful, and they sure complement the room."

Ruth followed me into the kitchen, where I complimented the dishes washed from breakfast; then I gushed over the table setting, and I thanked her for taking care of Debbie all day long. I continued to walk into the bedroom and the bathroom, praising everything I saw.

"What are you doing?" Ruth asked the obvious question.

"I'm doing what Howie Hendricks told me to do." I explained that I had fussed at her for the last time, and from now on I was going to compliment her instead.

I did the same thing the next night—and the following night, and the one after that.

After about a week of compliments, Ruth noted, "I know that you are insincere, and I don't like you to sound insincere, but keep the compliments coming."

When I saw how she responded to compliments, I determined to change. I began complimenting her on all the good jobs she did, while overlooking any faults.

My critical fussing had not corrected a single one of those faults. If anything, my critical nature hindered our relationship. To top it all off, all I had done was to stifle my spirituality—and hers as well.

Have you ever thought about how your criticism reveals what controls you and what is important to you? Criticism covers up the poison inside of us and keeps the good side from coming to the surface. Don't forget what Jesus said: "Judge not, that you be not judged. For with what judgment you judge, you will be judged; and with the measure you use, it will be measured back to you" (Matt. 7:1-2). Or, according to the *Phillips* translation, "You will be judged by the way you criticise others."

I want to go through life looking at all the good things people do, and forgetting their faults. I hope others will do the same for me.

Getting a University Education

At the end of my first year at Dallas Theological Seminary, I was still smarting from the rebuke I had received because of having a non-accredited college education. Being bold and pretentious, I went to visit Southern Methodist University—and thought about applying to the graduate school there. Since I was interested in teaching, it was only natural that I visit the School of Education, where I knocked on the door of the associate dean, Dr. G. C. Hoskins.

Dr. Hoskins immediately recognized that I was a fundamentalist, and he talked about his childhood in a fundamental Methodist church. As a young man growing up in West Texas, he didn't drink, smoke, dance or cuss, but now he announced, "I've taken my pilgrimage of life." Dr. Hoskins wanted to make a disciple out of me; he wanted me to take the same pilgrimage in life he had taken. So even though I had graduated from a non-accredited college and was attending a non-accredited seminary, he recommended to the university that they allow me entrance into their M.A. program on probation. He explained to me, "You'll first have to take 4 courses or 12 semester hours, and maintain an A to stay in the program."

The courses cost $50 each, and my father-in-law, Mr. Forbes, said he wouldn't pay for an education at a secular institution like Southern Methodist University. "They deny the Bible is the Word of God." So I eked out some savings to pay for four classes each summer for the next four summers.

Now We Were Three

On April 5, 1955, I had gone home tired, but stayed up late—until about 2:00 A.M.—studying for a systematic theology midterm I had to take the following morning.

Ruth poked me at 4:00 A.M. "It's time." I jumped up—no longer sleepy, but wide awake. The hospital was three blocks away, and within 30 minutes, Ruth was in the delivery room.

In those days, men didn't "share" the birthing experience; rather, they sat in dimly lit waiting rooms to wait for the announcement. I had just settled in to read an outdated magazine when Dr. Matinak burst in, shouting, "It's a girl."

I remember holding Deborah Jean Towns in my arms. She represented everything sacred in my heart—the promise of life, the hope of what I wanted to accomplish for God, and the dreams that God had placed within my heart. I was absolutely sure that she would do more for God than I could ever do. I prayed and dedicated her to God right then. But I also realized that the next 20 years of my life were going to be determined by all that I would have to do to raise this darling little girl: money, homes, bedrooms, clothes, and even Mary Jane shoes.

No man—not even Elmer—appreciates the unfathomable mystery of life that is formed within a womb—my womb. My child was conceived in love and grew within me, sharing my physical life. While I was pregnant, Elmer didn't fully appreciate the new life that would be born to us. He was too busy studying, working, moving mountains and killing dragons. Then Deborah Jean was born, and he held her in his arms—and I could see a change come over him. He was no longer just a husband and a servant of God—he was now a father. —Ruth Towns

Ruth and the baby were doing fine; Deborah was an amazingly strong girl from the beginning. We talked for a while, and Ruth said, "Listen." She was serious about my doing God's work. "You've already studied for that midterm exam, why don't you go and take it now?"

The seminary was about five minutes away from the hospital. Deborah was born at 6:00 A.M. At 8:00 A.M. I was writing the midterm exam for Dr. Charles Ryrie. I made an A.

Thirteen months later, we gave a repeat performance. I had studied until around 2:00 in the morning for a final exam in Dr. Dwight Pentecost's New Testament exegesis class. It took a little more time to get to the hospital this time, because we had a 13-month-old baby—Deborah—whom we had to take over to the apartment of Bud and Mary Strauss. We had previously arranged for them to take care of Deborah while we were at the hospital; Mary was due at almost the same time, so we were going to reciprocate and take care of their child when Mary was delivering.

Within 30 minutes of arriving at the hospital, Ruth delivered Stephen (Sam) Richard Towns—at around 6:00 in the morning. At 8:00, I was back at the seminary, taking my final exam.

Ruth delivered Stephen on Friday morning and came home early Saturday morning. The doctor had decided she shouldn't stay in the hospital on Mother's Day. The total hospital bill was $92, and the total doctor's bill was $75. Dr. Martinak's policy was to charge Dallas Seminary students $150 for a first delivery (he charged $300 normally). He charged only $75 for the second delivery, and the third delivery was free. God took care of us and provided for our financial needs in so many different ways.

He was such sunshine in our lives, the blessing of our newborn that day. He was a blue-eyed, handsome boy who seemed to snuggle in and be quietly satisfied. Behind the smiles of doctors and nurses was that look of "I have something to tell you." They talked about a muscle weakness called MD or muscular dystrophy. Our son was born with a disease that could cause early death or maybe never being able to walk.

I remember asking God, "Why me—why us? Was this my fault?" I didn't want to believe what we were hearing. I found myself deep in self-pity and self-blame. They told us that this disease comes from the mother to a male child. I was adopted—how could I have known that I carried this disease? Now I worried that my daughters would carry it. Wasn't there anything I could do?

Throughout Sam's life, I learned many important lessons: lessons about God's patience with me, His miracles, and His grace in my life. Sam? He lived to be 45. Why? Because he had an Aunt Mary who was an effective intercessor. I believe it was her prayers that gave him the additional 45 years. Sam was wonderfully used of God in teaching, counseling and daily living—this traumatic trial taught us more about God than we ever could have learned from a stress-free life. —Ruth Towns

Learning Journalism

Editor Homer Duncan stayed in our home during a missionary conference at Dallas Theological Seminary in the fall of 1955. He gave me a copy of his eight-page tabloid-sized newspaper, *The Missionary Crusader*, to read. As he left, he asked, "What do you think about my newspaper?"

I responded, "Don't ask me for my opinion unless you want to hear it." I've never been reluctant to share my beliefs.

"I want to hear it."

"Your newspaper has nothing to do with missions; you have sermons by great preachers of the past—Spurgeon, Moody, Wesley, and many others." Then I went on to explain that the newspaper was a devotional journal, but there was nothing about missions.

So he asked me, "What would you do to put more emphasis on missions in it?"

I answered straightforwardly, "I would turn the center two pages into a news section. I would report what is happening on the various mission fields of the world."

Homer Duncan nodded his head in agreement and then said, "All right, I'll need your first article on the last day of this month." He went on to explain that I would need to write approximately eight pages—typed double-spaced.

I suggested the title: *The Missionary World at a Glance*.

Once a month, for the next three years, I went to the seminary library around 10:00 P.M. to write my eight-page article, finishing around 2:00 A.M.

The library had a large rack filled with missionary newsletters from all over the world. The newsletters were not organized—not even sorted by country—just piled into this large rack, but it was a treasure chest of information for me. I took all the newsletters to a large table, stacked them by continents, and then put them in order based on priority of stories. I didn't think many people were interested in all missions, so I circled the material that seemed most important. Then, I would write summary paragraphs about what was happening on the various fields of the world.

This was a labor of love; I was not paid for my work. Over a period of time, I probably wrote 40 articles. This built up my résumé files to show people that I could write lengthy articles, but more importantly, I was learning journalistic skills of expressing action and stories in words.

Working Sunday School

During my second year at Dallas Theological Seminary, I left First Baptist Church to become the Sunday School Director at Southwestern Baptist Tabernacle, a church plant pastored by Ruth's cousin, Frederick Billings. For a while, the church, with about 50 members, was located in a storefront in Oakcliff, Texas.

The next year, the church exploded to more than 400 in attendance when it moved into a large recreational space in the administration building of a federal housing project. (When the houses were sold to individuals, the administration building was also sold.) In the new space, with the availability of adequate facilities, the church experienced rapid, New Testament-style church growth. In my role as Sunday School Director, I had opportunities to make innovative management decisions that contributed to this growth. I recruited Sunday School teachers and began new classes. Each new class produced 10 or 15 new church members. I learned that churches grow when new converts are discipled, trained to serve, and then put to work. I told Frederick, "As the leader, you make all the decisions—good and bad—and I get the privilege of learning from your decisions without suffering any failure."

Another Inner-City Pastorate

At the beginning of my third year of seminary, I was called to pastor Dennison Street Chapel, a mission of the Scofield Church. (C. I. Scofield, editor of the *Scofield Reference Bible,* had pastored the church.) Dennison Street Chapel was a small Sunday morning mission, made up of about 10 adults (students from Dallas Bible College) ministering to about 15 children. The Chapel's facility included a mostly empty 100-seat auditorium, plus five Sunday School rooms. White paint covered all the windows.

"Why?" I asked.

"So the neighborhood children won't peek into the windows to disrupt Bible teaching."

I told my new congregation, "If they can't look in, they won't walk in." Remembering how we had painted Westminster Presbyterian Church in Savannah, Georgia, in one day, I held up a piece of blue chalk on Sunday morning and announced, "With this chalk, we can paint the whole church in a whole day." As before, it happened just as I predicted: We scraped the windows clean and painted the church in one Saturday.

I realized that as long as the church was a mission of Scofield Church, it was not an indigenous congregation. The people didn't feel like the church belonged to them. So, I organized a strategy to give the church (building and ministry) to the community.

First, we changed the name to Faith Bible Church. We wrote a new constitution for our renamed congregation, and we voted on it.

Second, we appointed deacons. Some were students at Dallas Bible College, and others were fathers of the children from the neighborhood who had been converted.

Third, we constructed a basketball court behind the church building. Then we built a baseball field, installing a huge backstop. I became manager of the boys' team, and we entered the city leagues, playing baseball, basketball and soccer. I found out that when I organized 15 or so young boys to play baseball, I'd reach into 15 homes and touch more than 30 parents and other family members.

Fourth, I planned for the people of the community to build something of their very own. The church didn't have a bathroom; as a matter of fact, it didn't have any running water. For that matter, none of the homes in the neighborhood had running water or inside plumbing. Every house, even though built after World War II, had a spigot in the front yard, where people filled buckets of water to carry into the house. Each house had a Biffy in the backyard for toilet purposes. I felt the church could do something about this situation.

Raising Money

The City told us it would take $4,000 to bring the water pipe 500 yards to the church. Using a borrowed camera, I took a number of slides of the boys playing different sports, and then I took slides of the various families whose lives had been transformed by Christ. About a third of the congregation were second-generation Mexicans, another third were Chickasaw and Choctaw Native Americans, and the final third were "Okies" and "Arkies" from Oklahoma and Arkansas.

Scofield Church had a number of ladies' home Bible classes, many of them meeting in the elite upper-class Highland Park area of Dallas. I visited the various ladies' groups and with a slide projector showed them pictures of West Dallas families getting saved in the mission Sunday School their church had started.

On each occasion, I would look around the living room, find a large vase, put it in front of the ladies, and then say, "Fill it up so we can evangelize West Dallas."

Once the water line was installed, I arranged the purchase of a large older home that was being moved to make way for a highway. A foundation was built next to the church building, and that house provided six additional Sunday School classrooms– enough space for 60 people.

I announced to the church, "All men show up on Saturday to build a breezeway across the back of the church—plus we'll be building two bathrooms, one for men and one for women."

One of the students from Dallas Bible College argued, "Preacher, we've got to put doors on the breezeways to keep people from the neighborhood from dirtying up our bathrooms." He reminded me, "They don't have bathrooms in their homes."

"He's wrong," I told the deacons. "If they come to church to use the bathroom, maybe they'll come to church to get saved."

When the men appeared early on Saturday morning, I asked, "Alright, which one of you is a carpenter who knows how to lay out rafters and cut joists?" Then I added, "We'll also need a carpenter to help frame the doors."

There were more than 20 men there, but none of them had ever been a carpenter or even a carpenter's helper. Remember, I had been a carpenter's helper in the shipyard, and I had worked for two months as a carpenter for my father-in-law during the summer of 1954. Since I had always been bold to try something, even when I didn't know what I was doing, I decided I would be the carpenter. I announced, "Together we'll build these bathrooms."

Within three Saturdays, the rooms and breezeway were built. I had only seen plumbers do work, but I figured I had learned enough to lay the pipes, lead the seams, and set the commodes.

Then came dedication Sunday. Visitors came from Scofield Church, and some of my friends from seminary were there. Almost all of the families of the men who had worked on the buildings came, plus an enormous number of children. More than 200 people flooded the church grounds, and many couldn't get packed into the auditorium that only seated 100.

After the service, as we were standing drinking punch, Bernice Holt said to me, "Preacher, this is the greatest day in the life of the church!"

"No," I told her. "We'll see greater days than this when the altar is filled with people getting saved."

A Revival Greater Than Expected

The days I hoped for arrived that summer. We held a revival meeting—which was truly the greatest day in the life of the church thus far. It all began earlier that spring, when Reverend Jack Hyles, pastor of Miller Road Baptist Church in Garland, Texas, spoke in chapel at Dallas Theological Seminary.[1]

As he ended his challenge to the students, he asked, "Do you want a burning heart for lost souls?"

Hyles gave an invitation for students to come dedicate themselves at the altar. I was one of the first young men to go forward. Later, Hyles was criticized severely by seminary faculty members for suggesting a soul-winning church model that was different from the Dallas Theological Seminary model. Dallas taught a Bible expositional ministry where the Word of God was taught to believers. After chapel, I made an appointment and drove out to invite Pastor Hyles to come preach a revival at Faith Bible Church. He said he didn't have time, but he would send his associate pastor, Bob Keys.

On the first day of the revival, Bob Keys preached with great power—and he also started a buzz in West Dallas by his unusual approach to evangelism. He said things such as: "I'll preach standing on the piano if it will get people saved."

Keys couldn't stand on the upright piano, because the ceiling of the church auditorium was too low, but he sat on the piano to tell two or three illustrations. Later, he preached standing on the communion table. Finally, he gave an invitation while walking up and down the aisle. At that time, four or five individuals came forward to be saved.

The next night, people came to hear Bob speak and see his antics; so many came, we couldn't get them in the building. They stood around all the open windows to hear the sermon. When he no longer was sensational by standing in the pulpit chairs, he went into the middle of the auditorium, asked people to move, and preached standing on a pew.

The next night, we held services at 6:00 and 8:00. Half the people at the early service were children, and of course, many of the people came to both the early service and the later service.

I was thrilled by all of those who were making decisions for Jesus Christ, and I would have loved to continue ministering in that community, but I had made a previous commitment to begin teaching at Midwest Bible College in St. Louis, Missouri. So almost immediately after the revival, I left for St. Louis.

St. Louis Calling

Just as Jack Hyles preached a soul-winning sermon at Dallas Theological Seminary, I had preached the same kind of sermon on soul winning at Midwest Bible College earlier that year. I too gave an invitation to students to come forward to dedicate their lives to soul winning. At that time, about half of the 150 Bible college students came to kneel at the altar. Based on that one sermon, I was hired to be a Christian Education Professor at Midwest Bible College.

So, we left Dallas in the fall of 1958, turning the church over to Arvis Griggs, who was a student at Dallas Theological Seminary and had been my associate at Faith Bible Church.

My last year in seminary, things really began to pile up. Not only was I taking a full load at DTS, but I also had to take one class at Southern Methodist University (SMU) to finish my requirements there. I was writing two theses at the same time—one at the seminary and the other at SMU.

At the beginning of that year, the president of Dallas Bible College had phoned to tell me of an urgent need. Their professor of missions had left in an emergency. Because I was writing monthly for the *Missionary Crusade*, I was asked to teach two of his classes: History of Foreign Missions and Introduction to Philosophy. That meant preparation time in addition to teaching two nights a week. All of this came on top of my afternoon activities with the Boys Club at Faith Bible Church. I committed myself to getting it all done, because I felt that God was leading me to do it. I remembered the young Elmer Towns standing before the McFaddin granite memorial, listening to my mother say, "Remember, you've got McFaddin blood flowing in your veins. You can do more than anyone else."

My husband came home one day to find me sitting in a chair looking outside. "What'cha been doing?" he asked.

My answer was, "Oh, watching TV and eating chocolate," but the TV wasn't on and no chocolate was in sight. I was just resting, but I realized I had married the "energizer bunny." He just kept going and going, from one job to the next. I couldn't do as much as he could.

As we both grew older, I became more like Elmer, going more quickly from one task to another, and he takes more time now to reflect and sit looking outdoors. Isn't God amazing to put people together who need each other?
—Ruth Towns

I graduated from Dallas Seminary on May 8, 1958. In my vanity, I arranged for most of Faith Bible Church to show up at graduation and applaud me. I'd seen on previous years that graduation was a popularity contest. When the name of a graduate was called, people would applaud and on a few occasions some would whistle and yell. Obviously, those with the loudest cheers were the most popular. I wanted that recognition, so I instructed my church members to stand in unison when my name was called, applauding and cheering loudly. It happened just as I had hoped—I got the most cheers. But those cheers were empty.

I knew that they did not arise from genuine recognition; rather, they came from my selfish coercion.

A Life-Changing Thesis

After I graduated from Dallas Theological Seminary, I began to work seriously on my thesis for Southern Methodist University. Dr. Hoskins urged me to write on the history of teaching morals in public schools. He probably wanted me to see how public schools got rid of the Bible, thinking this would dilute my conservative roots. The topic was approved, and I conducted research throughout my last year in Dallas. But I made the mistake of not checking in with Dr. Hoskins on a regular basis.

I gave him a completed copy of my thesis around the second week of August. I was supposed to graduate two weeks later. He took it home to read, and the next day he told me, "No . . . no . . . no . . . you've done this all wrong."

My world crashed down around me. I thought I would not graduate. I had already signed a contract to teach at Midwest Bible College, and I wondered if they would break the contract if I didn't receive my M.A. degree.

Dr. Hoskins explained that I had used deductive logic to build the arguments in each paragraph. He wanted the opposite; he wanted me to build every paragraph inductively. He could see that I was crushed. So he said, "Be at my house tomorrow at 5:00 A.M." He lived about seven miles away from my home, out in the country; that meant getting up at 4:00 and leaving at 4:30. I didn't want to be late.

When my headlights reflected the house numbers on his mailbox, I saw him trudging outside in an old rumpled bathrobe to get his morning newspaper. He told me, "The moment my wife comes to the kitchen, clear the table and leave." Then he instructed, "I'll teach you what to write—you write—and I'll read the morning paper."

For the next two hours, we turned around every paragraph in the first chapter to write inductively: Begin each paragraph with evidence, then show more evidence, and at the end of the paragraph, draw a conclusion or make a point. The last sentence in each paragraph should be a conclusion drawn from facts. That's what Dr. Hoskins wanted me to do. I had done the reverse at DTS.

It wasn't enough to reverse the order of the sentences; he wanted to make sure I also reversed the order in my thought process. What I learned from Dr. Hoskins, I used to teach a course in logic for the next eight years in both St. Louis and Winnipeg, Canada.

By the time the revisions were finished, I had Scotch taped paragraphs together, Scotch taped footnotes in their places, and written a number of paragraphs on 3x5 cards—then Scotch taped those to their proper places.

I had paid Charlotte Sandburg (the wife of my friend Darryl, who went to Northwestern and Dallas with me) $20 to type my entire Dallas Theological Seminary thesis. Dr. Hoskins said to me, "My secretary types, and she will do a perfect job. She will charge you $60 to re-type this thesis." He went on to say, "It's three times what you would pay another typist." But he explained, "If my secretary types it, I don't have to read it again. I know it will be perfect, and I'll give you an A."

So, I wrote out a check for $60 (I had made $30 a week at the church). I handed the stack of Scotch-taped papers to him. The next time I saw my thesis was at my oral defense. Dr. Hoskins told the other professors in the room, "Gentlemen, I have read the thesis, and I want to give him an A. There are no mistakes in the typing, footnotes or format. You may ask him any question about educational philosophers that you wish, but stay away from his documentation."

Because I knew church history and educators, I could give rich details about the struggles that went on during the evolving secularization of the American school systems. I passed.[2]

The experience in Dr. Hoskins's kitchen absolutely changed my approach about research. Later, I would work with the graduate students at Trinity Evangelical Divinity School, mentoring young men who were presenting their theses to the faculty of Trinity. Later still, when I became Dean of Liberty Baptist Theological Seminary, I would spend time with students developing the argumentation for their doctoral dissertations.

6

The Midwest Bible College Years

(1958–1961)

Because Ruth was expecting our third child—Polly, born October 2, 1958—her parents flew her to St. Louis early so she could get settled and not have to deal with all of the stress and strain of moving our furniture to St. Louis. When I had graduated from Northwestern College four years earlier, I purchased a trailer for $25 to haul our furniture behind my automobile. When I arrived in Dallas, I sold the trailer to a student for $25, and when I got ready to leave, I bought the same trailer back—again for $25. It carried all of our belongings back to St. Louis, and once again I sold it for $25.

I finished my oral exam for my thesis at Southern Methodist University on the final Friday of August 1958, and my first class at Midwest Bible College (MBC) met on the first Tuesday morning of September 1958.

Dr. Hoskins, my advisor at SMU, told me, "You'll be teaching by the seat of your pants." By that he meant that every night I'd be preparing lectures to deliver the following morning. Boy, was he right! That year became the toughest year of my life. Each day was like final exam week. I'd stay up late every night to prepare for my lectures the next day. The first semester I taught 18 hours (10 classes), and the second semester I taught 19 hours—an impossible schedule by today's standards. But I was so thrilled to teach the Word of God to students that I didn't mind the late nights of preparation. I wanted to do the best job possible the following day.

My class schedule that first semester:

- Personal Evangelism, 2 hours
- Youth Camp, 1 hour
- Vacation Bible School, 1 hour
- Principles of Teaching, 2 hours
- Systematic Theology, 2 hours
- The Gospel of John, 2 hours
- The Book of Acts, 2 hours
- Introduction to Philosophy, 2 hours
- History of Missions, 2 hours
- Youth Ministry, 2 hours

Midwest Bible College belonged to IFCA (Independent Fundamental Churches of America) and was part of the "religious right" of American Christianity. In its day, it was much like Bob Jones University is today. The college had strict rules of personal holiness and a narrow doctrinal statement. I had no difficulty living by the strenuous rules required of the students, and I agreed with the doctrinal statement.

The college had a faith policy in fundraising, which meant "full information without solicitation." The college president sent out a monthly letter detailing the needs of the school and asking for prayer. Then the administration prayed for God to touch people's hearts to send money to support the school. There was no stewardship department to organize fundraising programs, nor did the school hold fundraisers to solicit money.

If the money did not come in, the faculty was not paid. Sometimes salaries were delayed for one, two or three weeks. Needless to say, my mother-in-law kept groceries on the table, so we were never in desperate need.

The college also had a rule that all honorary income received by faculty members from ministry had to go to the college. The idea was that no popular faculty member should receive more money than the others; it was "equal sacrifice/equal blessing."

Because of the popularity of my youth courses, I received a lot of invitations to speak at youth meetings and preach as a guest at local churches. Many pastors knew about my book of humorous stories, so quite often I was Master of Ceremonies at youth banquets. Often the pastor would give me a check, saying this was not ministry, and that this check should not go to Midwest Bible College. Those requests seemed marginal to me, so I gave the money to the college, even though those MC jobs paid only $5 or $10 for an evening.

Another teacher and I signed up with the St. Louis public school board as substitute teachers; they paid $22 a day. The president of MBC didn't consider this an honorarium for ministry, so we were allowed to keep our public school pay.

I found that there was an excessive teacher absentee rate at the inner-city schools of St. Louis, because of the difficulty of dealing with a growing teenage rebellion against authority. Those rebellious students tested me, because I was only there one day a week (Midwest did not have classes on Mondays, so that was the only day I could substitute).

To help keep order, I developed a technique of lecturing from the back of the room, where I could watch the students' notebooks and see what they were doing—but they couldn't see me. If they couldn't see my face, they wouldn't anticipate what I'd do. I'd keep a seating chart handy so I could call students by name before any potential problems got out of hand. Today, I still walk to the back of the room while lecturing at Liberty University.

One day, I ended up teaching a kindergarten class. That was the hardest day of teaching I had ever experienced. Those little tykes had minds of their own and would not obey. It was like herding cats. At the end of that day, I was so physically exhausted that I vowed never to teach kindergarten again.

Writing My First Book

I wrote my first book during my second year at Midwest Bible College. I went about publishing the book the wrong way, so don't follow my example. I produced the book along with about 9 or 10 students in my class on youth ministry.

One of the best courses I had under Howard Hendricks at Dallas Theological Seminary was Introduction to Youth Ministries. It became one of my favorite courses to teach; I used the principles I had developed at New Brighton Community Church in Minneapolis. But the textbook we used had been written for the YMCA—it included vague Christian principles, but nothing about local church ministry—so I decided to write my own resource textbook. I assigned nine students to write term papers/chapters that basically flowed out of my nine lectures (which included many of Howard Hendricks's ideas as well as my own).

After I had edited and expanded the term papers, we planned an evening work session in the third-floor attic of the college, using the school's business machines. I purchased 10,000 sheets of paper with my own money, plus 200 cardboard covers and 100 plastic binders.

Some students typed the chapters onto mimeograph stencils, other students ran the mimeograph machine, and another student punched holes for the plastic binders. In about three hours, we assembled 100 copies of our first textbook, which we called *Teaching Teens*.[1]

I organized a youth clinic to be held on the college facilities on a Friday night and Saturday morning. I invited youth workers from the greater St. Louis area to come learn the principles contained in that book. Representatives from Gospel Light and Scripture Press taught workshops on using their curricula. I also led workshops and delivered a general message from the textbook. We sold our books for $5 each and made enough money to pay for the stencils, paper and cardboard covers, and to give a free copy to all of our workshop participants and the students in the class. The rest of the money went for a class pizza blast.

Then an idea struck. I carefully packaged the stencils and took them home. Later I bought another 10,000 sheets of paper, plus plastic binders and cardboard covers. One weekend I took the college mimeograph machine home and ran off 10,000 pages for the book. Another weekend I took home the binding machine and punched holes in all of the pages. But then I needed help to collate the pages. I formed a long assembly line around our basement, with papers stacked on the washing machine, dryer, Ping-Pong table and storage boxes. Around the basement, Ruth, Debbie and I walked, collating *Teaching Teens*.

I spoke at local churches and conducted clinics on reaching their young people, where I sold *Teaching Teens* for $5 each. The school determined that profits from the book were not the same thing as an honorarium, so they allowed me to keep the money.

I bribed my daughter Debbie: "If you will help put books together, I'll take you and the family to McDonald's."

Later, on occasions when we were broke and couldn't go out for hamburgers, Debbie would beg me, "Let's walk around the basement and make a book so we can go to McDonald's."

When we had family prayer, I always reminded the children that whenever their daddy was away, he was serving the Lord, and they should pray for him. I wanted them to have a part in my ministry, so they wouldn't feel neglected when I was not home.

Two years later, I went to Winnipeg Bible College where the students had a yearbook room, complete with an architectural drafting table. I arranged for a printing company to typeset *Teaching Teens* (instead of using a typewriter). Bob Butts, an evangelist out of Calgary, Alberta, drew the illustrations for the book (in return, I gave him 50 free copies). I laid out the book in the evenings on that architectural drafting table. Then the book was printed at a cost of about $1 each. I continued to sell them for $5 apiece until DeLoss Holmes, a representative for Christian Publishing in Harrisburg, Pennsylvania, paid $500 for the rights to publish the book. When Baker Book House in Grand Rapids saw the book, they purchased it from Christian Publishing and began paying me royalties. I had never heard of royalties, nor did I know anything about publishing a book through a publishing company until I began working with Baker Book House.

As I had with so many other projects, I just did what needed to be done to get a book published. I didn't know how to approach a publishing house, nor did I understand contracts, royalties and publishing rights. Thus, my career in writing began in a very crude way. Doesn't great passion seek out skills and knowledge to get a job done?

Beginning a 40-Year Ministry

Another favorite course at Dallas Theological Seminary was Sunday School Administration. This course, along with Introduction to Youth Work, molded my future ministry to local churches.

In St. Louis, I taught local churches the principles and methods Southern Baptists used to build Sunday Schools, drawing on my experiences at First Baptist Church, Dallas, and Southwestern Baptist Tabernacle, as well as my studies at DTS.

Pastor Wes Hunt at First Baptist Church, Pittsfield, Illinois, heard about the excitement in my Sunday School administration class. He invited me to come to his church on a Saturday morning in October 1958 to teach his Sunday School teachers how to build a Sunday School.

When I arrived on Friday afternoon, we stopped for a cup of coffee at the Cardinal Truck Stop right outside Pittsfield. Harold Willmington, pastor of a small church nearby, joined us, and Harold became one of my lifelong friends. Fifteen years later, I invited Harold to help begin Liberty Bible Institute in Lynchburg, Virginia. There he wrote his famous *Willmington's Guide to the Bible.*[2]

I had never done a Saturday Sunday School seminar for laymen, so I simply planned to teach four 50-minute classes, just like I taught at Midwest Bible College. We began a class at 8:00, followed by a 10-minute break, and so on. Approximately 12 teachers attended, bringing their own pencils and paper, and I taught identically to the way I taught at the Bible college.

That church was averaging approximately 60 students in Sunday School at the time; three years later, the program had new facilities, and attendance had increased to more than 300. Pastor Hunt attributed the organizational growth to my seminars, but I believe Pastor Hunt's powerful preaching and soul-winning outreach were the driving forces for the growth.

About a month later, I held another Saturday Sunday School conference, this time at Tyng Memorial Church in Peoria, Illinois. I followed the same format of teaching four classes on Saturday morning, and then remaining to preach on Sunday. For the next 40 years, I gave Saturday Sunday School conferences all over the United States and Canada (in all 50 states and 10 provinces). Over the years, the format changed, and the focus was sharpened, but what I began during my first year out of seminary gave me a lifelong ministry to churches.

Learning from Your Children

Growing up, I always wanted a swing set. I had seen one in *Children's Activities* magazine: a tall set of red pipes that held aloft a swing on chains, a blue sliding board, and a yellow teeter-totter. This kind of structure is called a swing set by modern families, but in the old days it was also called a jungle gym. When I was a child, we were too poor for a swing set, so I planned for my daughter to enjoy what I never had. When Debbie was six years old, I scraped together all the extra money I could find and bought a Sears and Roebuck jungle gym for $9.99.

The backyard was dark when I got home that evening. So by the light of a flashlight (and leaving the dining room blinds open), I assembled the red pipes, chains and sliding board before going to bed. I expected my kids to rush out before breakfast to play on the jungle gym all morning. I expected them to fuss when we called them in for breakfast.

Yes, they ran out to swing, slide, and bump on the see-saw, but when called for breakfast, they obediently came in without a whimper. They didn't have a passion for a red jungle gym.

Two days later, Debbie came home with muddied feet, a bruised elbow, and buttons torn from her playsuit. "You should see our rope," she loudly proclaimed for all to hear. "We swing a mile."

Outside our subdivision, she had found an old apple tree from which a rope swing hung gracefully over a weed-covered ditch. The kids could swing from one high dirt bank to the other.

Debbie's swing in the apple tree taught me that it doesn't take money to make your kids happy. Another thing I learned is that your kids don't always have fun doing the things you dreamed of doing, so don't try to live your dreams through them.

Embracing the Sunday School Movement

In October 1959, I attended the National Sunday School Convention in Indianapolis, Indiana. Two events took place in Indianapolis that influenced the rest of my life. First, I attended the Research Commission of the National Sunday School Convention, made up of professors of Christian education from Bible colleges, Christian colleges and seminaries all around America. I sat in a room for two days with the greatest leaders in the Christian education movement. Before this, most of them had only been names in my textbooks and heroes of yore: Henrietta Mears, the founder and editor of Gospel Light; Mary and Lois Lebar, sisters who taught at Wheaton College and authors of several prominent books;[3] Howard Hendricks, my Christian education professor at Dallas Seminary; Drs. Ed and Lois Simpson, professors from Northwestern College; and Gene Getz, teacher at Moody Bible Institute.

Being around these perceived giants made me realize I could walk on an equal footing with them, even though I was young and fresh out of seminary.

Second, all of the convention participants were invited to an evening meeting to discuss accreditation for Christian education programs in our colleges. We wrote up a list of objectives for Christian education, and then began to develop plans for individual courses and the standards by which they would be implemented in all Christian colleges.

I brought along a pad of paper that evening, and I was taking copious notes when they decided to put together a steering committee to implement the group's suggestions through the Accreditation Association of Bible Colleges (AABC).

Once all of the influential names were suggested for the committee, Ed Simpson said, "Hey, let's put Elmer on our committee. He's been taking notes for us this evening. He can do all our 'donkey' work; we'll make him secretary."

Appointment to that committee soon led to my being sent to Western Canada to lead Canadian Bible colleges toward accreditation. That was intimidating, as I was only 26 years old and 2 years out of seminary. But I took on the challenge, and through that assignment, I was introduced to Winnipeg Bible College—where I eventually became president. Being a part of the AABC also gave me the needed background to lead to the accreditation of Liberty University.

Another benefit of the days I spent in Indianapolis was my exposure to large Sunday School conventions. I was impressed with the way thousands of Sunday School teachers came from all over America to be trained for their task. Immediately upon arriving back at Midwest Bible College, I wrote a letter to Dr. Clate Risley, executive secretary of the National Sunday School Association (NSSA), congratulating him on the outstanding job he had done. Dr. Risley got my letter and immediately phoned me in St. Louis. When I picked up the phone, I heard him say, "I need your help."

Clate Risley went on to explain that the next year's Sunday School convention, to be held in Kansas City, Missouri, was in trouble. The group in Kansas City had backed out of sponsoring the national convention.

Dr. Risley asked me, "Can you organize the pastors of St. Louis into a strong committee, and then motivate them to raise the money to sponsor a national Sunday School convention in St. Louis?"

What a staggering request for a 26-year-old neophyte! I was new to St. Louis, and I had no idea how many evangelical churches there were in the city. I had no experience organizing pastors on such a large scale, nor did I understand what it would take to raise the money to sponsor a national convention. Yet I knew that God had led me up until that moment, so I immediately said, "Yes, I can get it done."

Today, I realize how naive I was, and how recklessly I lived. Like a teenager standing on a bridge high above the Wilmington River, I felt I could dive four stories into the dark, threatening water below and not get hurt.

We had less than 51 weeks to make the St. Louis Sunday School Association a strong and viable entity. I planned a citywide pastors' luncheon to be held two weeks later at the downtown Salvation Army. So now, in addition to daily teaching and nightly preparation, I jumped immediately into an organizational mode to get the city ready for that luncheon.

Midwest Bible College had a list of approximately 50 churches with which we worked. To that list I added all the Pentecostal churches in the Yellow Pages of the telephone book. Then I began working through the Presbyterian, Baptist and other evangelical organizations. Within three or four days, I had a list of more than 200 churches. A letter went out from Midwest Bible College to invite the pastors to a luncheon, followed up with a second letter from Dr. Clate Risley at NSSA headquarters in Chicago.

More than 50 pastors showed up for the luncheon, pledged their support to a citywide Sunday School association, and elected me secretary of the St. Louis Sunday School Association. I went downtown and reserved Kiel Auditorium, St. Louis's 4,000-seat convention center. When I signed the contract guaranteeing the payment of $4,000, it was the biggest step of faith I had ever taken in my life. Obviously, I had doubts. *What if the convention doesn't materialize? Will I have to pay the $4,000?* Also, I thought to myself, *Suppose the convention is poorly attended because we are planning so late. Will I have to pay this myself?*

We organized 13 different committees to help plan the Sunday School convention. That involved 13 different pastors, each one organizing a piece of the infrastructure of the convention. We rented a huge billboard, located along the expressway leading to downtown, and advertized a national convention coming to town. We also put together a Saturday parade in downtown St. Louis (in those days, people still went downtown to shop on Saturdays). There was a Salvation Army marching band, as well as floats from various churches and Christian organizations.

Because I was the secretary of the convention, I brushed shoulders with national speakers who were leading evangelicals of the day.

I taught three workshops at the convention—including one titled "The Laws of Sunday School Growth," which had become my sugar-stick message. I had gone throughout the churches of St. Louis preaching that same sermon—explaining that there were laws for building greater and more powerful Sunday Schools.

Henrietta Mears sat on the second row of my workshop, and Bernice Cory, editor of *Scripture Press*, sat on the opposite aisle. These icons in the evangelical world should have intimidated me, but I had delivered the message so many times that the presentation went well.

Henrietta Mears told me after the workshop, "You must preach this sermon all over America. This message can change the churches of our nation."

"I can do it," I said under my breath. Later, I learned this was the way she motivated all young people. But on that day, I thought she meant me only, so I was honored—and she did succeed in motivating me.

Because of the success of the Sunday School convention, Clate Risley put pressure on me to resign from Midwest Bible College and move to Chicago to become the associate director of the National Sunday School Association. He appealed to my ego when he said, "You'll be traveling to all the great churches of America. You'll be speaking in conventions all over the country . . ."

Ruth and I traveled to Chicago, we picked out a house, and I tendered my resignation to Midwest Bible College.

About three weeks later, I woke up violently in the middle of a black night. Something was wrong. I began to sweat all over.

"Lord, what is it?" I asked.

The Lord was in the room. He did not appear physically, nor did I see a vision, nor did I hear an audible voice, but I knew that the Lord was standing by my bed to warn me of something.

I thought immediately of a burglar, and that prompted additional fear. Then I thought perhaps there was a fire, or someone I knew was in danger or dying. I prayed several times, *"Lord, what are You trying to tell me?"*

Then the Lord spoke to my heart, telling me not to take the new job I had just accepted with NSSA.

It was a perfect job: travel, influence, ministry in many churches, and national recognition. But as I lay in bed, I knew God was telling me, *"Don't take the Sunday School job."*

I wrestled with the Lord in my bed throughout the night, because I knew the Sunday School job had great potential. It would be exciting, I would be well known, and I would influence a lot more people than I could teaching at Midwest Bible College, which had only 150 students at that time.

"Don't take the job," God kept saying.

As I wrestled with God, I reviewed my long-range priorities. I asked myself what those priorities were. I also asked what my strongest gifts were and how I could make the greatest contribution with my life. I confessed to the Lord that I was ego-driven. Ever since entering Bible college as a freshman, I had wanted to be a Bible college president. I rationalized with the Lord that night that traveling for NSSA would open up a door into a Bible college presidency somewhere, sometime. But every time I gave God a different excuse, I got the same feeling: *"Don't take the Sunday School job."*

After a couple of hours of praying, I surrendered before the Lord. I told Him that fame was not important. I surrendered my reputation, and even said, *"God, if I never become a Bible college president, Thy will be done!"*

When I finally surrendered my will to God, I thought I heard Him say, *"Don't take the Sunday School job . . . but within a year, I will give you a college presidency."*

By faith I accepted God's will for my life. I signed a contract at Midwest Bible College for the coming year, and I resigned the new position with the National Sunday School Association.

7

The Canadian Years

(1961–1965)

About two months after that dark night when God said, "No!" to Chicago, God intervened in my life to allow me to become a college president. On a snowy winter day in 1961, I took a longer way home from Midwest Bible College—because the longer way was along flat roads. My usual route home included some steep hills, and I knew I couldn't make it in the snow. Driving past my church, I saw tracks in the snow up the front drive; I looked back to see the pastor's car in his usual parking spot. It was unusual for me to backtrack in the snow, but I did. I turned around to go back just to chat—and maybe catch a cup of coffee.

Pastor Robert MacMillan asked me, "What is your ultimate goal in life?"

"I want to be a Bible college president someday."

Pastor MacMillan was very close to the ministry of Midwest Bible College and had served on the committee that led to its accreditation. He jumped at my words, interrupting me to immediately reinforce my lifelong goal by saying, "That's wonderful!" He even jumped from his chair to pour more coffee. "A man like you has the drive and ability to be a Bible college president. I think that you will make a wonderful college president."

Just then the phone rang. Dr. Stuart Boehmer—a pastor in Toronto, Canada, and a close friend to MacMillan—was on the line. After they greeted one another and exchanged pleasantries, the Canadian asked MacMillan, "Do you know where we can find a young man to be president of Winnipeg Bible College?"

MacMillan almost swallowed the phone. "Your man is sitting right here," he told his friend.

In the predetermined will of God, there is no such thing as a coincidence; all things work together for the good purposes of God. Frank Frogley, chairman of Winnipeg Bible College (WBC) in Manitoba, had driven 1,200 miles to Toronto to ask Stuart Boehmer about a president for the college. While I was talking to Pastor MacMillan about becoming a college president, Frank Frogley was asking Stuart Boehmer to help him find a college president. So, Stuart Boehmer said to MacMillan, "I have a man here in my office who is looking for a president. Let's put them on the phone together and see if it's a match."

For approximately 30 minutes, Frank Frogley and I talked about Winnipeg Bible College. We discussed strategy, purpose and theology . . . but most of all, we discussed the will of God. While we were talking on the phone, I could hear the voice of God whispering in my other ear, *"See . . . I have a college presidency for you."*

The board at Winnipeg Bible College had rejected a number of candidates, but when Frank Frogley recommended me, I got the position.

I stayed in Canada for five years, and God blessed my ministry there. The college became accredited with the Accrediting Association of Bible Colleges (AABC), but more importantly, the Province of Manitoba granted it power to award baccalaureate degrees in religion and authorized the school to begin a theological seminary. While I was there, the college never grew beyond 100 students, but 25 years later—because of Manitoba's Province recognition—it became the largest evangelical college and seminary in Canada.

Not long after that first phone conversation with Frank Frogley, I flew up to meet with the board of directors of Winnipeg Bible College. I was interviewing for the presidency of the second oldest Bible college in Canada.

I had taken a course at St. Louis University in governance and college administration, and I had done research into some of Winnipeg's problems—why it wasn't growing, why it was experiencing financial difficulties, and why it had been called "the college that wouldn't die." (That epithet was the title of an article written to describe several "fights" between the board and students over doctrine and issues of separation from sin. The college lived through a multitude of crises, which included fire and flood as well as the clashes between directors and students.)

As I read minutes from previous board meetings, I was appalled that the board involved itself with such little things as how much electricity was used in the dorms, how many loaves of bread were served in the college dining room, and other petty items. So, I prepared a paper called "The Future Governance of Winnipeg Bible College." In it I declared that the board must set policy and doctrine, and involve itself with executive decisions. Then, I determined that the board had to delegate the daily administration of the college to the president and give him power over spending money and the budget.

On that freezing Sunday afternoon in 1961, I met with the board of directors in the living room of Mr. Frank Frogley's home—an apartment overlooking the Assiniboine River. They grilled me on every question that I could have conceived, and I answered each one as honestly as I could. Then, someone said, "We're satisfied with this candidate; now let's vote on him."

"Wait a minute," I stopped them. "You may approve of me, but the next question is, do I approve of you?" Then I added, "I've got questions to ask you."

I explained to them that hiring a president is a two-way street. I had to find out if they would trust me, if they would give me freedom to lead the college, and if I could spend money within the budget they approved. Then, I passed out the three-page proposal for relationships between the college president and the board that I had prepared.

I read them my proposal regarding what they must do as a board. I told them that I would act under their authority, but would need the freedom to lead the college according to their principles and doctrine. Then I concluded, "Don't vote for me as president unless you approve my principles of governance for Winnipeg Bible College."

I told them that I had read their past board minutes and felt that they had been functioning as an administrative board, not as an executive board. I explained that the college could never be accredited by the AABC unless they changed to normal standards.

The vote was 14 to 0 to offer me a contract as president. I looked around the room and wondered what my future held. There was not a single young man at the table; they were all more than 60 years of age. I knew I would have to recruit younger board members with energy and vision. I also knew that I would have to recruit board members with wealth to help support the college. I was not sure that the men in the room had the resources needed to help Winnipeg Bible College become what I dreamed. But I knew that God had called me, and I knew that God could do anything.

He said, "We're moving to Canada." God had answered our prayer, and Elmer had been asked to become president of Winnipeg Bible College, much to my surprise. Have you ever prayed for something but were surprised when it happened? As we made the transition to Winnipeg, many things about this new phase of our life surprised me. I was surprised going through customs. I was surprised at how flat the land was. I was surprised at how quaint the buildings seemed. I was surprised at the lovely Canadian accent. I was surprised at the depth of the snow and the length of the seasons.

I also had many things to be thankful for as we settled into our new home. I was thankful for answered prayer. I was thankful for a college that would hire a very young man to be the president. I was thankful for ladies who taught me customs different from mine (such as pouring tea and removing my shoes upon entering someone's house). I was thankful for my mother's prayers and encouragement. —Ruth Towns

A College with No Money

After about six months, the delightful taste of being a college president turned sour in my mouth. I found myself meeting with salesmen, which sapped my time. Each day I had to review the grocery list for the students' dining room. If I could shave $10 or $15 from the grocery budget, I didn't have to raise that money. WBC didn't have a business manager; it had one young lady—Alida Metzer—who was the school secretary and bookkeeper.

The first young man I recruited to the board was Bart Crunwell, treasurer for Reimer Motor Lines, a large Canada-wide trucking company. He took one look at the schools' books and announced, "Starting Monday night, I want you to come into the college office every night immediately after dinner—around 7:00—and we're going to work until 9:00. Within a week, I can give you a crash course in cost-fund accounting and bookkeeping."

Up to that time, Winnipeg Bible College had a bookkeeping system much like the family checkbook, listing only checks and deposits.

Crunwell taught me cost-fund accounting, and he upgraded our financial statements to a professional accounting level. As the bills came in, I had to "spread the account"—which means I had to assign each bill to a bookkeeping column. The same was true with income—all incoming money had to be listed in the appropriate "source of income" column.

It was a tough, mean, laborious week—but in the end, I had a firm grasp on the finances of the college. I knew where the money went, and I knew where it was coming from.

But there was still a problem: There was not much money coming in. We were a faith institution. Going back to the early 1900s, many Bible colleges and mission boards were established in faith. These organizations employed a very different strategy than did denominational colleges and missionary boards that received operational funds through denominational budgets. Like Midwest Bible College, WBC was a faith institution that depended upon people to send in monetary gifts to keep the doors open and held to a policy of "full information without solicitation." Therefore, I wrote a prayer letter each month to send to about 800 people on our mailing lists. I shared what God was doing, described projects, and asked for their prayers—without explicitly asking for money.

Each Friday, all the faculty and staff gathered around my office desk at approximately 2:00 P.M. Alida had a sheet of paper with three numbers on it. The first number told us how much money we had in the bank. The second figure indicated how much we owed in bills. The third number was the amount of money left to pay salaries.

We always paid our bills first; it was the Christian thing to do. Almost never did we have enough money to pay all the salaries, so every week I would say, "Everybody write down exactly how much money you *must* have today." The nine of us (faculty and staff) trusted one another, so we didn't write down things that were superficial, and no one seemed to fudge. We wrote down expenses like rent, utilities, and then gasoline for our cars.

After we paid all the college bills, we paid the necessities for the faculty and staff, and then divided the rest of the money equally.

We did one thing differently than Midwest Bible College had done: We allowed faculty to keep their preaching honorarium income. Many times, I didn't pay myself, but would put necessities on a credit card, because I knew I was going out the following Sunday to preach. As I was coming home from the church service, I would stop by a grocery store, cash the check, and bring groceries home for the family.

As a college president, I was paid $3,600 a year. That means I only got $300 a month, or $75 a week, and everything had to come out of that. Needless to say, we lived from hand to mouth. Yet, we never went lacking. God took care of all our needs.

"Ruth . . . why orange?" Elmer came home to see that I had painted the focus wall in our living room orange—Halloween orange. He wasn't mad, but he thought I might be. He thought the conservative Canadians might think their new American Bible college president was crazy.

I had two orange armchairs in my modern living room ensemble. "They match the wall perfectly," was all I could say.

But that orange wall became the talk among the churches. Everyone seemed to like it, and many leaders asked me for advice on their home decorations. God can even use home decoration ideas to establish leadership.
—Ruth Towns

Because Winnipeg Bible College was an old school with a storied history, we had a lot of elderly people on our mailing list who included WBC in their wills. Every three or four months, a lawyer would call me to say that someone had died and left a bequest in his or her will for Winnipeg Bible College. I listened carefully and expressed an appropriate amount of grief, but then I had two questions:

1. How much did they leave the college?
2. When can I get the money?

That's how it was; every few months, we would receive a check large enough to bring all the salaries up to date. Sometimes when I prayed, I felt guilty because I would ask God, "Isn't it about time for You to bring some of Your children home so You can enjoy their presence, and WBC can use their money?"

Winnipeg Bible College got most of its funding in four different ways. First, students paid their bills in the fall, and again in January. Second, WBC got bequests that ranged from $3,000 to $15,000. Third, people mailed gifts to the college. Fourth, there was the July wheat harvest in North Dakota.

Winnipeg was only 60 miles from the U.S. border, and the vast wheat fields of North Dakota lay just on the other side of that border. North Dakota had all kinds of churches, with tall steeples, towering over the flat wheat fields. These congregations seemed to be ignored by their denomination, but not by me; I knew there was money in those churches. So, each summer I recruited four young men, always Mennonites, to form an *acapella* quartet. We put together a 35-minute musical program, beginning with classical music, moving to contemporary, and ending with a spiritual from the South. Then, I would preach for about 30 minutes—the same sermon every night for the 30 days of July.

People from the churches provided overnight lodging, usually the evening meal, and the next morning's breakfast. Sometimes they would send us off with a boxed lunch to eat between locations. If they didn't, we would stop by some farm store and buy two pounds of bologna, a loaf of bread, and five Coca-Colas. Then I would tell my four singers, "Today it's bologna in the bush." That became one of our points of humor, and the way we sacrificed to get the work of God done: "Bologna in the bush."

The farmers harvested their wheat and were paid immediately from the co-operative. I knew their pockets were full, so I would say each evening, "You see these four young men? They're going to serve God around the world. Wouldn't you like to have a financial part in preparing them for ministry? Make a big offering tonight to help Winnipeg Bible College train young people for the mission field."

Most of the money came in cash, not checks. Every three or four days, I would stop by a Western Union telegraph office—and by the miracle of wire communications, sent money back to WBC to pay the bills, meet salary requirements, and get us through the difficult summer months until the students returned.

Elmer was gone again for another 30 days, and he'd taken our car for college transportation. I was stuck at home for a month, depending on the Hindmarsh family for transportation to and from church. Our children turned our basement into a fort, a playhouse, a racetrack, a castle and a battleground for soldiers. There was a lot of educational television—there were not many cartoons in Canada.

The kids had their neighborhood friends for play, and I had my friends from church for coffee klatches.

I believe God gives us lonely epochs in life so we'll seek His presence and talk to Him more often. I spent a lot of those lonely nights praying for Elmer's team, so that souls would be saved. I always added, "Help Elmer raise a lot of money so we can get paid."—Ruth Towns

Three Crises with the Board

I faced three crises with the board of directors at Winnipeg Bible College; each one was so severe that I could have been fired. When I think back to the possibility of being cut loose in Canada with no place to go, and no money to get back to the United States, I realize what a bold move it was to take on the board the way I did. Remember how I said we live recklessly in our youth? If I had not felt that God wanted me to take a strong stand, doing so could have been a foolish move.

The first crisis arose when, in my first year, I put Elizabeth Clee in the same room as Elizabeth Penner. The problem: Clee was a Canadian Indian, and Penner was an Anglo from a Baptist church in the lake head. I understood the animosity in the South between whites and blacks, but I never understood the animosity between the Canadian English and the Canadian Indian. Why? Perhaps because I had pastored a number of Native American Indians at Faith Bible Church in West Dallas, Texas. Their skin perhaps was a little darker, but I never treated them differently, nor did they seem different to me. Isn't the sin of racial prejudice primarily a matter of perception?

A meeting of the board of directors was held to examine the "integration" problem at Winnipeg Bible College. This was eight years after the Supreme Court of the United States had banned segregation in public schools. I remember explaining to the board, "I see absolutely no difference between the two girls, and I did what Jesus would do—He would put them in the same room together." Theoretically and morally, I was right, but culturally I was skating on thin ice.

I think the board was shocked at my bold approach. They were afraid to speak against the biblical truth of integration, so they kept asking, "Will this damage the reputation of WBC?" and "Will this hurt recruitment?" Finally, they dropped the issue, and it went away. The youth at the college were not as prejudiced as the elderly board members were.

The second issue came up in my third year. I had hired Leslie K. Tarr, a Baptist General Conference pastor from Main Street Baptist Church, to teach a course on journalism. Leslie was a published author, and he wrote an article for *Maclean's*, one of the largest magazines in Canada, titled "Let's Give Our Churches Hell."

A meeting of the board was held to terminate Leslie Tarr. I thought the board was foolish, and Tarr needed to be protected. The night before the meeting, I couldn't sleep, so I spent a long time interceding for the coming confrontation. I was going to stick up for Leslie Tarr, even if they fired me.

Dr. Weir, a professor from the University of Manitoba, led the charge. Leslie Tarr was accused of profanity unbecoming a faculty member. He had used the word "hell."

The atmosphere was highly volatile, and a wrong step could have brought about angry words or even a dismissal of Tarr and me. I began the discussion by asking Dr. Weir, "Have you read the article?"

"No." Then he went on to say, "I didn't get a chance to read it, but I know what's in it."

"No, you don't," I rebutted. "Tarr didn't use the word 'hell' as an expletive, but rather was criticizing our churches for changing their doctrine on eternal punishment. The main point of the article was: 'Churches ought to preach more on hell.' "

"Oh . . ." was all Dr. Weir said.

"Let's move on to the next item," I suggested, and we did. A potentially damaging fire had been quickly extinguished.

The third crisis involved changing the board's concept of "faith giving." The faculty and I were missing paychecks. The college was being built on the sacrifice of its faculty, not the board of directors or the Christian public.

Knowing it was a sensitive issue, I prayed long, and then approached the board to explain that our small income was keeping us a small college. "We'll never achieve our dream of building a great college without a great abundance of money."

I informed the board that on the following day, I would begin a personal strategy of appealing to individuals for money. I already had a luncheon date for the next day with Gordon Smith, an influential grain futures broker. Then I explained, "I'm not going to let you vote on this change of strategy, because you'll argue and fight. I'm just going to do it. I need your prayer support and backing."

Doug Hindmarsh, the youngest board member, gave his support. Then the rest of the men voiced agreement. That was a turning point for Winnipeg Bible College. From that point on, I went aggressively after financing.

A Governmentally Approved Seminary[1]

My daughter Debbie went bowling every Saturday morning with Marcy, the daughter of a lawyer, Don McCarthy. Don was a member of Elim Chapel, a leading evangelical church in Winnipeg. As we were watching our daughters bowl one Saturday morning, Don turned to suggest, "Now that you've got the college accredited, let's get a charter from the government of Manitoba so you can offer recognized degrees."[2] This was an unusual proposal, because no Bible college in Canada had ever been chartered by a provincial government or even given governmental authority to offer liberal arts courses. At the time, I had no idea of all the benefits that would come to Winnipeg Bible College. But I thought Don's idea was a good one, so we discussed it with the executives of the board of directors. Don then wrote up a bill to present to the provincial legislature.

On a snowy afternoon, I waited my turn to be interviewed in the Manitoba legislative building by the Progressive Conservative Caucus, the party in power. I had a copy of the bill in my hand, and I was told to stand on the dais and answer any questions from the delegates.

Americans need to understand that getting a bill passed through a Parliament-style government is different from getting one approved by a legislative body in the United States. A Parliamentary bill has to go through three readings. The first reading is to inform the opposition of the bill. The second reading debates the strengths and merits of the bill, and perhaps changes it or even dismisses it. The third reading announces any changes made to the bill, and a pre-determined vote by the majority party approves it.

Before the first reading, I took my position on the dais, and the secretary at the table next to me said, "Gentlemen, I am not going to read this bill. You have a printed copy before you. If you have any questions, you may ask President Towns." I had been told there would probably not be any questions.

A few seconds went by, and then a Frenchman from one of the cities along the Red River put up his hand to ask a question. There were several French sections of Manitoba, and they were almost all Roman Catholic. This delegate asked, "Where is the theological seminary?"

I launched into an extended response, observing that Roman Catholic priests have to go to a four-year college and three years of seminary before they can be ordained. I explained that many of the old-line Protestant denominations did the same thing. But Winnipeg Bible College represented the new evangelicals; much like Mennonites, they ordained men for the ministry with a Bible college education and didn't require a seminary degree.

"I don't understand that; where is the theological seminary?" the Frenchman continued.

I repeated my explanation of why evangelicals do not have theological seminaries. This time, I did add that I had a theological education, and there were many evangelical theological seminaries in the United States, but there were no evangelical seminaries in Canada.

A third time, the Frenchman inquired, "You still haven't answered my question. Where is the theological seminary?"

I turned to the secretary and asked, "Would you change the bill to read: 'Winnipeg Bible College and Theological Seminary'?"

He nodded his head and began to write. I thought to myself, *I just started a theological seminary without a vote of the board of directors, or anyone else's approval. This will probably be shot down.*

When I went back to the college, I was reluctant to tell any of the teachers what I had done. I certainly didn't tell any of the board members. I was going to let matters play out.

I had sat in the gallery of the large legislative assembly—it was just across the highway bridge from the campus of Winnipeg Bible College, both being located on the Assiniboine River—as the secretary announced to the delegates, "You have the bill printed in front of you. I will not read it; I move its adoption." A delegate seconded it, there was no opposition, and they voted, "Yea."

A few days later, I sat in about the same spot in the gallery for the second reading of the proposed legislation. Again the secretary said the same thing about not reading the bill. I was sure this was when the fireworks would break out; there'd be all kinds of opposition. But no one said anything. Then I heard the delegates vote "yea."

Since I knew it would pass, I didn't go back for the third hearing of the bill. God used my friendship with a lawyer to get the bill written up and passed by the legislature—and He used the stubbornness of a French delegate to add the phrase *Theological Seminary.*

Years later, Winnipeg Bible College changed its name to Providence College and Theological Seminary and became the largest evangelical theological seminary in Canada. One of the reasons for its prominence is that it was the first Bible college able to give provincial college credit that could be transferred to any college or university in Canada.

There was a second factor as well. Bill Eichhorst—two presidents after me—went to see R. R. Robertson, Minister of Education for Manitoba, and told him, "Because Winnipeg Bible College is provincially approved, it should receive funding from the Department of Education like other colleges, such as the Episcopal College and the United Church College." Almost immediately, the college began receiving approximately $450 per student per year. With that amount of money and accreditation in its pocket, the college began offering classes in counseling in neighboring provinces, such as Ontario, Saskatchewan and Alberta. In His wisdom, God used minute events to bring about a large and powerful move of His hand to train many young people in the Dominion of Canada for Christian service.

In 1992, President Eichhorst oversaw the construction of two new dormitories on the new Providence campus—one men's dorm and one women's dorm. Eichhorst named the women's dorm the "Elmer Towns Dormitory" in recognition of the role I had played in changing the direction of the college and getting it accredited.

In 2003, I spoke at the college's graduation. While there, I walked into the lobby of the Elmer Towns women's dormitory and stood there as several girls came and went. None of them recognized me or knew that I was the namesake for their dormitory. That experience convinced me that a person's greatest influence is in the lives of the students who sit before him, not in a building named after him. As a matter of fact, the girls at Winnipeg, if they live on the second floor of that dormitory, say "I live up towns," while those who live on the first floor live "down towns."

Elmer determined to make our kids "winners," so he played games with them to develop their competitive edge—Monopoly, Parcheesi, Chinese Checkers. But he wasn't the usual dad who made "dumb" moves to let his kids win. Elmer played to win; the children caught his spirit and they too wanted to win. He played just a little bit better, so he could barely win, or he played a little bit poorer, so they could barely win. Then came the time when they would sell one another Monopoly property cheaply, so one could beat Dad. Or they moved their marbles to help another beat Elmer in Chinese Checkers. Elmer always rationalized, "Whether I win, or the kids win, either way I win." —Ruth Towns

Raising Money

On the college's fortieth anniversary, I received a $25,000 challenge from the M-P Foundation in Toronto, Canada. ("M" and "P" were McClintock and Pitts, two men who were building a large expressway around the city of Toronto.) They promised $25,000 to WBC if we could raise an additional $25,000. That was more than twice the money ever raised for the college in one year.

"Students," I said to the entire student body, "I am going to need every one of you to help me raise $50,000." I explained that I wanted each of them to take a brochure to a donor who was already giving money to the college and describe the school's planned building projects. I told them their purpose was to be a spiritual blessing to the donor, and then to give him or her a pledge card.

Then an ingenious thought crossed my mind: *Maybe each donor would give his or her same gift the following year.* I had a small box placed at the bottom of the pledge card: "I will donate the same amount next year to WBC." That way WBC could have two years of financial stability.

All the students were taken to the college dining room. All the givers' names were typed on 3x5 cards and spread out on dining room tables. Some students took the names of people they already knew; others volunteered to make a presentation to business people in the community.

Three older single college girls contacted Mrs. H. L. Hunt for an appointment. Mrs. Hunt's husband was a multi-millionaire who owned the *Winnipeg Free Press*. Mrs. Hunt told the girls to wear gloves and hats, and to be prepared for English tea. They dressed accordingly and walked out the front of the college, prim and proper—dignity on parade.

Two hours later, they had lost all their dignity; they returned to the school and commenced screaming, stomping and yelling in the college foyer. When high heels stomp on wooden floors, the echo resounds all over the building. As all three jumped like cheerleaders, one of the girls waved in her hand a check for $5,000. Enthusiasm is infectious, and many other students were motivated to make their calls and bring their gifts back.

The money was used to build out our chapel (when the educational building was originally completed, the college ran out of money, so for years the chapel sat as a cold, isolated room without heat in the winter). In addition, two classrooms were built, and other modifications made around the school (such as installing overhead projectors in each classroom).

When I looked at all the pledge cards, I saw something I had never seen before. Enough people had checked the box at the bottom of the card, pledging the same gift for the following year, that I didn't have to worry about next year's budget. I immediately sent a letter to all pledgees thanking them for their commitments. I didn't know it at the time, but God was orchestrating a convergence of several factors . . . because He was preparing for me to leave Canada.

Back to the United States

I had invited Dr. Ken Kantzer, the dean of Trinity Evangelical Divinity School, to give lectures at WBC on the threat of neo-orthodoxy to evangelical churches, which was a hot topic at the time. Dr. Kantzer had studied under the world-famous theologian Karl Barth.

Dr. Kantzer must have been impressed with the new chapel and successful fundraising activities. He saw in my office that I had written and published *Teaching Teens* and a second book, on the Gospel of John, titled *The Deity of the Saviour*.[3] I also showed Kantzer a manuscript of more than 300 pages that I had written as a potential textbook for youth work.

To save money, Dr. Kantzer slept in my son's bedroom. He took copies of these three books to skim that night. The next morning, he charged out of the bedroom, fully dressed, to announce, "I want you to resign and come teach Christian education at Trinity Evangelical Divinity School in Chicago."

That's a thunderbolt announcement before breakfast. Dr. Kantzer told me about the great things Trinity would do, and that I was the man he needed in the department of Christian Education. He went on to tell me that there were many colleges and seminaries in Chicago where I could finish a doctoral degree. I listened carefully and then objected, "I can't come and teach for you this fall; I own this house. It would be impossible to sell it . . ."

The phone rang, interrupting me mid-sentence. On the other end was Paul Charack, a prosperous commercial photographer who attended church with me at Grant Memorial Baptist Church. Over the phone, he said, "I want to buy your house!" That's more than a coincidence. That's the hand of God. Charack offering to buy my home within minutes of my saying I couldn't sell the house was a clear indication that God was leading in my life.

Then Paul asked, "May I come and see your house at 8:00 this morning? I want to bring my wife before I go to work." He went on to explain that he had driven by our house several times and liked it—in fact, it was a dream home for him.

Ken Kantzer and I left around 7:45 A.M., as he had a TV appearance in downtown Winnipeg. Meanwhile, Ruth and the kids "ripped" through the house. (Whenever Ruth wanted to get the house in perfect order in record-breaking time, she would tell the kids, "Let's rip!") Paul Charack walked in the front door and, without seeing anything else, said, "I'll take it."

I told the kids we were moving back to the States, and Sam let out a terrific "Yippee!"

My response: "I thought you liked living in Canada."

"I do," my nine-year-old son answered, "but I like living where God wants us to live." That pretty much summed up the family's attitude about the move. A supernatural coincidence involving a phone call got us to Canada, and another coincidental phone call led us out.

I didn't know how to sell a house, especially in Canada. My lawyer friend, Don McCarthy, began working out the details for Paul to assume the loan and purchase our house.

Another coincidence: The following week, a friend in church asked if I knew anything about Trinity Evangelical Divinity School. No one knew about my resignation, so I choked down a smile to reply, "Yes."

My friend went on to say, "I am driving my truck down to Trinity—empty—and I am going to purchase . . . [I forget what] to bring it back to Winnipeg." Then he asked, "Can you get me directions to the campus?"

It didn't take me long to answer his question with a question of my own: "Can I go with you?"

I explained to him that I was moving to Trinity and asked, "Would you move my furniture?"

He agreed to move my furniture, get it through Customs, and deliver it to the school if I would pay for the gas. What a great answer to prayer. So, that summer of 1965, my family and I moved to Deerfield, Illinois, and I began work at Trinity.

The Seeds of Liberty University in Canada

I never built Winnipeg Bible College's enrollment past 100 students. When I spoke with prospective students or potential donors, WBC always seemed to be fourth or fifth in terms of their loyalty. People had greater loyalties to other organizations than to Winnipeg Bible College. Their churches came first, and the Bible colleges their parents (or they) had attended came second. Then people gave to sensational ministries like the Billy Graham crusades, Youth for Christ, or a popular Christian radio program. Only a few crumbs—if any—were left for WBC.

Then there were huge Canadian Bible institutes with powerful presidents as leaders. Students wanted to study under these spiritual giants, and Christians wanted to give money to their compelling causes.

I wrote an article that summarized my frustration and reflected my dream of a perfect college; it was called "A Bible College Is the Extension of a Local Church at the Collegiate Level." There was a subtitle: "Everything a Church Does to Produce Effective Followers of Jesus Christ, the Bible College Does the Same to Produce Effective Christian Workers."[4]

While I was dreaming in the snow-covered prairies of Western Canada, God was preparing me to begin a Christian university that would influence the world—Liberty University. The greatness of Liberty is a reflection of the biblical power of Thomas Road Baptist Church—the local congregation that gave birth to the school.

I had another thought about great Bible colleges. The two biggest Bible institutes in Canada were built by two of the greatest Western Canadian leaders: L. E. Maxwell started and built Prairie Bible Institute, and Henry Hildebrand started and built Briercrest Bible Institute. Both Bible schools were built in the middle of nowhere, which means they

At Columbia Bible College (1951).

Jimmy Breland, my first Sunday School teacher.

Ruth and I dating at Columbia Bible College (1951).

Northwestern College graduation picture (1954).

Ruth and I at Columbia Bible College.

Exchanging rings at our wedding celeration (August 21, 1953).

Our children (left to right) Sam, Polly and Debbie (December 1958).

The president's Christmas photo for Winnipeg Bible College, taken during my first year in Canada (1961).

Winnipeg Bible College student body (1962). I am third from the left in the last row.

At the president's desk at Winnipeg Bible College (1962).

Radio broadcast from Winnipeg Bible College (1962).

Preaching at Akron Baptist Church, the largest congregation in America at the time (1968).

Receiving my first honorary doctor's degree from Baptist Bible College, Springfield, Missouri (1970).

My daughter Polly with Jerry Falwell (1972).

Standing in front of Liberty Baptist College before the name was changed to Liberty University (1976).

Meeting with the Prime Minister of nationalist China (1980).

(Left to right) Me; Yonggi Cho (pastor of the world's largest church); his wife, Grace; and Jerry Falwell (1983).

Preaching at Young Nak Presbyterian Church in Seoul, Korea (1983).

Teaching (1975).

(Left to right): Me, B.R. Lakin (a well-known evangelist), and Jerry Falwell (1981). Jerry Falwell named the School of Religion after Lakin to keep evangelism in the hearts of Liberty's students.

Dedication of the B.R. Lakin School of Religion Building. (Right to left) Me, Jerry Falwell, B.R. Lakin, his wife, A.T. Humphries, Pierre Guillermin (president), Ed Hindson, Sounds of Liberty (1982).

Blowing out candles at my fiftieth birthday celebration (1982).

Teaching at Liberty University during the 1990s.

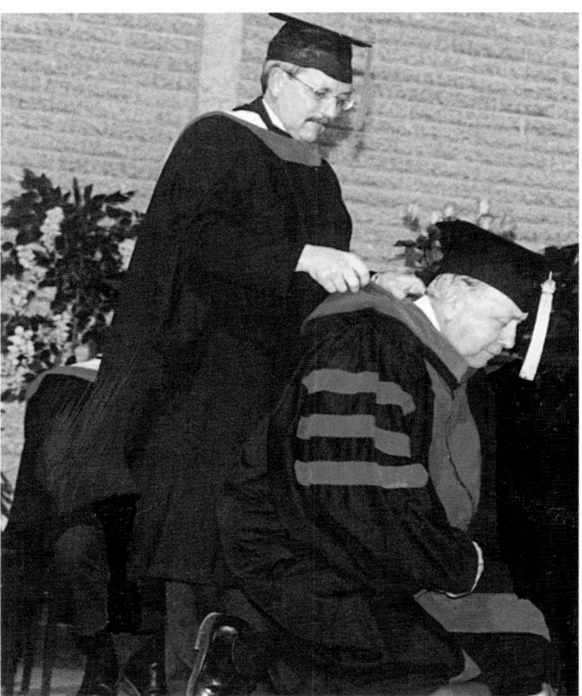

Receiving my honorary doctorate degree from Providence College and Seminary, Winnipeg, Manitoba (2002).

Me with Jerry Falwell (2003).

At an event with John Maxwell (2005).

In 2009, I preached at the largest Baptist church in the world in Seoul, Korea, with Pastor Daniel Lee.

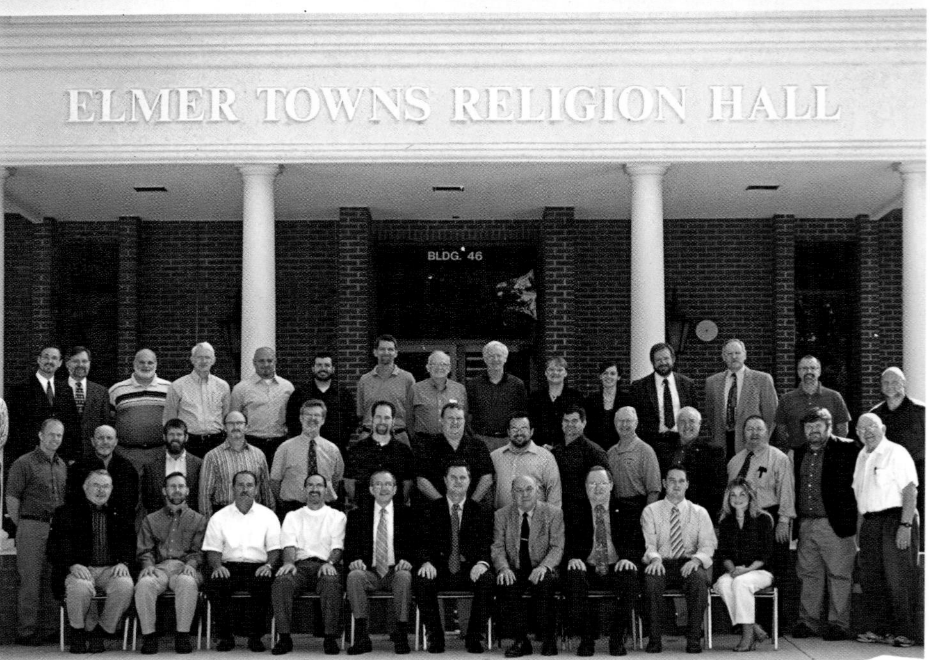

The School of Religion faculty at Liberty University (2008).

Ruth and I at our fiftieth wedding anniversary celebration (2003).

Me with my grandchildren Collyn Towns and Bradford Elmer Towns.

Playing golf with (left to right) John Gregory, Steve Wingfield and Tom Rice (Augusta National, 2003).

Answering questions for students at Fudan University in Shanghai, China. I was invited to lecture at this prestigious university by the faculty in 2009.

Having a discussion with Jerry Falwell, Jr.

Speaking with a seminary graduate.

Ruth and I at a Liberty University event with Glenn Beck (2010).

Me with my grandchildren Bradford Towns and Collyn Towns at Liberty's Homecoming Parade.

The 2012 commencement ceremony at Liberty University.

were not built on a population of people; but great men attracted students and money to their causes.

When I left Canada, I realized I was not a "great man," but I had the idea in the back of my head that somewhere there was another Charles Spurgeon who would build a great college, and perhaps I could help.

I thought perhaps that person might be Ken Kantzer, who was building Trinity Evangelical Divinity School in greater Chicago. Little did I know it would be Jerry Falwell, and the school would be Liberty University—and I would help.

8

The Trinity Evangelical Divinity School Years

(1965–1971)

When I left Canada for Trinity Evangelical Divinity School, I had no idea what kind of seminary Dr. Ken Kantzer was building—and I didn't know why God had chosen me to be a part of its faculty. But I was convinced He had called me to be there, and it wasn't long before I was caught up in the vision for this fledgling educational institution. Perhaps because Ken Kantzer was a *dreamer*, I too became a dreamer.

The name Trinity Evangelical Divinity School was shortened to TEDS by all who worked there, and we were all told by Kantzer that this was not a usual seminary—hence the phrase "Divinity School." He planned to build a university environment of biblical studies, where world-class scholars would produce world-class students.

Kantzer felt that most American seminaries were weak academically, narrowly limited themselves to professional training, and were cookie cutters turning out average men to pastor average churches.

TEDS would be a university of great ideas, where great thoughts by great scholars would capture young minds and produce ministers who would change the world. Some of these giants only taught one semester a year, or a couple of weeks a year. Because TEDS was only 20 minutes from O'Hare Airport, visiting lecturers could fly into Chicago to teach one day a week, then return to their universities and seminaries.

Wilbur Smith, a recognized expert in English Bible exposition, left Fuller Theological Seminar for Trinity. So did Dr. Gleason Archer, a double doctorate from Harvard and Princeton. Other Trinity faculty included J. Edwin Orr, an authority on revivals; John Warwick Montgomery, double doctorate in Church History; J. Oliver Buswell, former president of Wheaton College; Carl F.H. Henry, an authority on systematic theology; Lloyd Perry, an authority on homiletics; Richard Longnecker, an authority on the New Testament; and Kenneth Scott LaTourette, world-renowned church historian.

These great thinkers were hired for their scholarly value, but they only taught; they did not hold faculty committee positions, nor did they do any of the everyday work involved in running a seminary. (They were, however, all on the cutting edge of research and publishing, so I endeavored to become like them by producing a "cutting edge" book.)

Kantzer had hired about five of us to grease the machinery, solve problems, and do the daily work of the seminary. We were not known authorities, nor did we have our doctorates. I understood my role and accepted it gladly. In addition to teaching in the Christian Education department, I was chair of the Graduate Studies Committee, which oversaw the theses being written by the students. This stretched my academic thinking far beyond any course I could have taken.

I met with students to hammer out their objectives and strategies, and then I helped them write their theses. Once they were written, I had to present each thesis to the faculty of eminent scholars, who seemed to know something about everything in every thesis.

Faculty meetings began at 3:00 P.M. on Wednesdays and usually extended into the dinner hour, ending around 6:00 or 7:00 P.M. These great giants debated every thesis, pouring their knowledge into the topic. It was my duty to take notes and report back to the student what the faculty had said.

Trinity was a marvelous place to be during that season. If anything great was happening in the evangelical world, it was happening in Chicago—and I got to be in on it.

One faculty meeting ended early—around 5:30 P.M.—and someone gave me tickets to that evening's dedication of the *New Scofield Reference Bible*. The original *Scofield Reference Bible* was one of the biggest Christian publishing events of the 1900s. For the dedication of this edition, Oxford University Press of England had sponsored a banquet at the Drake Hotel. I had to attend. I phoned Ruth, she got a babysitter and got dressed, and we walked in just as the banquet was starting; the only space left was at one of the head tables down front.

As we talked about the new reference Bible, an executive from Oxford Press casually mentioned that they had changed or updated about 100 words from the original *King James*; these were obsolete words that meant the opposite in the contemporary world.

"You can't do that," was my reaction. "No one can change the *King James Bible*. It's copyrighted."

"No." The executive gently reminded me that the *King James* had never been copyrighted. He explained that there had been five editions of the *King James Bible*—the first revision coming within two years after the initial printing. Also, he mentioned that since the majority of the market was in the United States, the *New Scofield Reference Bible* would follow the *Webster's Dictionary* spelling used in the United States and not the *Oxford Dictionary* spelling used in England. "Dozens of words have different spellings."

That information became valuable, because a few years later I would share it with Sam Moore, president of Thomas Nelson Bible, and it would lead to the translation and publishing of the *New King James Bible*.

When we moved to Trinity, I was asked to supervise the missionary closet, where hand-me-downs were donated for the needy seminary students. But maybe I was chosen for the job because of my marginal wardrobe and those of the children. After five years on poverty wages in Canada, everything was worn or out of date.

Trinity was surrounded by wealthy homes whose occupants brought loads of donations, still stylish and in good condition. They suggested, "Why don't you try on that one?" or "This dress is you!" The girls and I received some of the best "styles" we ever wore, and the donors were not treating us like missionaries. Everything went to the closet, and because the girls and I worked hard, more went to student families than would otherwise have reached them.

When Elmer wrote a best seller, we depended on the missionary closet no more, but we still worked there for the students. —Ruth Towns

Dr. Kantzer had a policy for faculty: "Publish or perish." We had to write at least one significant journal article each year—or one significant book could take the place of the journal article.

Obviously I asked Kantzer the question "What is a significant article or book?"

He smiled and said, "Because I am the dean, I'm the one who determines what is significant." I began to pray that God would lead me to a significant book. God answered in an unusual way.

Getting a "10 Bestselling" Idea

Late one afternoon, I was teaching a large class—60 students—and our discussion got off the original topic and onto the largest churches in America.

"First Baptist Church, Dallas, Texas, is the largest in the world," I boldly maintained. "Dr. W. A. Criswell has led that church to double its size since he's been there, and they have more than 4,000 in Sunday School attendance."

"I don't think it's the largest," replied Ron Rynn, one of my brightest students. Rynn went on to explain, "Jack Hyles in Hammond, Indiana, has the largest Sunday School in the world."

"I don't think so," I argued back, explaining that Jack Hyles had around 2,700 in Sunday School attendance, and Criswell had more than 4,000 in attendance—therefore, Criswell's church must be the largest.

But Rynn wouldn't give up. He declared, "Jack Hyles says he is pastor of the largest church in the world."

To that I snipped, "You can't believe it every time a pastor brags." The class laughed.

"You're both wrong," another student spoke up from the back of the room. He mentioned there was a "hillbilly" church in Akron, Ohio, that had more than 6,000 in attendance. This student went on to say that he had attended that Sunday School as a boy, and he remembered it having great crowds.

I ended that conversation, went on to another topic, and forgot about our discussion of the largest Sunday Schools until the next Sunday afternoon. I was reading the Sunday *Chicago Tribune*'s listing of the 10 best-selling books, and I thought to myself, *If the 10 best-selling books are important to readers, a list of the 10 largest Sunday Schools would be too.* Right then, I made a life-changing decision to find the 10 largest churches in America, although I didn't actually start my research until the following day.

At the time, I was the Sunday School editor for *Christian Life* magazine, which was the largest Christian magazine in the evangelical world. I had contracted with editor Robert Walker to do three short articles in each issue. The first was "News and Views in Sunday School," a news article about what was happening in Sunday School; second was an in-depth article on new trends; and third was a personality article on a Sunday School newsmaker, whether a well-known person or someone doing a significant job.

So, I started my research by advertising in the pages of *Christian Life* that I was looking for the largest Sunday School in America. Next, I wrote to evangelical denominations asking them for lists of their largest Sunday Schools. Then, since I had access to a list of citywide Sunday School conventions of America, I wrote to the leaders of these conventions, asking for information on the largest churches in their areas. I even used a non-scientific tool: I began phoning church leaders in major cities and asking for their knowledge of great Sunday Schools.

When I began this research, I found out that almost no church kept worship attendance records. So I determined that I couldn't find the largest worship service, because those statistics weren't available. But I might be able to find the largest Sunday School, because almost every church kept Sunday School attendance figures to report to their denominations.

A New York newspaper reported in 1959 that Sunday School was "the most wasted hour of the week."[1] That was probably true in New York, particularly among mainline denominational churches. Those were probably liberal churches that no longer accepted the inerrancy of Scripture. If the Bible is not relevant, why attend Sunday School to learn it?

But as I traveled the hinterlands and suburbia of America—out in the Midwest, the South, and even on the West Coast—I found large, vibrant Sunday Schools that were the driving force of their congregations. I knew about big Sunday Schools and churches, but the general public didn't know about them.

The first article on the 10 largest Sunday Schools appeared in the October 1967 issue of *Christian Life* magazine. *Shazam!* The listing jarred the church people of America. "The news of the ten largest Sunday schools hit America like a thunderclap," said Robert Walker, editor of *Christian Life* magazine.[2]

How did it happen? An editor of the *Los Angeles Times* printed the list of the largest Sunday Schools in his newspaper. (The tenth largest Sunday School was at First Baptist Church, Van Nuys, California—in the greater Los Angeles area.) Then he put the list on the *Associated Press* wire, and it went out to newspapers all over the country. News of the largest Sunday Schools appeared in many of the larger newspapers throughout the country, and the deluge began.

Preaching All Over the United States

Within two years, I had expanded the list from 10 Sunday Schools to the largest 100. I didn't realize it, but that brought even more attention to the listing. When newspapers saw churches from their areas on the list, they turned it into a local story, bringing more attention to the list. I began getting invitations from all over America to speak at Sunday School conventions, denominational conventions and local pastors' meetings.

The first year the 100 list came out, the last church on the list—the hundredth largest Sunday School—was First Baptist Church, Bossier City, Louisiana. Pastor Devon Vaughan called to ask me to speak there on a Sunday. As we chatted, he asked, "Could you have a plaque made to present to my church, recognizing that it is the one hundredth largest in the United States?"

"Yes," I answered, "it would be an honor."

About 10 minutes after we hung up, he phoned again to ask, "What will be on the plaque?" We worked out a few things that could be engraved on the plaque. After another 10 minutes, he called back a third time to ask, "How much are you going to spend on the plaque?" He didn't want a cheap little plaque, but one worthy of his church. We agreed to let him purchase the plaque, and I would present it to the church.

I kept a large map of the United States on the wall of my garage, and each time I went to speak in another city, I put a pin on the map. To me, it was almost like a war map, where a general would place pins to indicate locations of advancing army divisions.

I was invited to speak at the New England Conference on Evangelism, sponsored by Jack Wyrtzen, president of Word of Life Ministries in Schroon Lake, New York. I was one of five leaders who spoke in five states in five nights. Each of us changed churches for each succeeding night. During that conference, I spoke in Connecticut, Massachusetts, Maine, New Hampshire and Vermont.

Later, looking at my map, I realized only one state didn't have a pin—Nevada. The only thing I knew about Nevada was Las Vegas, which was famous for gambling and sin. So I looked through a church directory and found Las Vegas Baptist Temple, a church that belonged to the Baptist Bible Fellowship. I phoned the pastor and confessed to him my ego, saying, "It's not the right motive to come to preach in a church to have all 50 states under my belt."

He interrupted, "I want you to come speak, Dr. Towns, no matter what the motive."

I knew Elmer had a pen name, but he wouldn't tell me, or anyone. When asked, he'd say, "No, I can write and publish my poems with more freedom if no one knows my pseudonym." Then one fateful day, the whole family was riding across Northern Minnesota listening to Elmer enjoy the song, "Dream a Little Dream of Me."

Debbie asked Elmer, "Why do you like that song?"

He told us it was the way girls sang when he was a kid. Then he described Mama Cass as about 5'2" tall, blond, with her hair in a flip, and skinny. The kids rolled in the back seat with laughter. Then we seemed to all be honest, on the same page, so Debbie asked her dad to tell us his pen name. He agreed and made the kids promise not to tell anyone. So Elmer explained his pen name was Remle Snwot. It was his name spelled backwards. Again the kids rolled with laughter, and when they got home they told everyone. So Elmer now has another secret name to publish his poetry, and he won't tell anyone. That secret will die with him. —Ruth Towns

I agreed to pay my airfare and motel there. My flight from Los Angeles into Las Vegas had engine trouble, and instead of landing early Saturday evening, I arrived around midnight. We drove down the Las Vegas strip so I could see the dazzling lights.

Viewing Las Vegas from the air late on a Saturday night was like seeing a small atomic bomb explode: It was a huge, glistening ball of light on the desert floor.

"You want to walk through some of the casinos?" the pastor asked.

"No, I don't approve of gambling or drinking; also I don't approve of public displays of nudity." Then I explained that if I went into a casino even one time, someone could whisper behind my back that I had compromised with gambling. Following the same reasoning, for the rest of my life I never ate meals in bars; if I had no other alternatives, I would fast. To me it was a matter of being true to Jesus Christ.

Preaching at the World's Largest Church

Finally, I was invited to preach at the world's largest church—the Akron Baptist Temple—and all week long, Ruth and I talked about the great honor of preaching in the world's largest church. I had been a young kid from Savannah, Georgia, who was not sure he could make it through Columbia Bible College; now I was preaching for Dallas Billington, pastor of the world's largest church. As I was getting in the front seat of the car to drive to the airport, Ruth said, "Don't get a big head, or God won't use you." Therefore, that whole night, I prayed and dedicated the opportunity to God. When I arrived at the church, I unrolled a 3' by 6' scroll of paper on which I was gathering statistics to compare each of the largest churches in America. (These statistics were part of my research for the book *The Ten Largest Sunday Schools in America*.)

Before the service began, three or four secretaries hovered around my chart, filling in all the statistics I needed. I glanced over the chart before walking to the pulpit to preach, so I said in my sermon, "I see by the statistics I gathered earlier that you only had 150 baptisms last year. I would expect the world's largest church to have more baptisms than that." I was bold in my preaching: "If you are going to remain the largest church in the world, you're going to have to give attention to winning people to Christ and baptizing more people."

As soon as the morning service was over, Dallas Billington yelled to his pastors and staff, "Who the h— told this kid preacher that we only had 150 baptisms last year?" He snapped the words: "Everyone get in my office immediately."

I was shocked, because that was the first time I heard a man of God curse. (I wish I could say it was the last time, but I have heard a few other cursing preachers, and anytime I hear it, I say, "Don't curse in front of me.") Dallas Billington taught me two things. First, we "have this treasure in earthen vessels" (2 Cor. 4:7). Even the best of us fail—and sometimes we fail at our strongest point. We all saw his feet of clay on that special day when Dallas Billington was recognized for pastoring the world's largest church.

Dallas Billington was a man of simple tastes, yet he also had his moments of frivolity. After church was over, and we had been to lunch, he drove me to the edge of his four-story Sunday School building and put his '98 Oldsmobile in neutral. He revved the engine. His eyes glistened. Turning to the back seat, he said to his wife, "Honey, you and your mother, buckle up."

He turned to me. "Buckle up, Preacher." Then, with a sly grin, he said, "I'm gonna show you a really big Sunday School." (This was the second lesson.) He hunkered down over the steering wheel like a NASCAR driver, revved the engine two or three more times, and then dropped the gear into drive. The tires squealed; rubber burned as he floor-boarded the accelerator.

"Yell when I get to 100 miles per hour," Dallas instructed.

The Oldsmobile roared into action, whistling past the Sunday School building, only a few feet away from windows and doors. I was scared someone might step out through a door and cause a catastrophe.

"Yiyeeee . . ." I yelled, "We're over 100 miles per hour!" The Oldsmobile skidded to a stop, rocking back and forth from its momentum. Smoke from burning rubber drifted into the front seat. Billington looked over at me and laughed. "Now go back to Chicago and tell them you've seen a really big Sunday School."

I didn't realize at the time that I was walking in the shadow of a giant. As a matter of fact, I could tell stories about several other giants in other churches; these were men who banged on the windows of heaven, who boldly attacked the gates of sin, who won multitudes to Jesus

Christ and built huge churches to the glory of God. Yes, these were giants for God. They stretched me to think big for God, and later I dreamed with Jerry Falwell of building the largest Christian college in evangelicalism.

My First Best-seller Surprise

My new book, *The Ten Largest Sunday Schools and What Makes Them Grow*, was a small, 163-page paperback (costing $1.95) that people could read in one sitting.[3] Baker Book House gave me a 50 percent discount, so I would order anywhere from one to four boxes to sell in churches where I preached. I'd sell the books for $1. It was more important to me to get the message out than it was to make money off the book.

Each month I looked into the *Christian Bookstore Journal* to see whether my book made a list of the 10 best-selling Christian books. When I was talking with Robert Walker, the editor of the *Christian Bookstore Journal*, I asked why my book didn't make the list of best-selling books. Then I showed him a card with the numbers:

September: 550 copies
October: 675 copies
November: 625 copies

As Walker looked at the sales numbers, I explained, "These were just books I sold at the back of a church auditorium." Then I added, "A lot are also being sold in bookstores."

Walker reached for the telephone and called a friend at Baker Book House, inquiring how many copies were sold. Their numbers were larger than my numbers.

Then Walker picked up the inter-office phone to advise a writer at the *Christian Bookstore Journal*, "Next month put in the best-selling list Towns's book, *The Ten Largest Sunday Schools*." Then Walker pulled a number out of the air: "Let's put it at number seven."

That was when I learned that the listing of the best-selling books was not scientifically accurate, but was publicity filled with politics and guesses. For five years, I had a best seller each year, and I'd like to say that I got on the list without any politicking. But that's not the case. When I sold copies of my books at the back of church auditoriums, I always made sure to get the numbers to Robert Walker. These best-selling books, some of which I co-wrote with Jerry Falwell, each sold about 100,000 copies: *The Ten Largest Sunday Schools*, Baker Book House, 1969; *Church Aflame*, Impact Books, 1971; *America's Fastest Growing Churches*, Impact Books, 1972; *Capturing a Town for Christ*, Fleming-Revell, 1973; *Getting a Church Started in the Face of Insurmountable Odds with Limited Resources in Unlikely Circumstances*, Impact Books, 1974; *The Successful Sunday School and Teachers Guide*, Creation House, 1975.

Could I Influence America?

Honestly, I felt I could change the United States by motivating churches to "capture their towns for Christ." I went everywhere in my effort to spread that message. My sermon, based on *The Ten Largest Sunday Schools*, challenged pastors and congregations to double their efforts, double their outreach, and double their attendance. If they didn't already have an aggressive Sunday School bus ministry, I challenged them to purchase a fleet of Sunday School buses to bring children to the house of God. I exhorted them to go door to door to reach every person in their "Jerusalem" with the gospel of Jesus Christ.

I taught all my classes at TEDS on Tuesdays and Thursdays. From Chicago, I could fly to most major cities in America, preach one sermon, and return home that night or early the next morning. There were a couple of weeks when I preached seven straight nights.

Late one Saturday evening, I preached in Jamestown, New York. Pastor Charles Hand of the Open Door Baptist Church in Marion, Indiana, insisted that I preach at his church the following Sunday morning. He personally drove me all night across several states while I slept. Arriving after dawn, we followed Sunday School buses as they picked up children in the poor sections of Marion.

I had great hope—but a flawed hope—that my preaching in every major city of America could produce aggressive soul-winning churches that would bring evangelism and revival to each city. I naively thought I could change the face of America's Christianity.

What I didn't realize was the spiritual frailty of some church leaders. They were not as pure in motive as I thought they were. I knew of two who went to prison for stealing, and a few who were hounded out of office because of sinful sexual conduct. Some wanted to retire, while others wanted promotions to cushy denominational positions. Just about the time a church became powerful for the gospel, something usually diluted its outreach.

I should have known that Satan is a crafty deceiver. He hates soul-winning churches that snatch lost people from the certainty of hell. When Satan can trip up a soul-winning pastor, he destroys the church's evangelistic outreach.

I loved The Ten Largest Sunday Schools*—it provided money for us to live normally. Before this, we were always saving to pay the demanding bills—light, rent, phone, water—and we never went out to a restaurant, or had a color TV set, or even had gas money to just go for fun rides, vacations or a picnic. So while Elmer was traveling all over America to preach in the largest churches, I finally had money to spend on the kids for clothes, or fun things to do, or just kids' stuff—but their father wasn't there to enjoy all of that with us. Isn't life a trade off? Elmer's trips were both a win and lose situation for me and the kids.*
—Ruth Towns

The greatest thing about the 10 largest Sunday Schools was that they were more fundamental in doctrine than the average church; they certainly were not liberal, nor were they drifting towards compromise. The pulpit ministers thundered, "Thus saith the Lord!" in a world of uncertainty and confusion. They didn't speak in theological abstracts, nor were they trumpets giving a wavering sound. These pastors believed that the Word of God always had been and always would be the answer to the basic needs of humans. They were ardent, enthusiastic, unapologetic biblicists who knew they had a relevant message for every man and woman on earth, especially children; therefore, they poured their lives into their Sunday Schools. Within the limitations of time, space and opportunity, these pastors made every effort to communicate the message of the Word of God to people in their own ways.

These churches were separatists from sin, and people were warned not to live like the world. The pastors did more than give lip service to Christ as pre-eminent; they strove to magnify the risen, living Christ as a personal reality in every aspect of the church program. To lost people, they offered a loving Savior who could indwell the lives of individuals and transform their churches.

These pastors believed that God could do miracles and answer prayer, and they were committed to winning their cities for Christ.

The Most Powerful College in America

In the third year of the Sunday School listing, I decided to add a question to my survey: "What college or seminary did you attend that equipped you to build one of the largest churches in America?"

I expected the responses to include recognized evangelical schools, like Wheaton, Moody Bible Institute, and all of the other great evangelical schools. But they were not there. To my shock, other great schools, like Biola, Nyack, Columbia Bible College and Northwestern College, also didn't make the list. A few pastors attributed their great churches to various Southern Baptist seminaries. But 23 of the pastors were graduates of, or otherwise associated with, Baptist Bible College in Springfield, Missouri.

I've got to find out why that college is so great, I thought.

I flew to Springfield, Missouri, unannounced, rented a car, and drove straight to 800 East Kearney Street. The first place I visited was the library; I figured a great, influential college would be driven by a great library.

What a shock to find only one room with bookshelves on the four walls. There were no stacks, and fewer than 5,000 books.

"Where are the stacks?" I asked Mrs. Noel Smith, the librarian.

"You're lookin' at 'em." It was a jaw-dropping experience.

Then I asked about the reference room for encyclopedias and other reference books.

"They're right here!" The reference section occupied two shelves.

I had taken great Bible classes at Columbia Bible College and Northwestern College, so I was sure that the classes at Baptist Bible College would be even greater. After all, out of these classrooms had come some pastors of the largest churches in America.

But the classes were normal—not any better, nor any worse, than my college courses. Apparently, it wasn't the classroom experience that produced great preachers who built great churches. As I walked around the college, talking to students and faculty along the way, I still couldn't understand why this school—whose buildings were mostly converted World War II barracks—produced such great leaders.

Then I went to chapel. Dr. John Rawlings, pastor of Landmark Baptist Temple, was preaching, and he said, "Young men, when you graduate, get in your jalopy, drive to someplace like Keokuk, Iowa, and *capture your town for Christ*." (Later I would write a book with Jerry Falwell titled *Capturing a Town for Christ*.)[4]

That was when I realized that the greatness of this college stemmed from the greatness of the speakers in chapel. To produce burning hearts for evangelism in its graduates, the school's leaders kept the chapel pulpit hot. (This philosophy later became the basis for greatness at Liberty University.)

Losing Momentum

The sermon on *The Ten Largest Sunday Schools* consumed my focus. I went everywhere preaching the same sermon. One week, I preached that sermon eight times—every day, and twice on Sunday. When you get caught up in euphoria, you think the words of the song: "Those were the days, my friend; we thought they'd never end."[5] But all things human will eventually end.

God gave me a thought that was important for a moment in time, but I didn't realize that time was slipping through my fingers like sand. After a few years, *The Ten Largest Sunday Schools* became old news—and no one buys old newspapers, except those interested in history.

The next event on God's calendar for me was the creation of a world-class Christian university.

Leaving Greater Chicago

I taught at Trinity for six years. It was the hot, prestigious seminary of the '60s. Potential faculty thought it was the position of a lifetime; *no one would ever leave it*. But I did!

My nation-capturing idea had introduced me to Jerry Falwell, the pastor of Thomas Road Baptist Church in Lynchburg, Virginia. This church had the ninth largest Sunday School in America, with 2,620 in attendance. Pastor Falwell asked me to leave TEDS and co-found Liberty University in Lynchburg, Virginia, with him. My resignation was announced in a faculty meeting, after which Dr. Ken Gangle confronted me publicly, thinking I was making a mistake.

"Elmer, why are you going to the Appalachian Mountains of West Virginia to start a Bible college?"

"I'm going to the Blue Ridge Mountains of Virginia to begin a liberal arts college," I countered.

He continued his attack: "A lot of mountain preachers try to start a Bible college, but most of them fail in a year or two, and they don't have the education to successfully start a college."

"But God has called me," I answered.

"Who is the pastor?" Gangle asked.

"Jerry Falwell."

"Never heard of him."

I told him that Jerry had built the ninth largest church in America in the shortest period of time. I said Jerry was one of the first pastors to preach on television every Sunday, and was the first to put all his church's records on a computer. I compared Jerry to Charles Spurgeon, and I predicted that the faculty would one day hear from him. (Fifteen years later, Jerry Falwell was invited to address the faculty of TEDS when he became *Good Housekeeping Magazine*'s Man of the Year in 1969.)[6]

Gangle wouldn't quit. "Chicago is the center of the evangelical movement. It has some of the greatest educational institutions, mission headquarters, publishing houses—and it's the crossroads of America." Then Gangle warned, "You will leave Chicago, bury yourself in the hills of Virginia, and never be heard from again."

There were a dozen reasons why I should have stayed in Greater Chicago, but only one reason to leave. God spoke to me and gave me the assurance that Liberty would be a great university. I am probably better known today for teaching at Liberty than I ever would have been for teaching at TEDS. Leaving TEDS was probably my greatest step of faith. Some called it a leap into the dark. But don't credit me with great faith—no. I have a great God, and I just obeyed His leading.

9

The Early Liberty University Years

(1971–1973)

I was preaching at Canton Baptist Temple (the sixth largest church in America) on the last weekend of January 1971. Pastor Harold Heninger was an astute financial manager; the church had a suite in the Sunday School building for visiting speakers, rather than lodging them in a local motel. That Saturday evening, I ate dinner at Harold's home, and he looked across the dinner table at me as he announced, "Jerry Falwell is going to start a college; I want you to talk with him and help him start it."

"He won't do it for six years," I answered Pastor Heninger. "Falwell has a Christian grade school through grade six, and he'll add a grade a year. He won't start a college for six years."

"No, he's going to do it immediately," Heninger disagreed with me, explaining that Jerry was impetuous and impatient. "You two—Falwell and Towns—are like two peas in a pod; you think alike, you dream alike, and you have the same passion in life."

"When you go back to your apartment," Harold told me, "I want you to pick up the phone and call him tonight—on my nickel." The apartment where I was staying had a phone system attached to the church switchboard. No one could call in, but I could call out.

"Okay." I nodded to him, but then forgot my agreement until I was leaving.

Harold poked me on the chest with his index finger, "Will you promise to phone him when you first walk in your apartment?"

"Yes."

I still had my overcoat on when I picked up the phone and dialed Jerry Falwell around 7:00 that Saturday evening. "Hello, this is Elmer Towns."

"Elmer, what are we going to name the college?"

Dumbfounded, I didn't know what to say at first. Jerry hadn't even said "hello." He just wanted to talk about the college. "Jerry, you don't start a college with a name," I finally explained. "You start with its purpose and philosophy."

"Okay," he said. "Let's discuss purpose and philosophy."

One Woman Prayed While We Planned

I didn't know this until after our phone call was over, but 15 minutes prior to my calling Jerry, he had called my home in greater Chicago and talked to Ruth. He told my wife that he wanted me to help him start a college, because he liked my spirit and vision, commenting, "Elmer gets things done!" After talking with Ruth for a few minutes, Jerry said, "I never ask a wife if her husband would come to work for me, but do you think that Elmer would come start a college for me?"

"He'd be perfect for the job," Ruth answered Jerry. She told him that I had been a college president in Winnipeg, and that I had been on the steering committee of the Accrediting Association of Bible Colleges. As they continued talking, Jerry sold Ruth on the college before he had talked with me. As a result, Ruth immediately began praying for the college and asking God to motivate me to phone her long-distance, so she could tell me all about it. For an hour, while Jerry and I were drawing mental blueprints for a world-changing college, Ruth was in the presence of God, interceding for our future. God's timing for spiritual advances is always perfect.

I liked Jerry Falwell the first time he talked to me over the phone. He was excited about the new college he wanted to start; it was going to be the "biggest and best" in all of Christianity. I liked the fact that he was a big dreamer, just like Elmer. Then Jerry complimented my husband, saying Elmer had integrity, spirituality, and was a "go-getter." Finally, Jerry told me Elmer was the kind of man he needed to start his college.

My heart raced with excitement. I knew this was where my husband ought to be. But Elmer was staying in a room at a church without a telephone. I couldn't talk with him or share how excited I was about the new college. So I began to pray that God would touch Elmer's heart about this new college. Then I prayed for the college's success, but most of all I prayed that he would phone me so I could get him to phone Jerry Falwell. I decided to pray until Elmer called. —Ruth Towns

"Jerry, the new college will be like a three-legged stool," I painted a mental picture. "The first leg will be *academic excellence*. I want this college to be greater than most Bible colleges; it will be a liberal arts college."

"No . . . not liberal." Jerry reacted to that hated term: *liberal.*

I explained that the phrase "liberal arts" meant a college that teaches the arts and sciences. I said we'd train educators, businessmen and engineers, not just people for ministry. "We'll even start a law school."

In those days, Wheaton College was committed to academic excellence, but it had co-ed dorms, so I added, "We don't want to compromise like Wheaton, but we want to build a college with *academic excellence* like Wheaton."

"The second leg of the stool is *cutting-edge creativity*," I explained.

Our college would be culturally relevant and attuned to the times. I wanted our college to minister in a world of computers and television, just like Jerry's church did. In those days, I thought Bob Jones University was the most creative in its outreach, so I said to Jerry, "Let's be as creative as Bob Jones, but let's not be swallowed up by legalism." He agreed.

"The third leg of the stool is *local church evangelism*." We both agreed that Baptist Bible College in Springfield, Missouri, was one of the greatest places to train pastors for ministry, and we wanted that passion in our college. I said, "Let's be evangelistic like Baptist Bible College, but let's not adopt its 'hillbilly' ways."[1]

Jerry agreed to the three-legged stool, and then I added, "I've got another innovation for our college that will be world-changing." I explained that I didn't want to start a school controlled by a denomination or fellowship, such as Baptist Bible College. I also didn't want an independent college with its own board of directors, such as Bob Jones and other independent schools. I shared with Jerry the philosophy I had written about while I was at WBC: "A Christian college should be the extension of a local church at the collegiate level. Everything a church does to influence its people, the Christian college should also do to influence its students, but at a college or university level." I told Jerry we would start a college where all of our students were members of Thomas Road Baptist Church and did their Christian service in the church. The spiritual dynamics of Thomas Road Baptist Church would infuse spiritual life into the college.

"I love that idea," Jerry agreed. Then he said, "Elmer, of course you'll be president . . ." He was assuming that since I had been a Bible college president, I would run the college.

"Absolutely not."

Jerry was shocked by my response, but I had come to the conclusion in Canada that "great men build great colleges, and average men build average colleges" (see chapter 7). I was an average man. Jerry was the great leader who would build a great college. That night I called Jerry a modern Charles Spurgeon (Spurgeon being the pastor who had built the most powerful Protestant church in London while England ruled the world). "Don't compare me to Spurgeon," Falwell protested.

"You did something few have done," I explained. "You started your own church and built it to become one of the largest in America." In addition, I reminded him that he had built a television empire that spanned the country. I felt the new college would be as large as the talents and faith of Jerry Falwell—and my opinion that night has been confirmed by the modern-day Liberty University.[2]

I arrived in Lynchburg on Monday, June 1, 1971, ready to go to work. I met David and Linda Rhodenhizer in my office at 9:00 A.M. David had finished one year as a student at Baptist Bible College, and he wanted to talk about transferring to Liberty University. I didn't try to talk him out of the Springfield school, but laid out the alternatives and let it be his decision.

"Baptist Bible College is a great college. They have produced some of the greatest church leaders in America, and you could become one of those great men. But on the other hand," I reasoned, "Liberty University is going to be greater. You'll get everything at Liberty that Baptist Bible College can give you, plus you'll get a passion for church growth and soul winning, and you will want to capture a town for Christ."

David and Linda enrolled in Liberty (they were the first married couple we had as students) and graduated. He planted Calvary Road Baptist Church in the greater Washington, DC, area in 1979 and was one of our first students to reach 1,000 in attendance at his church plant. Today David is a member of Liberty's board of directors.

Later that first Monday morning, I walked to Jerry Falwell's office and presented him with a budget of $152,000 to $160,000.

"Jerry, I'll need some seed money—$5,000—to open a checking account for Liberty University."

Jerry told me, "I don't have any money; the church is broke."

"What do you mean . . . broke? There was a great offering yesterday; more than $10,000 came in."

"We spent it all. The church had bills, and $10,000 wasn't even enough to pay all the bills."

"How are we going to start a college when we don't have any money?" I asked Jerry.

"Well, let's go raise the money tonight." Jerry was an eternal optimist.

Later that afternoon, we got into his Buick and drove about 100 miles west into the Blue Ridge Mountains to Mountain View Baptist Church—a large Southern Baptist church with attendance of about 300. Doug Oldham, the famous gospel singer, showed up in his bus and met us there.

That evening, there were about 150 people present, Doug Oldham sang for 30 minutes, I pitched a new college that would capture the world for Christ, and Jerry Falwell preached on the "Door Keeper" from a text about Solomon's Temple. Door keepers were the ones who made it possible for Israel to enter the house of God, so people could pray, worship and fellowship with God. Jerry appealed to the audience: "Will you be a 'Door Keeper'? Will you hold open the door to a new college that will carry the gospel to all the world?"

After the sermon, I went up and down the aisle, distributing ugly-looking stacks of envelopes held together by commercial staples. They were called "Door Keeper" packets, and each packet included 52 envelopes, one for each week of the year. People could slip a dollar into an envelope each week to help open the doors of Liberty University and equip students to reach the world for Christ.

As individuals raised their hands, I gave them each a package of envelopes. Jerry instructed them to tear off the first envelope and insert a dollar or more. I had dollar bills in one hand and envelope packets in the other. That evening, 75 people took packages of envelopes. Going home, Jerry told me, "Do you know what 75 people times 52 envelopes means? We raised $3,900 here this evening." But then Jerry went on to explain that Door Keepers represented more than a dollar a week; they were prayer supporters who eventually gave much more than $52 a year. Many high schoolers took Door Keeper packages that first summer.

They would later come to Liberty University and remind me of the evening we visited their church.

The next night, we went to Buena Vista, Virginia, where we recruited 35 Door Keepers from about 100 people. Wednesday evening we came home from Richmond with 150 Door-Keeper promises. Throughout that first summer—three or four times each week—Jerry, Doug Oldham and I visited various churches throughout Virginia looking for Door Keepers and raising money for Liberty University.

When Liberty University began, it did not own a stick of furniture, a piece of property, nor a building. I used a phrase "shared services" to describe the way Thomas Road Baptist Church and Liberty University shared facilities and other resources. Liberty used Sunday School rooms for its classrooms, the church gym, the church dining room—and for chapel we used the church sanctuary. Liberty Christian Academy had a large library that was shared by the new college.

I had lunch with Jim Moon, Jerry's co-pastor, one day, and he asked me, "How many students do you think we will start the year with?"

"We'll be lucky if we have 50," I said, reflecting my doubts and pessimism.

When I asked him how many he expected, Moon said his opinion didn't matter; it was what Jerry believed that was important. "Jerry expects 100 students."

Moon assured me that if Jerry said we were going to have 100 students, there would be 100 there.

"I'm not going to massage the figures, nor will I lie about the number of students," I immediately responded.

Jim came back quickly to explain that Jerry wouldn't lie, but I needed to learn something about Jerry Falwell's practice of "Say-it Faith." He set goals by faith, then worked to reach them. Jim said, "When Jerry Falwell sets goals, the church always meets them. So, we'll have 100 students." Liberty University opened the year with 154 students.

At the beginning, I was the only full-time teacher; all the rest were part-time. Jim Moon, a graduate of Baptist Bible College, taught Old Testament Survey. Two or three other pastors taught individual courses in Christian education, and Jerry Falwell taught the soul-winning course "Evangelism Aflame."

In addition, I recruited two former college presidents to teach part-time. The first had been president of Presbyterian College in Clinton, South Carolina, and had taught World History at Central Virginia Community College. The second was a former president of a Southern Baptist college, who was now teaching Introduction to Psychology at Roanoke College. Counting me, this small, unknown college had three former college presidents teaching classes.

Jerry and I set a goal of 5,000 students. That goal was just a little bigger than Bob Jones University and Tennessee Temple University, both of which averaged around 4,500 students at the time. We had a secret sign that I would flash to him when I walked onto the church platform. I'd hold up my thumb and pointer finger with a small space between them. That meant, "Liberty will be just a little bit bigger than those two universities." While Falwell didn't flash the sign to me, he'd throw his head back to smile in agreement.

The first year, only freshman courses were offered, and a year of classes was added each year until Liberty reached a four-year curriculum. I told the faculty, "Assign a quiz on the first day of class, and quiz the students the second time your class meets." I pushed to enforce the first leg of our stool: *Academic Excellence*.

Toward the end of the first year, Jerry Falwell saw that the academic excellence of the young people was different from anything he had seen in his classmates at Baptist Bible College. He knew God was doing something extraordinary in Lynchburg. At either the end of the first year or the beginning of the second, he upped his goal from 5,000 students to 50,000. (No one is quite sure when the goal was expanded, because we don't have documentation of the change.) Jerry had faith that God was going to build one of the largest Christian training centers in history. He had faith none of the rest of us had.

"You didn't talk to me about a goal of 50,000 students," I complained privately.

"No . . ." Jerry answered, "I talked to God." He went on to predict that we would have a great football program and play Notre Dame at Notre Dame . . . and beat them.

I couldn't believe the goal of 50,000; that stretched my faith too much. Yes, I wanted 50,000 students, and yes, I would pray for that goal, but that number of students was beyond the credible reach of my faith. So I prayed, "Lord, I believe; help thou mine unbelief" (Mark 9:24, *KJV*).

Let's go back to that first week in June 1971. I went to see Jerry with a deep concern, because we only had five applications (the Rhodenhizers would make seven if they applied). I warned him, "You're going to be embarrassed in front of your pastor friends if Liberty has only 25 or 30 students. Also, I'll be embarrassed in front of my faculty friends back at Trinity Evangelical Divinity School."

Jerry answered, "You said we should build a college the way we build a church, so let's have a contest. That's the way my church gets a big attendance in Sunday School."

We talked about different contests for college enrollment, but none of them seemed to apply. Then Jerry said, "I'm going to Israel; let's tell every pastor who sends us five students that he can go free with me to Israel."

"Jerry, I don't think that will work." I explained that if a pastor could get five people to go with him to Israel, he could get a free trip.

Jerry countered, "Then let's give the pastor a free trip if he sends us one student."

"No, let's give the free trip to every student who enrolls."

"GREAT IDEA! Let's do it," Jerry said, slapping me on the back.

The very next day, Jerry began announcing on the radio that every student who attended Liberty would get a free trip to the Holy Land (and the following Sunday, he began making the same announcement on television). I cautioned, "Let's make sure that the student is worthy of the trip," and suggested, "Students have to take a full load, pass their classes, pay their bills, and not have more than 50 demerits."

The free trip was announced at a pastors' conference at Thomas Road Baptist Church the third week of June; the next day, we received 16 applications. For the rest of the summer, applications kept showing up, until we had 154 students the first year.

The first week of February 1972, we took all our students to Israel and cruised the Mediterranean. Each morning, we boarded buses, and I lectured on "Following the Steps of Jesus in the Holy Land." All the students got academic credit for the trip.

Established colleges have traditional events scheduled throughout the school year to keep their students involved. Students look forward to these events, such as football games, Homecoming, traditional bonfires, and so on. Liberty University had no traditions, so I found myself having to create weekly events to keep students motivated and excited.

Dan Manley, our first basketball coach, had been the youth pastor at Thomas Road Baptist Church and a fairly good basketball player at Tennessee Temple University. I told him, "Put some wins under their belts." I explained to him that a new college didn't need to play established colleges that would "beat the stuffing out of us." We needed to play colleges that were not quite as good as we were, so we could establish a winning spirit in the student body.

That first year, Liberty played several military schools in the area (two-year colleges that included high school undergraduates). We also played John Wesley College in High Point and Piedmont Bible College in Winston-Salem, and ended up with a 6-4 record.

We were legalistic in those days, so when I was asked if girls could wear blue jeans or pantsuits to the basketball games, the answer was no. We didn't share that belief, but independent Baptist churches—whose pastors preached that girls could not wear pants—had influenced Liberty's beliefs.

At that first basketball game, I was standing on the floor, talking to our players, when I looked up into the stands and noticed the immodesty of our girls sitting in dresses with their knees apart. At the next chapel service, I announced, "From now on, we have a new rule: Girls must wear blue jeans or pantsuits to the basketball games. Girls must be modest."

That event gives an illustration of how the rules have been modified over the years. We didn't always recognize the cultural implications of our legalism; sometimes Liberty was more concerned with rule keeping than with our testimony to the world. Initially, male students could not have facial hair, but when we found deacons in Baptist churches had facial hair, we allowed it among our boys. The same thing happened with movies. When we realized that most of the people in our supporting churches allowed movies, we permitted our students to attend movies—

as long as they were not R-rated. However, some rules have never changed, such as: no swearing, no sex outside of marriage, and no alcohol or addictive drug use.

Sunday School attendance exploded at Thomas Road, because all the Liberty students were dumped into the church's workforce. Aggressive young soul winners brought a spirit of revival into the church.

During the heyday of its Sunday School bus ministry, Thomas Road had more than 100 buses, reaching out more than 50 miles from Lynchburg into the Blue Ridge and surrounding towns. The buses averaged 27 riders each, so there were about 2,700 in Sunday School because of the buses.

My son, Sam, and his buddy, Mark Grooms, were responsible for Buena Vista, a town in the Shenandoah Valley, 50 miles from Lynchburg. Every Saturday morning, Sam drove his car over the Blue Ridge Mountains, and the boys went door to door, meeting parents and children, and asking, "Can your children ride my Sunday School bus to Thomas Road Baptist Church tomorrow?" They passed out letters describing our church and providing phone numbers that parents could call if they had to check up on their children.

Because Jerry Falwell had a widespread daily radio ministry, and his televised church service was one of the first to blanket America, his name was "hot." People were ready to let their children ride a bus 50 miles to go to Sunday School at his church. So, on Sunday mornings, Sam and Mark would leave around 6:00 and arrive in Buena Vista around 7:30 to gather approximately 50 children to ride their bus. They arrived back at Thomas Road by 9:45, and the children went to Sunday School, then children's church. Afterward, Sam and Mark drove their bus back over the Blue Ridge Mountains, getting the children home by 2:00 P.M.

I've heard someone say that Colonel Sanders of Kentucky Fried Chicken supported Thomas Road Baptist Church. That's true, but not with money. He arranged for the church to get a discount on buckets of fried chicken. While Mark would drive the bus, Sam would tear the chicken into about 47 pieces, so each child had a little to eat on the long bus ride home.

Sunday School attendance at Thomas Road Baptist Church averaged a little more than 3,000 when Liberty University started. Within two years, attendance was averaging almost 8,000 each week.

Gordon Luff joined the faculty of Liberty University in the second year, and he also took over the youth Sunday School class. There were approximately 40 to 50 students in the youth department when Luff came; within two years, there were more than 300 high school students attending weekly, along with another 200 junior high school students. Then we started an explosive college and career ministry to young adults (not Liberty students, but those recruited from surrounding colleges). Another 300 attended that class.

Breaking the 10,000 Barrier

In November 1971, Jerry Falwell set a Sunday School attendance goal of 10,000—a goal he thought no one had ever reached (later research revealed that a church in Long Beach, California, had previously broken that record). Jerry and I had written a book, *Church Aflame*, that explained the concept of saturation evangelism, which means using every available method to reach every available person at every available time.[3]

To get ready for that big day, Jerry Falwell stood in the front of a prayer meeting with 108 pages from a Lynchburg telephone book. He asked individuals to volunteer to phone every number on both sides of each page and "invite them to the biggest Sunday School in history."

High school students took 5,000 posters and nailed them to every telephone post and put them in every store window throughout town.

Junior high school students took 10,000 flyers to place one under the windshield wipers of every car in town. Sixty one-minute announcements were aired on every one of the 13 radio stations in town, and an advertisement also ran on the ABC television outlet in Lynchburg.

On Saturday morning, more than 200 students and lay workers from the church canvassed every home in the city and surrounding counties, inviting people to attend the largest Sunday School in history.

The big day was called "Friend Day."[4] Every church member was asked to bring a friend to Sunday School. As an incentive, the one who brought the most friends would be given a brand-new *Scofield Reference Bible*.

This prize went to a first-year student, Steve Wingfield, who brought many of his relatives who lived in the area. Steve, who later became a city-wide evangelist, had 51 visitation cards in the barrel.

That morning, the 2,000-seat auditorium of E.C. Glass High School was filled for a gigantic youth rally; all those young people could never have fit into Thomas Road Baptist Church's auditorium.

There's always a question about whether the count at such an event is accurate, or if someone has padded the numbers. However, Sam Pate, the chairman of the deacons at Thomas Road Baptist Church, had the fire marshal count attendance in E.C. Glass, individual Sunday School classes and the church auditorium. Electricity went through the crowd when Jerry Falwell announced, "We have 10,187 present today." People knew that our church in the little city of Lynchburg, Virginia, had done something that was bigger than any other church in the nation. They knew that God was in our midst and rewarding our work with His success.

Church Aflame

Jerry and I wrote a book about the reasons that Thomas Road Baptist Church was growing so rapidly. One Sunday morning, Jerry Falwell announced to the congregation, "If you have found Christ at this church, take a visitor's card and write your testimony. Or use any type of paper in your wallet or purse and write down how you got saved. Give your testimony to Jeanette Hogan, my secretary."

When I arrived at church that night, Jeanette handed me a large cigar box filled with more than 100 pieces of paper. After church, I sat on the floor of Harvey's Motel to arrange the pieces of paper into different piles, according to where people were saved—jail ministry, Elim Home alcoholic ministry, Sunday School, door-to-door visitation, television, radio, tract ministry, and so forth.

As I sorted out the testimonies, I began to weep. It was then that I saw the strength of Thomas Road Baptist Church; God had used this church in a supernatural way to save lost people. This church was not growing because of transfer growth, i.e., Christians becoming members by transferring into the church. No, it was a congregation of converted drunks, prostitutes and other wayward people. God's presence rested on Thomas Road Baptist Church.

Dick Tate, a former pitcher with the St. Louis Cardinals, had been an alcoholic on the chain gang. When members of Thomas Road Baptist Church presented Christ to him, he prayed to receive Christ. Dick became a junior boys' Sunday School teacher and committed to keeping young boys from following his previous drunken example.

When Lynchburg's Chief of Police first visited the church, there was no room for him, so he had to sit on the stairs leading to the pulpit. As he looked out over the congregation, he said to himself, *Oh my! This place is filled with prostitutes and thieves. I'd better go back to my car and get my gun.*

Red Whit and his wife ran a bar and house of prostitution across the James River, and Red testifies to having been in jail 57 times, stabbed once, and shot twice. But when he got saved, he became a flaming witness for Jesus Christ throughout the area. His wife became an interpreter for the deaf at our worship services.

I loved Thomas Road Baptist Church because of Jerry's optimistic preaching. I anticipated going to every church service, knowing God would be there and that He would speak personally to me through Jerry's preaching. I always came away from church having been touched by God.

I also loved Thomas Road Baptist Church because my children loved the church. They wanted to get there early to be with their friends. Sometimes they wanted to hang out there on Sunday afternoon before evening church. My children loved the Lord, loved their Christian buddies, and loved serving God. I felt that Thomas Road Baptist Church was the best church in America, and God had privileged my husband to serve there; we were a happy family there. —Ruth Towns

Influencing the World for Christ

In February 1972, our students had taken their free trip to Israel, walking where Jesus had walked and studying about Jesus in the places where

He had performed miracles and preached His sermons. They saw Calvary, and then walked over to the Garden Tomb for communion.

The second year, the school gave away a free trip to England for all who enrolled. There we studied the revivals of the First Great Awakening and the ministry of John Wesley. A total of 420 students made the trip.

I lectured nightly on the influence of John Wesley and challenged the young people to reach the world for Christ in keeping with Wesley's words: "The world, my parish."[5] We visited Wesley's tomb at the foundry, and I spoke to them from New Chapel in Bristol, England. I reminded the students that the church-planting movement that was perhaps the greatest expansion of Christianity in history took place a generation after John Wesley died. When the Revolutionary War began in 1776, there were 243 Methodist churches. By the War of 1812, there were more than 5,000 Methodist churches. Then I reminded the students, "Liberty students can do the same thing that the followers of John Wesley did: We can influence the world for Christ."

This was not a new idea for Liberty University. Because Jerry Falwell had been unavailable for Liberty's first chapel on September 10, 1971, I spoke to the 154 students assembled at Thomas Road Baptist Church that day. I reminded them that they were part of the most unusual college in history—and also part of a long and glorious tradition. "Suppose you were a member of the first church in Jerusalem when the Holy Spirit came on Pentecost. Suppose you were a founding member of Spurgeon's great church in England that influenced the British Empire. Today, you are a charter member of Liberty University—a movement that will influence the world."

That first sermon was built on Matthew 28:19-20: " 'Go therefore and make disciples of all the nations, baptizing them in the name of the Father and of the Son and of the Holy Spirit, teaching them to observe all things that I have commanded you; and lo, I am with you always, *even* to the end of the age.' Amen."

Then I challenged them, "Let's change the world." From that first sermon, Liberty students received the commission to be world changers. I explained, "First, you must change your inner world; second, change the world around you; and third, reach out to change the whole world."

I ended chapel with my life verse: "Faithful is he that calleth you, who also will do it" (1 Thess. 5:24, *KJV*). I said to the students, "Every one of you is called, just as I was called. So, remember that our faithful God will help you accomplish the purpose for which He brought you to Liberty."

As I mentioned earlier, at the start of the first year of Liberty University, I was the only full-time faculty member. Falwell told the students, "Call me Jerry," as he wanted to be friendly and accessible to all of them. But he said, "Always call him Dr. Towns; he's the only educated dignitary we have."

That would soon change. Craig H. Lampe visited Lynchburg and was overwhelmed with the greatness of Thomas Road Baptist Church. As we chatted together, I hired Craig, who held a Ph.D. in physiology from the University of Florida, as Liberty's Registrar.

As we prayed for qualified faculty members, God was working on Dr. J. Gordon Henry, an administrator/professor at Eastern Kentucky University (EKU) and pastor of a Baptist church. At the university, his responsibilities included serving on the Faculty Senate (he was chair of the Committee on Committees) and as the president of the EKU Education Association. Dr. Henry had also been appointed by EKU's president to serve on the Kentucky Education Planning Commission. He had developed an interest in Jerry Falwell's work through the television ministry and was particularly interested in his plans for a Christian liberal arts college. He decided to come to Lynchburg and see first-hand what was happening.

Dr. Henry talked to me after a Wednesday evening service and expressed extreme interest in our fledgling college. When I offered him a position, he jumped at the opportunity to become the dean of Liberty University. For the next eight years, Dr. Henry led in the development of the academic infrastructure and the building of a strong faculty. He was invaluable in our gaining and maintaining accreditation with the Southern Association of Colleges and Schools (SACS).

Meanwhile, Jerry Falwell and I were talking about starting a Bible institute in addition to the four-year college. After all, Tennessee Temple had a Bible institute, and so did Northwestern College. I told Jerry that

Harold Willmington, my good friend, was one of the best Bible teachers I knew. At the time, Harold didn't have his doctoral degree and had never taught in a college, but I felt he had raw talent and could develop a great Bible institute. I invited Harold to come teach a one-week intensive on the Life of Christ. All students were required to attend, and all other classes were cancelled. Out of that week, Harold was hired, and for the next 40 years he taught in our two-year Bible institute. Harold recorded the entire Bible institute—first as audio tapes, next CDs, and finally videotapes—and the Liberty Home Bible Institute would eventually have more than 100,000 graduates—people who wanted to master the Word of God, and in many cases, who entered full-time Christian ministry.

I hired Joyce Wipf, who held an M.A. in English, to be the chair of the English department. Joyce formerly had been head of the English department at Bob Jones University. I instructed her, "Build a strong English department at Liberty so that our students learn to write well, speak fluently, and read widely." I felt that some of the best public speakers in the world came out of Bob Jones University. Her husband, Amos, with three earned doctoral degrees, headed up our science department, which included courses in math, biology and science.

Interviewing potential faculty was overwhelming during the second year, as enrollment exploded and we needed to hire 22 additional people. New faculty members were hired after I conducted long interviews, escorted them around Lynchburg (showing them potential homes to buy), and gave each one an in-depth tour of the church facilities. Hiring 22 meant I had interviewed more than 60 candidates. I barely got through the first year by the skin of my teeth. I was at my Liberty office from seven in the morning until nine o'clock in the evening or later. Because I had good physical stamina, I was able to endure that year.

But the next year was even worse, as enrollment continued to grow. I was constantly hiring more teachers. My duties as executive vice president became so demanding that I found myself missing classes and had no time to prepare new sermons or review my lectures. I didn't have time to think, much less write articles or books. I began assigning my classes to other teachers, including various pastors in the area. I was administrating a college and was no longer teaching. I had come to Lynchburg to teach large classes at Liberty University; my dream of having 300 students in one class was dying.

During Thanksgiving break, our family went to Savannah, Georgia, to visit my family. My brother Richard had a speedboat, and we cruised the various rivers surrounding Savannah. For some reason, we stopped at a beautiful, waterfront home on Rio Vista Island. It was for sale. The home was at the mouth of Moon River, a few doors down from Johnny Mercer, the songwriter of "Moon River." I fell in love with the home—it had four bedrooms, two stories, and was about a mile away from the intercoastal waterway. It would make a perfect second home—a perfect place to escape to and relax.

That night, I attended a service at Bible Baptist Church, in Savannah, where Cecil Hodges preached. Walking through the church, I shook hands with Silla Hair from Westminster Presbyterian Church and many other former parishioners.

An usher, Hayword Grooms, chatted with me, telling me he was a contractor. I asked him if he knew anything about the home on Rio Vista Island. He got a funny look on his face, and then he said, "I can't sell it." In talking with Hayword, I found out that the asking price for the house was $45,000. He could see in my eyes that I really loved the house, and then he dropped the bombshell: "I'll sell it to you for $25,000 cash, as is."

I reached for his hand, shook it, and said, "I'll take it." I didn't know where I would get the money, but I really wanted the house. He told me I would need to put $5,000 down, and he would arrange with the bank for me to get a loan for $20,000. Little did I know at the time that the home on Moon River would allow me to leave Liberty and write full-time.

Just as I left Winnipeg Bible College because of an overwhelming schedule of details and administrative work, the same thing happened at Liberty. I was co-founder of Liberty University, yet in the early days Jerry Falwell did not understand the necessity to delegate and build infrastructure. He was committed to big numbers—and there's nothing wrong with striving for a large student body—but he was not committed to hiring a staff to build an infrastructure to serve the growing student population. I found myself working harder and harder at things that were secondary to me, and I had less time to do the important things.

In the spring of 1973, I met with Jerry right before a Sunday morning service at Thomas Road. I handed him an official letter informing him of my resignation. He read it carefully, then said, "I know you, Elmer. I know this is final."

"Yes."

"So, I'm not going to try to persuade you to stay."

Then Jerry asked, "What are you going to do if you don't teach at Liberty?"

I explained that I had my home on Moon River, from which I would write, research, and travel around America to preach.

I was not worried about finances. In addition to the editing job at *Christian Life* magazine (for which I received $100 a month), I was writing a weekly series of back-cover articles for *The Sword of the Lord*, featuring "great soul-winning churches." I traveled each week to a great church, surveyed the congregation, interviewed the pastor, and wrote a compelling story, motivating readers to adopt the successful practices of that church.

As a matter of fact, I traveled so much in the year following my resignation from Liberty that I complained inwardly about not getting to enjoy my home on Moon River because I spent so much time in airports and motels. I soon discovered that I missed teaching classes on a regular basis. Little did I realize that within three and a half years I'd be back at Liberty in a new role, and that eventually I would teach classes larger than I ever dreamed.

10

A Desert Experience in the Interim Years

(1973–1977)

For three and a half years, I lived in Savannah, Georgia, writing books and magazine articles, and traveling to citywide Sunday School conventions and local church seminars.

Sam Moore, my roommate at Columbia Bible College, had become president and major stockowner of Thomas Nelson, Inc. He was excited about a title for a book: *Is the Day of the Denomination Dead?*[1] He asked me to write this book to expand Thomas Nelson's Bible publishing into book publishing.

When the book came out in the fall of 1973, a publicity agent arranged for me to be interviewed on *Good Morning, America*. In those days, the program was local, so I traveled to Dallas, St. Louis, Chicago, Philadelphia and Baltimore in one week, explaining why denominations were declining in attendance, membership, finances and ministerial candidates.

The thesis of the book was that conservative churches were growing in attendance and influence, and that many of the 100 largest churches in America were bypassing the need for denominational affiliation. The book asked if denominations were necessary for the future.

I'd like to say that the book was a great success, but in actuality it was a dismal failure. In spite of advertisement and a push from *Good Morning, America*, not many potential readers were excited enough to purchase the book. People were not interested in their denominations; they were interested in their own local churches. Liberals didn't buy the book because they didn't like the conclusion that fundamentalist churches were growing. Fundamentalists didn't buy the book because they knew liberal churches were dying, and they didn't care.

A few years later, my daughter Polly was going through my records and exclaimed, "Dad, did that book sell only 400 copies?"

I told her, "Don't ever tell anyone!" I was embarrassed by the low sales, afraid the book's failure would hurt my reputation. However, now I'm glad to tell everyone that I had several publishing duds. Sometimes the problem was that I chose the wrong topic; other times the fault lay in a misleading title, or poor publicity for the book, or the fact that I put the book with the wrong publisher.

A couple of years after it had come out, Sam Moore shipped me 9,000 copies of *Is the Day of the Denomination Dead?* that he couldn't sell.

My good friend C. Peter Wagner required it as a textbook for Church Growth classes at Fuller Theological Seminary. Each class had around 60 to 70 students, so over the next few years, Fuller Seminary Bookstore bought all the books out of my basement.

Elmer determined not to spend money on expensive Christmas gifts for the kids or grandkids. Rather than a gift they would probably forget, we give them family experiences they probably will never forget. Elmer would use his award miles from the airlines and rent a big van for all of us to travel, and we would get several rooms together on one floor of a motel. We went to such places as Disney World (Florida); Disneyland (California); Hershey Park in Lancaster, Pennsylvania; Dolly World in Pigeon Forge, Tennessee; Hawaii; and Myrtle Beach, South Carolina. We liked Myrtle Beach so much that we bought a place there and go back regularly. —Ruth Towns

Co-founder of Baptist University of America

In the fall of 1974, I was invited to Jacksonville, Florida, to meet with seven pastors, each of whose churches was struggling to build a fledgling Bible college. Each of these pastors wanted to do what Jerry Falwell had done with Liberty University. Each had only had a small amount of success, and all were struggling with finances and recruitment. At the end of the day, the seven pastors agreed to merge their seven colleges into one, call it Baptist University of America (BUA), and move their facilities to one central location.

They hired me at $100 per day consultant fee to merge seven colleges into one. I traveled to each campus, determined what furniture and equipment should be kept, and then arranged for shipment to the new location. I interviewed staff at each of the colleges to determine who would compose the faculty at BUA. Then I organized the consolidated faculty and staff and prepared for the 1974 school year. As I was leaving, they hired me as a part-time teacher—again for $100 a day—to teach every Tuesday.

The fledgling college soon got into trouble financially. It was impossible for seven pastors to manage a college through a board of directors. So they twisted my arm to become the executive vice president and academic dean. I had walked away from that position at Liberty University, and here I was in the same position a year later. My sojourn in Savannah was a desert experience, and I went through another dark, cold winter's night.

For the next two and a half years, I raised money from the seven churches and expanded appeals to fundamental churches throughout the South. I also found myself traveling to churches to recruit students.

Once again, I was not a happy camper; I had little time to spend studying and writing. The demands of a growing student body sucked up any creative energy. One of the reasons I stayed with BUA as long as I did was our son, Sam.

Sam came to BUA to be a business major, but during the first week of his first semester, God called him into full-time ministry. At BUA, he got an outstanding education. I had chosen the best teachers from seven colleges, so Sam received excellent academic training. I guided BUA into a balance between legalistic rules and the positive influence of the deeper Christian life, so Sam grew in his faith. I made sure BUA had a strong local-church approach to evangelism, and Sam adopted this biblical view of outreach. Ruth and I agreed that our sacrifice at BUA was for Sam.

The empty nest had a whole new meaning to me. Debbie got married and left home, Sam went off to college, and Elmer was away five days a week running BUA; sometimes he was gone on the weekends, too. My nest was almost empty—only our youngest daughter, Polly, was still home. I poured my whole energy into Polly, praying constantly that she would become all the Lord wanted her to be. —Ruth Towns

A Sunday School Museum

Sam went forward to surrender to God at the altar his first night at BUA. It had seemed an average sermon to me, but I could see in Sam's eyes a new determination and hear in his voice excitement about God's work in his life.

We went out for late coffee and banana splits. I had counseled many young men who had dedicated their lives to God, but this was different. This was my son. I challenged him to be a world changer. Then he turned the tables on me, asking, "What do you want to do for God the rest of your life?"

I quickly rattled off three goals. First, I wanted to help build a world-changing Christian training institution. Second, I wanted to build a Sunday School museum and research center. Third, I wanted to train at least one man to take my place.

"*A SUNDAY SCHOOL MUSEUM . . .*" Sam's thrilled voice repeated what I had just said. Since Sam had always read history novels, the idea of a Sunday School museum excited him. Before we left, he prayed, "Lord, give my dad a Sunday School museum."

God cherishes those who surrender to Him, and I think He delights in answering their first prayers—just to demonstrate His acceptance to them. The next morning, I flew to Philadelphia to speak at a Sunday School convention in the city's civic center. I mentioned, "The two-hundredth anniversary of Sunday School is coming in five years, and the Church must get ready for it." I told the story of Robert Raikes beginning the Sunday School in England. After I finished preaching, Gerald Stover, a friend who worked at the 150-year-old American Sunday School Union headquarters, drove me to a Philadelphia museum that had a copy of Robert Raikes's first published Sunday School lesson book. Seeing my love for Sunday School history, Stover offered to give me all his Sunday School treasure. "You're God's man to do something with Sunday School history," he said.

Stover told me that the American Sunday School Union had changed its emphasis, becoming the American Missionary Fellowship to minister to unreached rural America.[2] The mission had thrown all its Sunday School treasure into a barrel and left it at the curb as trash. Stover had gotten permission to take it home.

The next day, Stover opened the trunk of his car to show me some treasures from the past: the first Sunday School book printed in America, the charter of the Boston Sunday School Association, parts of a printing press used by the American Sunday School Union, and more than 50 early song books and other early Sunday School books. I cried at the discovery.

The following weekend, God continued to unfold His plan for the Sunday School museum. Ruth and I went to a concert in Savannah on Saturday evening, and I had to run by my office to pick up my Bible. (I had bought the original Bona Bella Presbyterian Church in Savannah and turned it into my local office.) A heavy rain was falling, so maybe that's why he didn't hear me coming. I opened the door to see a young man pilfering my desk. I shouted, "*What in the world are you doing in my desk?!*"

He was too startled to run, and I could see that he was too afraid to fight me. I decided to show authority: "*Sit down in that chair.*"

He obeyed. So I turned and yelled to Ruth, "Go across the street and phone the police. There's a burglar in here."

I sat beside the young man, told him I was a preacher, and pointed to my books, saying, "This is where I study my sermons and lessons to train young men like you to be preachers." He could have had a gun in his pocket; he could have attacked me—but I was not afraid.

I felt the presence of God falling on that conversation, just as we could hear the rain falling on the tin roof of that old church. I opened my Bible and began showing the thief the plan of salvation. After a few minutes, a police officer entered the room, followed by Ruth and the lady from across the street.

"You'll have to wait until we pray," I told the police officer. Later I found out that the policeman was a deacon at Calvary Baptist Temple in Savannah. He filled out the arrest papers for breaking and entering, and handed them to me to sign. I questioned the officer and found out that if I didn't sign, he wouldn't arrest the young man. However, I could sign the papers anytime in the next six months, and an arrest warrant would be issued. I looked at the boy and made him an offer: "If you'll go to church once a week for one year, I'll not sign this arrest document."

"Thank you!" he said multiple times.

The police officer disagreed with my decision, because the boy had been arrested twice before. But I stuck to my promise—if the boy would stick to his promise. Then I prayed, and the boy prayed to receive Christ. I don't know if a salvation prayer is valid when the sinner feels coerced—

only God knows. But the boy told me of other items he had stolen from my office previously. The next morning, there was a box full of my missing office equipment at the office door.

A week later, I looked at a two-story empty bank building as a possible site for the museum. The building was located in the heart of the historical district of Savannah, across the street from the Pirate House, which was the most visited restaurant in the city.

"That's too expensive," I told the bank employee when I learned they wanted $2,000 per month in rent.

A couple of days later, the bank president phoned to ask me to come see him. When I arrived at his office, I recognized his secretary as the lady who lived across the street from my office—the one who had called the police. The president told me that he was a Christian, and that his secretary had told him how I led the boy to pray to receive Christ. Then he asked, "How much do you want to pay for the building?"

"Two hundred dollars," I meekly told him. Even that stretched my budget for my proposed Sunday School museum.

The president told me that there was a drive-in teller window in that building, and they would rent the drive-in space back from me for $1,800 if I rented the building for $2,000. He explained that he couldn't do this for Christian purposes, but a Sunday School museum would be a natural tourist attraction, since the Chamber of Commerce advertised Savannah as the birthplace of Sunday School.

God supplied the money, and soon display cases were installed and a Christian bookstore was set up. I even had a film produced—*The Birth of Sunday School*—to show in a theater I had built in my new museum. I charged $1.00 for entrance, thinking 100 visitors (i.e., $100) a day could cover expenses.

The museum didn't even attract 100 visitors a month. My honorarium from preaching went to support its upkeep. Then I had a creative idea for a way to pay expenses: I mailed every pastor I knew an invitation to attend an all-day seminar in Savannah on *How to Build a Growing Sunday School*. I charged $25 per attendee. Fifty-six pastors came to Savannah, paying a total of $1,400—enough to cover expenses for one month. I was delighted with the success of my brilliant idea!

So I tried it again the next month—but only 10 people came, bringing in $250.

I decided to take my seminars on the road. I sent the museum secretary to nearby cities to phone churches she found in the Yellow Pages, and then mail reminders. I took the seminar to Holiday Inns in Augusta, Georgia; Macon, Georgia; Columbia, South Carolina; Jacksonville, Florida, and elsewhere.[3]

When the two-hundredth anniversary of Sunday School arrived in 1980, a huge celebration was held at the Michigan Sunday School Convention, with a large assembly of Sunday School memorabilia on display. Out of a delegation of 5,000 people, only 500 took time to view the historical exhibit. When I moved back to Liberty University, I closed the museum. I determined that people were not interested in the history of Sunday School; they only cared about the present Sunday School where they attended.

Some good things did come out of the Sunday School museum effort. For instance, we produced the *Bi-Centennial Sunday School Bible*, which sold 10,000 copies. Alongside the scriptural text, I told the story of Sunday School in features and special sections. Also, the city of Savannah held a bi-centennial Sunday School parade down Bull Street and invited me to be the parade marshal. More than 20 floats from local churches followed behind us. But as Ruth and I left the convertible we had been riding, I felt hollow. Everyone had waved at me, but so what? Being a parade marshal didn't match the thrill of teaching young people who could change the world.

Later, I was inducted into the Savannah Hall of Fame. Mayor John Rousakis presented me with an inscribed silver bowl in honor of the occasion. A plaque commemorating Savannah as the birthplace of Sunday School and me as its Sunday School son hung in the Savannah Room at the Pirate's House, alongside commemorations of other Savannah greats.

Return to Liberty University

On Thanksgiving morning, 1976, the telephone rang. Roscoe Brewer, mission director at Thomas Road Baptist Church and Liberty University, invited me to go with him and a team of Liberty students to feed those starving from a famine in Haiti. Roscoe wanted me to write a series of magazine articles about the outreach efforts. We planned to meet him in Haiti during the Christmas vacation.

Before hanging up, Roscoe brought up a subject that was on his heart: "Elmer, you ought to come back to Liberty University." He had been fearful to mention the idea, but did so anyway.

Once again, God worked in my life through a phone call. I was growing more unfulfilled in my administrative role at BUA. Sam had only one semester left there. Roscoe said, "Elmer, you should spend your time writing stories for our foreign missions outreach at Liberty." Then he added, "There are several magazines and newsletters at Liberty—you could write for them all."

My heart warmed to the idea. I was immediately willing to return to Lynchburg to research and write and help mold the entire ministry. I didn't need to run Liberty University; I would be satisfied in a journalistic position.

"Roscoe . . ." I affirmed him, "you can put this deal together." I asked Roscoe to talk to Jerry Falwell about my returning to Liberty. "If God is in this transition, you can pull it off."

A couple of days later, Roscoe phoned to tell me that Jerry wanted me to return, and that he had set a breakfast appointment for us on December 26, 1976. When we met, the only issue was my title. Jerry wanted me to be more than a news reporter; he gave me the title Editor-in-Chief of all publications.

Ministry in Haiti

Jerry Falwell had appealed for finances to save the starving multitudes in Haiti, and with that money, Roscoe bounded into action. He leased a 200-foot freight hauler that was docked in New Orleans, at the mouth of the Mississippi River. The ship belonged to a captain who loved Jerry Falwell, but the vessel itself was a rust bucket.

Roscoe organized about 50 Liberty guys to ride a school bus to New Orleans during the Christmas vacation, sleep on the docks in sleeping bags, and climb all over the rusty ship to paint it in four days. Working around the clock, these 50 tough, Marine-like servants of Christ hung from ropes, climbed poles, and crawled into tight spaces to convert an old, rust-corroded ship into a life-giving instrument for God.

Food was donated from many sources in the Midwest. When the ship arrived in Port au Prince, Haiti, there was such corruption on the docks—and prices for docks were so high—that Roscoe Brewer felt he just couldn't pay the price. Across the harbor, BP (British Petroleum) had a fueling dock where tankers came to unload fuel. God's provision continued, as BP allowed our ship to unload our food at their dock—for free.

There were literally tons of food to unload—thousands of boxes and sacks of grain. There were no hydraulic cranes to lift heavy loads, and no ramps to slide the cargo to the ground. The 50 willing Liberty servants attacked the cargo hold and began carrying the boxes and bags of grain to the shore—one at a time. Because we were feeding the starving and doing the work of Christ, the task seemed easy and was finished quickly.

There was a problem, though. We had a donated pick-up truck that was too big to get off the ship. The team prayed for wisdom and divine help. Then two dozen Liberty students hoisted the pick-up truck onto their shoulders and carried it to the dock.

Another problem! The boardwalk from the dock to dry land stretched more than 100 yards through a soggy marsh and was only wide enough for one walker at a time. How to get the pick-up truck down such a long, narrow walkway? The boys found a pile of old, heavy, creosote-coated railroad ties. They balanced about 24 ties on the narrow boardwalk and drove the truck about 10 feet. Then, moving the railroad ties from the back of the truck to the front, they were able to drive the truck gradually to safety.

Wallace Turnbull, a missionary with Baptist Haiti Missions, had alerted dozens of Baptist churches that food was coming. Deacons in each church built a small warehouse to protect the food from marauding bands that would have stolen it. Then that one pick-up truck made several hundred trips to fill up the warehouses. To make it happen, those 50 boys worked in shifts from first light until darkness each day.

We were high on a mountain one day, getting ready to feed everyone in a small village. Children with large bloated bellies were too immobile to attack us for something to eat or create a food riot. They sat listlessly in a near-comatose state; their emaciated arms reached out, begging for food. One lady had carried her 10-year-old daughter to hear the Bible stories. Suddenly, a shriek riveted the small gathering. The girl had died! A little later, Roscoe appeared on camera, crying, "She's dead . . . she just died a few minutes ago." Roscoe made one of his most passionate appeals—spontaneously. He forgot his script, but with real tears begged for money and prayer for Haiti.

That telecast prompted one of the largest financial responses to that date—more than a million dollars. Later, I had to answer the letters of complaint and skepticism—people suggested that we got a dead child from the morgue, or we casually waited until a girl died to start the tape rolling. But the critics were wrong. I was there, and I know the truth. God holds the keys to life and death; it was God who allowed the little girl to die at that precise moment, so that her death would be the key for many others to live.

I had spent three and a half years away from Liberty. Those were good years, and I had worked hard serving the Lord. I learned that you get stronger when you struggle, and that there is always a struggle before victory—otherwise the victory doesn't have as much satisfaction.

But when I wrote about Liberty's feeding campaign in Haiti, I felt I was back in the action. I was experiencing God's hand working around me. Returning to Liberty was like coming back into the manifest presence of God.

That trip to Haiti confirmed the will of God; I would return to Liberty to research, write and tell the story of what God was doing at Thomas Road Baptist Church, at Liberty University, and in the world. I was willing to forget about my role in founding Liberty—perhaps God had to humble me to prepare me for a bigger role of usefulness—and all I wanted to do when I came back was teach, study and write. I wanted to let the world know what God was doing through Jerry Falwell and at Liberty University, and I determined to use all of my ability to that end.

11

Great Ministry at Liberty

(1977–1999)

I returned to Liberty University with the title Editor-in-Chief of all publications for the university, the Old Time Gospel Hour (Jerry Falwell's radio and television ministry) and Thomas Road Baptist Church. That involved newsletters, a full-color magazine, a broadsheet newspaper, plus the printing and release of books as gift premiums.

Ministry in Southeast Asia

One of my first projects was reporting the story of refugees fleeing Communism after the fall of Vietnam. The Viet Cong were persecuting those friendly to the United States in Vietnam, Laos and Cambodia. Many were slaughtered, and most of those who escaped ended up in miserable conditions in Thailand. Jerry Falwell determined to help feed these refugees and take care of their needs. He sent Roscoe Brewer and me on an exploratory mission.

"Find out how severe the need is, and determine how much money is needed to help and how we can evangelize those in need," Jerry instructed us. Roscoe and I flew to Bangkok and met with the Minister of the Interior of Thailand, who gave us free reign to help in any way possible.

We found a 10-year-old girl—Mai Lee, an orphan from Laos—who became our "poster girl" to represent the needs of the displaced people of the Indo-China region. Mai Lee and other survivors from her extended family slept in one room in an abandoned military building. At night, utensils were removed from a shelf so that Mai Lee could sleep on it. I wrote the script, and Roscoe made the television appeal.

When Americans who watched Jerry Falwell's program saw Mai Lee and heard her story, the financial response was overwhelming. A team of 23 students, including the SMITE Singers, was sent from Liberty University along with camera crews to help minister to the multitudes. We visited all 12 of the refugee camps along the Mekong River, providing meat, clothing, blankets, New Testaments in survivors' native languages, and, since it was Christmastime, a toy for every child: a doll for each girl and a plastic airplane for each boy.

The United Nations agency UNESCO provided powdered milk—and nothing else—for the refugees, and people scavenged whatever vegetables they could, so our bags of cooked chicken were a prized delight. Each morning around 5:00, the Liberty boys built huge fires and began boiling water in 50-gallon pots. The girls plucked the chickens and threw them into the boiling water. While it was still hot, the students stripped the meat from the bones to fill plastic bags—one bag per family. Some days the young people spent five or six hours filling 10,000 bags. The bags were distributed after a gospel service where Christ was presented—or at least, that's the message we thought we were sharing.

During the first gospel service, Roscoe was preaching through an interpreter, an undersecretary from the Department of the Interior of Thailand. The listeners began grumbling; some even walked out in disgust.

Thinking the Laotians were rejecting Christianity, I began to pray. God answered by a tug at my sleeve; it was Prasha, a 15-year-old Thai boy we had hired as an interpreter.

"Dr. Towns . . ." He tugged again at my sleeve. "The man is messing up the sermon. He's saying Buddha created the world, not God the Father. He's saying Buddha had a baby whose name was Jesus . . ." The people were starving, and Buddha hadn't heard their prayers; they didn't want to hear any more about Buddha.

"Oh, no!" I panicked. How could I tell Roscoe the interpreter was ruining the sermon? If we offended the undersecretary, he could cut off our permission to visit the refugees. So, I determined to interrupt Roscoe. I would preach instead of him—but the undersecretary would mess up my sermon, just as he was corrupting Roscoe's.

"Have you ever interpreted a sermon?" I asked Prasha.

"No . . . I can't do it!" he declined.

"Yes, you can do it," I interrupted. "Let's pray and go . . ."

I walked up to Roscoe, tapped him roughly on the shoulder, and announced, "It's my turn; you're taking up my time."

When Roscoe looked at me, dumbfounded, I said, "One of the students will explain." I figured the undersecretary would pity our confusion over speaking and not be offended, when actually it was a charade. It must have worked, because we played out the same game 12 times.

I preached for more than an hour, beginning at creation and telling the story of the Old Testament. Then I told of an Asian girl—the Virgin

Mary—who gave birth to Jesus Christ, the Son of God. When I began preaching, the crowd returned. I preached Jesus' perfect humanity and full deity, and His death for their sins. Then I gave an invitation to become a Christian.

"If you will say Buddha is not God . . . if you will say Jesus is God . . . if you will say you're sorry for your sins . . . if you will accept Jesus Christ as your savior . . . if you will repent and stop cursing in God's name, and stop pinching another man's wife (that meant adultery) . . . if you will take the Bible and read it . . . if you will go to the gate and be baptized by the gospel church (the Christian and Missionary Alliance) . . ." Then I yelled my instruction: "STAND UP!"

Almost everyone in the crowd of 1,600 stood. I thought they didn't understand my message, or they didn't understand the appeal, so I instructed them to sit back down.

Then I gave the same appeal again. When I came to the climax, I shouted louder, while waving my arms, *"STAND UP!"*

Again they all stood. I told Prasha I didn't think they knew what they were doing. An elder from a gospel church interrupted me, "They understood; they will come to be baptized."

Some 20 years later, I told this story to a large class at Liberty University. All of a sudden, I was interrupted by a shout from the rear of the room: "I WAS THERE!"

Dara Suon was a 12-year-old Cambodian orphan when I gave that invitation to be saved to 1,600 people in Thailand. He was saved and baptized that day, and he told me that almost everyone in the crowd had gone to the gate to be baptized in water.

Dara and I met in the aisle of that Liberty class, hugged, rejoiced and praised God. After Dara came to America, he had heard Jerry Falwell say on television, "If you are from a foreign nation here in the United States and can speak English, get to Lynchburg, Virginia. I will give you a college education free." Dara rode a Greyhound bus to Lynchburg, worked as a janitor, and received his B.A. and M.A. degrees from Liberty. Today he works for the government of Cambodia in Phnom Penh.

In 2002, I went back to Bangkok, Thailand, to speak at a Christian workers' conference. Prasha introduced me to the Thai audience by telling the above story. As for his own story, Prasha finished college and the Evangelical Theological Seminary in Taipei, Taiwan. He has become head of the British Bible Society for all of Thailand.

Ministry on the South China Sea

The trip to Thailand to feed the refugees was an outstanding achievement by our students, and a great work of God. But the next three weeks, spent in the South China Sea, were even more spectacular.

First, our team traveled to the world famous harbor at Singapore. Roscoe had arranged to purchase a World War II destroyer that had previously belonged to the Australian Navy. The ship was now rusting away in a ship graveyard in Singapore. We paid $50,000—the price of scrap metal—for the ship and had a tugboat tow it into Singapore Harbor. The ship carried many memories; it had served in the Battle of the Coral Sea, where the Americans and Australians turned back a Japanese armada that was headed to invade Australia.

We had contacted three Aussies who owned a saloon in Sydney, Australia. They had been sailors aboard the destroyer during the war, and only a sailor knows the love another sailor has for his ship. These three closed their saloon and worked tirelessly day and night for three weeks to get that ship ready to sail. It was their labor of love. They wanted no pay—only expenses—to sail their ship again.

Next, we needed a captain with international papers to command the ship. The only one we could find was a drunken Korean captain. "Don't worry, mate . . ." one of the Aussies told us, "we can sail this ship without him. Let him drink his life away; we won't get lost." It's interesting how God put together a team: one drunken captain, three saloon owners who made no profession of Christianity, and 23 servants from Liberty. God used that team to help refugees who were lost in the South China Sea.

The steam boilers broke down twice; each time, we sat dead in the water for three days while the Aussies and the Liberty men plugged leaks in the steam boiler. We ran out of water, and we ran out of food—at least, we didn't have normal meals. We were running low on fuel, so there was no cooking, no water for baths, and no lights at night. But we never panicked, because we knew we were on a mission for God. We knew God would provide for our needs.

The ship ran on steam, but water escaping from holes in the boiler put out the fire that made the steam. So when the ship went dead in the water, our Liberty guys crawled through a hole 30 inches wide, into the water chamber, to plug the holes. Because of the intense heat, they could only work in that chamber for five-minute intervals, and they came out black from head to toe.

But when we saw the first refugee boat—with 16 people aboard—we knew our sacrifice was not in vain. God honored our faith. The women had been raped by pirates, several of the men had been killed, their possessions had been stolen, and there was no water. When you help save someone who is about to die, it's a life-defining feeling of accomplishment. You don't need appreciation, and you don't even want to be called a hero. The knowledge that someone will live because of you is its own reward. It gives new meaning to your life.

My parents loved to host guest speakers who came to my home church when I was growing up. They bought a beautiful double bed with an expensive Beautyrest mattress for me, but when these giants of the faith came to our home, I slept on the living room couch. There was Charles Fuller, who began Fuller Theological Seminary; Pat Zondervan, who began Zondervan Publishing; J. Edwin Orr, the revivalist who was Billy Graham's prayer partner; Oswald J. Smith, pastor of The Peoples Church, which was the first church to give one million dollars to missions; and Isaac Page, head of China Inland Missions. When I saw the title of this book—Walking with Giants—I realized the influence these men had in my life. When Elmer and I got married, we slept in that bed, and now 70 years later we still use it. —Ruth Towns

Building a Mailing List

As Editor-in-Chief of Jerry Falwell's publications, I wrote several political stories during the early days of the Moral Majority. I'd show my press card at the nation's Capitol Building and get access to the Senate lounge. Then I'd send a page for one of the senators who might be listening in the chamber. They always came, because press coverage was vital to their influence. Jerry Falwell was the *Good Housekeeping* Man of the Year in 1979, and senators wanted that positive identification.

I began the *Journal Champion* newspaper for Jerry Falwell, and because his mailing list had grown so large, the paper was mailed biweekly to more than one million homes. Approximately 400,000 copies were mailed to pastors. The power of the press gave Jerry tremendous political leverage.

One of the first things I had done as Editor-in-Chief was to help Jerry expand his mailing list to pastors. Everyone knew that John R. Rice, editor of *The Sword of the Lord*, had the largest mailing list of pastors in America, especially independent and fundamentalist pastors. Before coming back to Liberty, I had been a regular speaker at *Sword of the Lord* conferences—Rice's weekly conference held all over America in large soul-winning churches.

When I returned to work for Jerry Falwell, he asked me to contact John R. Rice, with the view of getting his mailing list of preachers for the Old Time Gospel Hour. It was rumored that Rice had a mailing list of more than 400,000 preachers, and he sent his magazine, *The Sword of the Lord*, free to all of those preachers. I had written for his magazine on a regular basis.

Dr. Rice invited Jerry and me to come spend a day with him at his farm in Murfreesboro, Tennessee. The first thing he did was take us to his stable to feed Rice's horse, MacArthur—named after Douglas MacArthur. As we headed to the stable, Rice cautioned, "Be careful of MacArthur, he has a foul attitude, and he does not like visitors."

I was standing in the stall near MacArthur's left hind leg when he suddenly bolted sideways, pushing me against the wall. I pushed him back and refused to move; I had never let a horse tell me what to do.

You may recall that during my boyhood summers, I lived on my grandfather's farm, and the field hands let me plow with Lightning. This mule had been fierce when he was young, but I had plowed with him when he was older. A field hand brought a pocket full of sugar up to the barn and had me feed sugar to Lightning. The mule liked sugar, so he liked me.

A second time MacArthur bolted and pushed me against the wall; I was not afraid, because a horse cannot kick sideways. But apparently I jabbed him in a nerve, something like our funny bone that really hurts, and he began to get agitated. I did not have any sugar with me, but I had half a Milky Way in my pocket—so I broke off a small bit and behold, MacArthur liked Milky Way candy bars. I patted him on the forehead and gave him a second bite. I don't remember—I may have given him three or four bites.

As we left the barn, Dr. Rice said, "You are the first preacher that MacArthur likes; I bet he would let you ride him gracefully." But I did not ride him that day.

Toward the end of the day we went back by the barn, and it was very evident that MacArthur liked me—he immediately began nosing around my pockets for more Milky Way bar.

A little later that afternoon, Jerry Falwell and I carried heavy cassettes of data tape containing a list of more than 400,000 preachers out of a bank vault in downtown Murfreesboro. We loaded the tapes onto a plane and flew back to Lynchburg. Those 400,000 preachers were the ones who gave power to the Moral Majority, and Jerry rallied them to support Ronald Reagan for the presidency rather than the liberal Jimmy Carter. Isn't it strange to think that God used a little Milky Way to help put Ronald Reagan into the presidency? Obviously, there were many other forces that got President Reagan elected, and I was one of millions who supported his candidacy.

Becoming Dean of Liberty Baptist Theological Seminary

About a year after my return to Liberty, Jerry took me for a ride up into the mountains and said, "When you take over the seminary, there's some things I want you to do . . ."

"*Wait a minute!*" I interrupted Jerry, reminding him that I came back to be an editor and writer, not to run the seminary. I pointed out that academic management was the reason I had left before. Jerry explained his quandary: "I've got problems with Robert Hughes, dean of the seminary, and I know he won't last long." Dr. Hughes was the founding dean of the seminary and held a doctorate from New Orleans Baptist Theological Seminary. He was a recognized authority in Southern Baptist circles. However, Hughes was an avid anti-Calvinist, and launched forays against Liberty University, attacking some teachers he perceived to be Calvinists.[1]

Dr. Ed Hindson was a very popular and gifted Bible teacher, but he had used a hyperbole, claiming he wasn't a "five-point" Calvinist, but rather was a "six-point Calvinist." Hindson said he was not a Calvinist but used the term as a diversion against hyper-Calvinism. But in a huff, Hughes had said that Hindson—who had earned his Doctor of Ministry under Jay Adams, an avid Calvinist who taught at Westminster Theological Seminary (Calvinistic) in greater Philadelphia, Pennsylvania— would never teach in his seminary.

Jerry Falwell usually didn't solve his problems behind the scenes. In chapel, he announced publicly, "Dr. Hindson is going to teach a counseling course this fall in the seminary." Ripples spread throughout the college and seminary. Not only was Hughes against the perceived Calvinism of Ed Hindson, but he was also against counseling.

About a week later, Hughes had a heart attack. It probably came from self-induced tension over his perception of the problem. When Jerry and I visited Hughes in the hospital, Hughes said, "Jerry, I want you to reverse your announcement."

"I can't do that," was Jerry's kind answer, and he dropped the subject. Hughes was left to chew on the results.

Two weeks later, Robert Hughes dropped off copies of a letter at many of the lunch counters in Lynchburg. The 15-page letter accused Falwell of compromise. On almost every page of the letter, Hughes accused Jay Adams of heresy because he said as a reformed Christian, "Counselors must not tell any unsaved counselee that Christ died for him, for they cannot say that. No man knows except Christ himself who are his elect for whom he died."[2]

The letter sent gossip rippling through Lynchburg. No one talked about Calvinists; they were shocked that Jerry Falwell was accused of *compromise*. The local ABC television station announced a live interview with Dr. Robert Hughes on the 11:00 evening news, promising to "get to the bottom of this compromise." It probably was one of the most widely viewed late news programs in Lynchburg.

I sat on the edge of a stool, staring into a black and white television, anticipating a blowup. The news person began the interview by asking Dr. Hughes, "How has Dr. Falwell compromised?" The interviewer got one answer.

"Calvinism."

"No . . . I mean what about money, or sex, or lying . . . or . . . ?"

Hughes interrupted to say, "Falwell is not guilty of these issues." Falwell was squeaky clean. Hughes began to explain about compromising with Calvinism. Probably no one in the city—except a few theologians—understood what Hughes was talking about. Surely, no one cared.

Then the announcer interrupted Hughes and said, "We'll be right back after these announcements."

But he was wrong. He came back after some commercials, but Hughes did not. Not another word was said about Robert Hughes . . . or compromise . . . or Calvinism . . . or anything else related to the letter. The issue was dead as far as the city was concerned. So was Hughes.

The next morning, Robert Hughes received a letter of termination.

Several things had happened during the night. Security and janitors showed up at Dr. Hughes's office and packed all of his books, carefully inventorying each so no one could say that anything was lost.

Also in the middle of the night, security had awakened my secretary, Shelly Hunt. She went to my office and packed my books and other belongings. She tells the story of sitting on boxes of my books, riding on a dolly being pushed through the halls, singing the Air Force theme song: "Off we go into the wild blue yonder . . ."

Hughes expected a revolt within the student body, and for many within the community to follow him, but only his secretary and one student left the school. Even Dr. Hughes's son, Charles, didn't leave school but stayed to graduate with a B.A. from the college, an M.Div. from the seminary, and eventually, a Doctor of Ministries degree. Charles stills works at Liberty University 32 years later.

I arrived at 8:00 on the morning following Dr. Hughes's television interview, surprised to see my books and files all set up in my new office, ready for business. At 9:00 A.M., Bill Sheehan, a deacon at Thomas Road Baptist Church and lawyer for the seminary, showed up at my office with a legal document. "Sign this," he instructed. He proceeded to tell me that the document was a legal transfer of funds. With the knowledge of only a select few, Dr. Hughes had opened a secret bank account where he was gathering finances to move the seminary away from Liberty University and house it in a small town a few miles from Lynchburg. Several seminary graduates made monthly contributions to the seminary from their churches, but none of them realized how their gifts would be used.

Sheehan informed me that the account was in his name and the name of the dean of the seminary, Dr. Robert Hughes. But since Hughes had been fired, and I was the new dean, this document would allow us to withdraw the money from the secret account and deposit it back into Liberty University's account. Bill Sheehan was embarrassed that he had been duped into undermining Jerry Falwell.

Falwell asked me to make several changes in the seminary. First, Hughes had not allowed women into the M.Div. program because of his bias. I changed the purpose of the program from training pastors only to training missionary translators, administrators and counselors. That opened up the M.Div. program to all. Second, I allowed divorced students into the seminary. Even though I was not in favor of ordaining a man who was divorced into the ministry, I felt that there were many evangelical churches in America that would accept a divorced man as pastor, and I believed Liberty Baptist Theological Seminary ought to serve all evangelical churches, not just the churches that agreed with me and/or with Thomas Road Baptist Church on ordination. Third, the seminary had been incorporated separately from the university and had its own board of directors. Immediately, I led the board to vote to dissolve the corporation and merge the seminary into Liberty University. All of the seminary board members became board members of the university.

Finally, Dr. Hughes had done an outstanding job of building a theological library for the seminary. Prior to 1970, accrediting agencies had insisted on separate libraries for theological seminaries connected with universities. However, this opinion began to change in the '70s, as people recognized that many reference books could be part of a shared-services approach. I led a study group that showed that Liberty could save approximately a million dollars over the next five years by merging the seminary library with the university library.

With these moves, the seminary began to grow. Within four years, the student body had doubled in size, to more than 300 students. In 1984, the seminary received Associate Membership in the ATS (Association of Theological Schools); two years later, it received full accreditation from SACS (the Southern Association of Colleges and Schools).

Teaching Church Growth

When I became dean of the seminary, Dorm Landtroop, our registrar, insisted that I start teaching courses on church growth; up to that time, I had only taught Bible and systematic theology. Landtroop had developed an evangelism/church growth minor about the time I began writing books on church growth.

The Complete Book of Church Growth, written with John Vaughan and Dave Seifert, was instantly received by the academic community as the standard church growth textbook in the seminaries of America.[3] When John Vaughan and I began writing the book, we assumed there was only one way to grow a church—the way Baptist churches grew. But our research revealed that Bible churches were growing, even though they didn't have evangelistic visitation, nor did they have evangelistic altar calls, nor did they do the other things that soul-winning churches did.

Next, we began to see that some Pentecostal churches grew as a result of spiritual dynamics, not by using the methods of Baptist churches. Many Pentecostal or charismatic churches were growing because of signs and wonders—a phenomenon we called "power" evangelism.

The Complete Book of Church Growth is unique in that it suggests that there are seven growth models found in American churches, and each model has a different dynamic that causes both health and growth in churches.

Church Growth Institute

In 1981, I became friends with an older Liberty student named Larry Gilbert. He had owned a sign-painting company in Maryland and had been an avid church worker. He developed a *Spiritual Gifts Inventory* and wanted to spread it among the churches.[4]

Larry decided to borrow money and print 10,000 copies of the inventory, using an expensive printing method. I assured him, "I can sell these in my Sunday School meetings." As Larry went to my Saturday seminars with me, he heard me teach the idea of Friend Day. (You may recall that Friend Day was a one-Sunday evangelistic event where all members were encouraged to bring an unsaved friend to church with a view of getting them saved.) Larry and I developed the first *Friend Day* packet.[5] Although the idea of Friend Day was not original with me, I had seen it effectively used in many Baptist Bible Fellowship churches.[6] I told pastors everywhere about Friend Day, because I wanted other churches to experience the same success.

Larry suggested putting all the ideas into a notebook; he would draw promotional artwork so that churches could copy letters, tracts, a calendar and other materials to help make Friend Day successful in their churches. Bill Bryan, educational director of First Southern Baptist Church of Del City, Oklahoma, had "Friendly Freddie" drawn for a Friend Day in his church. He graciously allowed us to use the image for the cover of our *Friend Day* packet. I wanted to sell the notebook for $9.99, but Larry insisted on selling it for $59.99. He argued that if people paid a good price, they were more likely to use it. I decided to let him try to sell it until proven wrong. But Larry was right. That price then included enough profit that we could build up resources to develop other outreach programs. (*Friend Day* was used primarily to build the Church Growth Institute up to a $2.5 million a year business.)

We assembled the first batch of 100-page *Friend Day* packets in 3-ring binders and took 60 packets to the Michigan Sunday School Convention. More than 10,000 delegates had registered for the convention, held in Cobo Hall in Detroit. Hysteria broke out in my workshops when I held up the *Friend Day* binder. All 60 copies were sold in one meeting, plus we took orders for additional copies that we shipped later. To save money, Larry and I were sharing a hotel room. We were so fearful of losing about $3,600 (more money than we had ever seen in book sales) that we secured the cash overnight in the hotel's safety deposit box.

Next, I decided to market my Saturday Sunday School seminars. Rather than just going to churches and giving three or four classes on a Saturday, I decided to put all my messages into one unified program. I prayed about the task and looked for an opportunity to write up the program.

A couple of weekends later, I had a speaking engagement in Virginia Beach, Virginia—200 miles away. Larry drove, while I sat in the front seat with a Dictaphone and began dictating everything Sunday School leaders needed to do to grow their attendance and enrollment. There was late afternoon light when we left Lynchburg, but it was dark when we arrived at our destination. The following Monday, the typist began typing out my points. There were 154 major suggestions I gave to grow a Sunday School, so we called the program *154 Steps to Revitalize Your Sunday School and Keep Your Church Growing.*[7]

For the next 10 years, my Saturday seminars followed the "154 Steps" program. Larry began buying church mailing lists, and we targeted metropolitan areas. We charged $19.95 per person for the seminar, but if a church wanted to bring all of its Sunday School teachers and workers, they received a group rate of $99.

The Church Growth Institute was organized in Lynchburg, Virginia, under a board of directors made up of Larry Gilbert and some of his friends. I didn't want the responsibility of running an organization and meeting payroll every Friday. I wanted to write church growth material and let the Church Growth Institute publish and distribute it.

After we developed *Friend Day* (more than 60,000 copies sold to date), I developed a second packet, *How to Go to Two Services* (more than 15,000 sold).[8] I described how churches could grow by beginning a second worship service and/or Sunday School. I began developing a new resource every three or four months until I had developed 25 packets for the Church Growth Institute.

After several years, Larry came to me with an idea even greater than the *154 Steps* seminar. He made me promise that if I wrote and presented this new seminar, I would do it with the Church Growth Institute. I agreed.

Larry had read an article about the influence the baby boomer generation would have on the Church of the future. I did my research in the library as thoroughly as I would for any term paper or journal article. I developed a one-day seminar on *How to Reach the Baby Boomer.*[9]

This time, the Church Growth Institute charged $99 per person (in other words, the cost for one pastor was the same as what we had previously charged for an entire church staff). This was an innovative method—charging top dollar to train pastors for the future. The largest seminar, held in greater Los Angeles, drew 327 pastors. Over the next two years, I taught the seminar in most major cities in the United States, equipping pastors to adapt their worship services and Sunday Schools for the influx of boomers coming into the church.

The Church Growth Institute purchased a three-bedroom home on Waterlick Road in greater Lynchburg to use as its headquarters and manufacturing facilities. Then the Institute expanded the facility five times; the throttle was wide open. The Institute was in the driver's seat to influence church growth in America, yet neither Larry nor I realized that American Christianity would eventually cool down to church growth and that the sales of church growth materials would begin plummeting.

Perhaps we were our own worst enemies. The first packet, *Friend Day*, was a great success, and we received complimentary letters from pastors all over the country, describing how *Friend Day* led to growth in their churches. So we produced a follow-up packet, *Second Friend Day*, and then the *Friend Day Tune-Up Kit.*[10] With these and all the other packets I produced, pastors ended up with resource packets on their shelves that they didn't use, or that weren't successful.

Although the seminars are now a thing of the past, the Church Growth Institute continues today and still supplies churches with Friend Day resources. This event is a classic that consistently gets results. Larry's *Spiritual Gifts Inventory* has also stood the test of time; it's the best-selling resource of its kind in the nation, with more than five million in use.

Ministry in Korea

Ruth and I observed our twenty-fifth wedding anniversary in 1978, but we could not agree on where to celebrate. So, I suggested that we each make a list of 10 places, and then compare our lists. We included exotic places like Hawaii, the Bahamas, the Florida Keys, and resorts in California. But, out of our combined 20 suggestions, the only place that appeared on both of our lists was South Korea. We agreed that we would spend our anniversary focused on ministry, rather than pleasure. Our life together had been about ministry, so why not celebrate with ministry? Neither of us had any idea what door would open in South Korea.

Korean Airlines was offering a special price—$400—for a package including round-trip travel from Washington, DC, to Seoul, South Korea, and accommodations at the Presidential Hotel. At the hotel, we found the Liberty YouthQuest singers and Liberty SMITE singers (a foreign mission team), who were there for ministry at the same time. I became the official speaker for all of their events. At each high school rally, I presented the gospel, and many young people stood to accept Christ as Savior. Because the Spirit of God was so evident in these gatherings, I was invited to speak to approximately 400 of Korea's top military generals and officers—the equivalent of America's Pentagon.

I announced that my topic was not political or Moral Majority, but God's concerns. I told those Christian officers, "The Great Commission challenges you to reach your nation for Jesus Christ." I concluded, "The secret to evangelizing South Korea is not Christian television, nor radio, but church planting."

Around 10 o'clock that evening, a knock came at our hotel room door. It was a high-ranking officer in uniform who told us that Vice President Kim, the second in authority under the president of South Korea, would meet Ruth and me for breakfast in his office at 7:00 the following morning. I explained to the officer that I would show up, but I was not sure if Ruth would come. I told him, "In South Korea you may tell a woman what she must do, but you cannot tell an American woman what she must do."

"Oh, she must come," the officer pleaded. Then he explained, "She cannot turn down the vice president of South Korea."

"Tell him I'll be there," I heard Ruth say through the bathroom door.

The following day, we were at Vice President Kim's office in the National Legislative Building at 7:00 A.M. Vice President Kim had invited me to breakfast because he wanted to tell me about his church-planting activity. Kim had also been the commanding general of the United Nations Army that turned back the Communist North Korean Army during the invasion of 1950. (Kim was commander in name only; the United States' Douglas MacArthur was the power behind the army.)

Kim explained that as the Communists took each city, they burned the churches and shot the pastors in the city streets. More than 2,000 churches had been burned, most of them Presbyterian. Then Vice President Kim said, "I filled out invoices to use Yankee money to rebuild South Korean churches." We laughed about his access to U.S. money to rebuild the nation and how he set aside funds to rebuild churches. With each new church building, Kim de-commissioned a chaplain from the military to pastor the congregation. Then he noted, "I've helped plant more than 200 churches throughout South Korea."

Vice President Kim also told me that a few years earlier, as an elder in a Presbyterian church, he had helped to plant Riverside Presbyterian Church in Seoul. He wanted me to know that my sermon on church planting was what the nation needed.

Preaching at the Largest Church in the World

I had an appointment with Pastor Yonggi Cho of Full Gospel Church, also called the Yoido Island Church, which was then (and is still today) the largest church in the world. Attendance was averaging more than 70,000 people weekly at that time. That was the biggest attendance I had seen in a church.

As I met Cho at his office door, he indicated that before he would give me the interview, I must promise to write, "The Yoido Church is the largest in the world because of the baptism with the Holy Spirit and speaking in tongues."

"Why are you making this demand?" I asked, honestly not understanding where he was coming from.

Pastor Yonggi Cho, who spoke very clear English, said, "I've read all of your works, especially those articles on Pentecostal churches." Then he explained that I had made Pentecostal churches sound like Baptist churches when I wrote that they were growing by door-to-door soul winning and evangelistic preaching. He then made his demand again: "You must tell everyone that the Yoido Church is the largest in the world because of the baptism of the Holy Spirit and speaking in tongues."

Pastor Cho went on to explain that he did not use the growth methods used in America. He also thought I was an honest man, and that I had written exactly what Pentecostal pastors had told me. He explained his concern: "Many Pentecostal pastors want to be number one—BIG SHOT. They want to be the big man, so they tell you they are like Baptist churches so you will write a story on them."

"I will write exactly what you have said." Then I clarified my promise, explaining to Pastor Cho that I would write, "Pastor Cho *said* his is the largest church in the world because of the baptism of the Holy Spirit and speaking in tongues." Notice, I quoted him accurately without necessarily agreeing with his observations.

Even after writing hundreds of stories about local churches, I don't remember ever being criticized by anyone who said that my article was not accurate. I think I am more objective than many contemporary news reporters and television announcers. Why? Because I learned to use quotations accurately in term papers. Perhaps it goes back to Ms. Logan, the seventh-grade teacher who taught me to write quotations on index cards. Perhaps it goes back to the vast number of term papers I wrote at Dallas Theological Seminary.

Based on my interview with Pastor Cho, I wrote an article titled "The Biggest Little Church in the World." I wrote that the church was big not because of dynamic preaching or human techniques, but because of the work of the Holy Spirit in the region. The church had more than 10,000 small groups at that time. These small groups met in living rooms, laundry rooms of apartment buildings, and restaurants all over the city. Most of the groups met on Friday night, and each had approximately 10 people present.[11]

From that first meeting, Yonggi Cho and I have been close friends. We've had breakfast together on many occasions. At one of these meetings, he explained to me, "Dr. Towns, I usually pray two hours early every morning. But when I have breakfast with you, I will set aside my prayer time until the afternoon."

He added, "I want to learn everything I can about church growth from you." That statement humbled me, because this man has experienced more church growth than any other person in the world.

About the third time we met for breakfast, I told Cho I wanted to learn the secret of his spiritual power. I asked, "Dr. Cho, what can you tell me that will make my ministry more powerful and effective for God?"

Dr. Cho later wrote in an introduction, "I didn't want to tell Dr. Towns some Pentecostal thing to do, so I told him to pray the rounds each day."

I am a student of Church history, so when Pastor Cho said "pray the rounds," I understood that he was referring to the Lord's Prayer. Cho went on to say, "Each day I pray the rounds five or six times, just as a jogger will run around a racetrack five or six times to keep physically conditioned. So I pray the Lord's Prayer each day five or six times to keep in spiritual condition."

When I heard Dr. Cho say that, I committed myself to praying the Lord's Prayer each day for the rest of my life. Before I get out of bed in the morning, I throw the covers down to my waist and pray the Lord's Prayer over the events of the coming day. Then after I've eaten breakfast and read the newspaper, I go to my office for prayer and begin again with the Lord's Prayer. I have practiced this daily for 30 years.

I have gone back to South Korea 18 times to teach classes for Liberty Baptist Theological Seminary and preach in various churches. It's been my privilege to preach two times in the Yoido Full Gospel Church–the largest church in the history of the world. I preached in the Young Nak Presbyterian Club in 1982, when it was the largest Presbyterian church in the world. In 2010, I preached in the Suwon Church, the largest Presbyterian church at that time. I preached for Billy Kim when he pastored the world's largest Baptist congregation (Central Baptist Church); then I preached in Global Mission Church in 2007, 2008 and 2011, when it became the largest Baptist church in the world.

An Innovative New School at Liberty

In the summer of 1985, Dr. Ron Godwin, who worked as an executive assistant to Jerry Falwell, came up with the idea for LUSLLL, which stood for Liberty University School of Lifelong Learning.[12] Godwin proposed that we videotape Liberty courses so that students could take an accredited course at home by learning through their VCRs. Liberty professors wrote supporting educational materials, and their lectures were taped. Students watched the tapes, read the textbooks, studied and took their exams at home.

When Godwin presented the concept to the deans, I immediately saw the long-range implications of educating thousands of people—especially those who could not come to Lynchburg—in their homes. I jumped on the bandwagon, although several of the deans argued against what they called "watered-down education" or a "glorified diploma mill."

I volunteered to put my courses on tape, and that summer I spent four hours each morning carefully outlining my lectures and another four hours each afternoon videotaping the lectures. In three months, I turned out four courses: Old Testament Survey, New Testament Survey, Systematic Theology, and Church Growth and Evangelism.

The idea of LUSLLL exploded, and our online school was off the ground and running. Within five years, more than 14,000 students were studying from their homes, in addition to the 5,000 students who were on campus. Jerry and I had promised that Liberty University would reach the world, and LUSLLL was another way of doing it.

But not everyone was happy. I had led Liberty Baptist Theological Seminary to receive Associate Membership in the Association of Theological Schools (ATS), the accrediting agency for seminaries. Dr. Marvin Taylor, executive secretary for ATS, said to me, "Now, ATS will accredit your resident program, but we will pretend that these online courses do not exist." Dr. Taylor thought online courses were not credible education. Some educators were so blinded by their tradition that they couldn't see the future.

Two years later, the Southern Association of Colleges and Schools (SACS) extended accreditation to Liberty Baptist Theological Seminary. Hence, our young seminary had what many other seminaries didn't have: accreditation by both ATS and SACS.

Sam Towns and Liberty University School of Lifelong Learning

Our son, Sam, had recently gotten married in California and was teaching at Arlington Baptist College in Texas. The college was undergoing a theological battle between Calvinists and non-Calvinists. A Calvinistic pastor became chairman of the board and decided to purge the school of all teachers he perceived to be non-Calvinists. So, in one day, eight faculty members were fired, including Sam. On Friday evening, he cleared out his desk at the campus, and on Monday morning, he found work in a store at the mall. I phoned Sam with an idea: "There is a new school starting at Liberty called the Liberty University School of Lifelong Learning [LUSLLL], an online educational program."[13]

I explained that LUSLLL could be shot down in flames, or it could be the biggest thing Liberty had ever done. I arranged for Dr. Tom Diggs, the new dean of LUSLLL, to phone Sam. Without coming to Lynchburg to be interviewed, Sam became the second person hired for our innovative new program.

Immediately after moving back to Lynchburg, Sam enrolled in the Doctorate of Ministry program at Fuller Theological Seminary. He had earned three master's degrees: a Master of Arts in Theological Studies from Dallas Theological Seminary, a Master of Religious Education from Lynchburg Baptist Theological Seminary, and a Master of Education from Longwood College in Farmville, Virginia.

Sam decided to write his doctoral dissertation on me, titling it: *Elmer L. Towns, A Biographical and Chronological Presentation of His Writings*. His research was thorough, and he wrote a review of every book, pamphlet and resource packet I had produced. I told him I had written more than 70 books.[14] He said, "No, you've written only 48 books." He would not count any pamphlet of less than 100 pages.

I told him that I had written for one magazine—*Christian Life Magazine*. "No, you've been on the mastheads of eight magazines." When I counted, I only thought of *Christian Life Magazine* because of its importance and size. But his research found a listing of all the magazines in which my name had appeared on the masthead: *The Missionary Crusader, The Evangelical Witness, The Evangelical Christian, The Bible Expositor and*

Illuminator, Christian Life Magazine, Faith Aflame, Fundamentalist Journal, and *Journal Champion.*

Sam became dean of the School of Religion for LUSLLL, and he enjoyed reminding me that he had more than 2,000 students in his school, while I had only 600 students in the resident program.

In 1992, Liberty University faced its 10-year accreditation renewal with SACS. This affected my life in two different ways. First, I had been a vice president and member of the board of directors without a specific designation. During the first SACS visit, it was felt that my influence on the board of directors was crucial because I was a co-founder of the university. However, 10 years later, things changed. The accreditation team said, "It is a conflict of interest to teach for a university and be on the board to determine its policies." So, I was dropped from the board and stripped of the vice presidency.

The team also felt that I couldn't give adequate leadership as both dean of Liberty Baptist Theological Seminary and dean of the college's School of Religion. During the financial crisis, I had saved a vast amount of money by administering a merger of the two. Teachers with strength in one discipline, such as Church history, could teach both undergraduate and seminary classes, as long as the classes and students were never intermingled. However, for the strength of the seminary, there had to be a complete organizational break between the School of Religion and the seminary. That posed quite a dilemma for me: Should I keep the seminary or the School of Religion? I loved them both.

My secretary, Judy Forlano, did a two-week time assessment of my work schedule, keeping track of every task I did for both institutions. The assessment showed that I spent 75 percent of my time on the seminary, because the seminary did not have its own infrastructure, such as a dean of students. I was involved in managing every aspect of the seminary, and a lot of my time was spent on paperwork. However, the undergraduate School of Religion did not take as much of my time, because I had support from the entire university infrastructure. The decision was a no-brainer: I gave up the theological seminary and kept the School of Religion. That freed up much of my time. In the next 15 years, I did more research, writing, and developing of courses than at any other time in my life.[15]

Becoming Teacher of the Pastor's Bible Class

The first Sunday of February 1986 was another one of those days that changed my life. For 30 years, I had spent many Sundays away from home, preaching in the morning services in local churches. These sermons helped Winnipeg Bible College, Trinity Evangelical Divinity School, and Liberty University. Earlier, Ed Dobson, dean of students and teacher of the Pastor's Bible Class at Thomas Road Baptist Church, irritated Jerry.

Ed Dobson had been invited to preach in some of the greatest churches in America, especially those without pastors. Each church begged him to become a candidate to be their pastor. Every time, Eddie returned to Liberty asking everyone to pray about whether he should become a pastor in Baltimore, or greater New York City, and finally Grand Rapids, Michigan. While this was a legitimate prayer request, Eddie didn't realize how much it irritated Jerry Falwell—because it meant Eddie's primary loyalty was not to Liberty. His desire to pastor away from Lynchburg raised a question over personal loyalty to Jerry. As an illustration: If a man tells a woman that he is thinking about a divorce, she's not going to let him in her bed anymore.

That Sunday morning, Jerry Falwell stood and announced to the Pastor's Bible Class, "Next Sunday Dr. Elmer Towns will begin teaching this class." That was it! No discussion! Eddie was not given a chance to explain or repent, and I was not consulted. That's the way Jerry did business—out in the open, make a decision, and make it work.

About a week earlier, Bobby and Carol Smith had taken Ruth and me to the Crown Sterling Restaurant for a steak dinner. During the meal, Bobby said, "When you teach the Pastor's Bible Class, I get so much from the Bible." He knew Jerry was going to make a change in the class, so he asked me, "Will you come off the road and make a commitment to teach at Thomas Road Baptist Church every Sunday?"

Bobby's question shocked me. *How did he know?* God had been speaking to me about taking over the Pastor's Bible Class, but I hadn't mentioned it to anyone—not even my wife. As a matter of fact, I would rather teach the Bible than run all over the nation challenging churches to grow. Bobby's question seemed to be a sign from God, so I said, "Yes, if Dr. Falwell asks me." For the next 26 years, I taught the Pastor's Bible Class without pay, because I love the ministry. But that meant giving up honorariums I could otherwise be receiving.

Let me tell you about pulpit honorariums. When I first started preaching in pulpits while teaching at Midwest Bible College, I usually got $10—occasionally as much as $25. When I went to Canada, they gave about the same amount—except for Elim Chapel in downtown Winnipeg, which paid $50 a Sunday. That was quite a bit for a college president who was only making $75 for a whole week of work.

After my move to Trinity Evangelical Divinity School, a black congregation in inner-city Chicago gave me a sealed envelope when I preached at their church. In the parking lot, I opened the envelope to see a check for $100. I was shocked and could hardly wait to get home to tell Ruth. When you work in faith colleges that don't pay on time, pulpit honorariums are a necessary way of life. But when I took over the Pastor's Bible Class, without honorarium, God rewarded me in a much greater way.

I was forced to write a new lesson each week—something that would be relevant to lay people, something they needed to hear from God, and something practical to help them live for God. Many of my books on spirituality and prayer were first taught in that class and then compiled into manuscripts. The books I've written are a much greater reward than any money I might have received for preaching anywhere else.

When I started teaching this Sunday School class, there were about 3,000 in attendance, packing the auditorium to capacity. Two years later, the IRS ruled that Liberty University and Thomas Road Baptist Church were in conflict of interest. The university could no longer force students, faculty and staff to join and attend Thomas Road and pay tithes to the church. In the IRS's opinion, one leader—Jerry Falwell—led both, and the deacons of the church and the board of directors of the university were co-mingled. The IRS said the university had to be an educational institution, and the church had to be a ministering institution, if both were to maintain charitable status to receive tax-deductible gifts.

Immediately, the faculty, staff and students were allowed to join any church in Lynchburg and attend wherever they chose. Some loved liturgical worship, so they went to Presbyterian churches. Others preferred small Baptist churches, some liked Southern gospel music, and still others wanted to go to the denominational churches of their childhoods. Within two years, attendance in the Pastor's Bible Class dwindled from 3,000 to 1,000. For the next 20 years, I had an attendance of about 1,000 weekly.

While preaching in Hamilton, Ontario, Canada, one time, I saw great potential in a young man named Doug Porter who had planted a church in his hometown and rallied a huge crowd for a Moral Majority-type rally. I told Doug if he could get to Lynchburg, I would take care of his tuition, room and board. Doug lived with us for the next year. I gave him two goals: He had to lose 100 pounds (because he weighed more than 300), and he had to go on a date a week until he got married. A year later, he moved out when he married.

Doug was a relentless researcher. At night, his light was on as he poured over his books; the next morning, he was up before me, studying the Word. I shared with him my writing topics, and he did research for me. Even after he moved back to Canada, Doug continued as my research associate. Every time Doug helped me with a book, I gave him credit in the Preface or Introduction. Then Doug became my co-author, writing a number of books and study guides with me.[16] Several years later, Doug became the second person to get a doctorate from Liberty Baptist Theological Seminary.

I planned to write a book on the names of Jesus, and my research found that Charles Rolls had written three books, published by Moody Press, on that topic. Doug looked Rolls up in the Toronto, Ontario, phone book, and they chatted about his list of the names of Christ. Rolls had found 327 different names for Jesus. He told Doug, "I believe there are twice as many names of Jesus in the Bible as I have published." Rolls explained that he was too old to do any more research, and he challenged us to study and write more on the names of Jesus. We found more than 700 names, titles, offices, similes and metaphors for Jesus and listed them in the book *The Names of Jesus*.[17]

That series went so well that I did the research and found more than 100 names for the Father. I taught those in a 12-week series and then published them in *My Father's Names*, which went through several printings.[18]

Since I am a Trinitarian, I decided I would also teach a series on the names of the Holy Spirit, and then write those into a book as well. It was the first time there had been a book on the Holy Spirit's names. In 1995, *The Names of the Holy Spirit* received the coveted Gold Medallion Award from the Evangelical Publisher's Association and the Christian Bookseller's Association in the Bible Study category.[19]

Hard Times at Liberty

While the Church Growth Institute was prospering, Liberty University fell on hard times. In 1985, Jim Bakker, host of the extremely popular PTL television show and network, fell into sexual sin. Jerry Falwell called all the leaders of the church and university into his office to say, "Tomorrow [March 20, 1987] the *Charlotte Observer* will announce that Jim Bakker has committed adultery, and will print the name of the lady with whom he has committed adultery."

At first the other leaders and I didn't think Bakker's problem would affect Liberty. Then Jerry explained, "Because of his success and the great respect that America's television audience has for him, I predict that all Christian television shows will fall on hard financial times." Jerry proved to be an accurate prophet. His television program did fall on hard times, along with shows hosted by Billy Graham, Robert Schuller of the Crystal Cathedral, and others. Many Christian television programs completely disappeared.

Financial support for the Old Time Gospel Hour, which had risen to $27 million per year, decreased by $25 million within two years. As the university began to fall into debt, several things were done to prop it up. First, Liberty began to borrow against its assets, and when it couldn't repay the loans, assets were lost—such as the acreage on Liberty Mountain, the headquarters of the Old Time Gospel Hour located in the former Shoppers' Fair, the Liberty Broadcasting Network, and the executive headquarters and warehouse known as Craddock-Terry.

Debts continued to accumulate, but no one could actually take away Liberty University property by court action. Previously, Liberty had tried to raise money through a bond offer, but the Virginia Supreme Court ruled that Liberty was a church, so the university couldn't sell tax-free bonds. During these financial hard times, loan holders tried to force the sale of Liberty on the courthouse steps and liquidate our assets, but an ancient law in the original constitution of the Commonwealth of Virginia stated that a church could not lose its property by lawsuit. That law saved Liberty. Eventually, Liberty University amassed a debt of more than $104 million—an unheard-of debt among Christian organizations, especially educational institutions.

In the early '90s, a multi-millionaire—or perhaps a billionaire—named A. L. Williams stepped in to help save the university. On two or three occasions, A. L. Williams made payroll when Liberty was broke. But he eventually told Jerry, "I am not going to keep making payroll for the university. The salaries and expenses must be cut below income."

A. L. Williams sent five certified public accountants (CPA) to audit Liberty's finances. Using a cost-fund accounting analysis, they functionally put a dollar mark on the forehead of every teacher, administrator and other staff member—right down to the lowest-paid janitor—to represent how much each person cost the university for their services. That number included salary, vacation, supplies, and so forth. Then the CPA team conducted a second assessment, putting another dollar mark on every forehead. This number represented the amount of money each person brought into the university.

I called the day the dreadful news about layoffs came down "Black Friday." At the time, I had a total of 34 faculty members teaching in the School of Religion and the seminary. After the pinks slips went out that Friday evening, I had only 17 teachers. Those who had large enrollment in their classes were safe. Some faculty members with doctorates from the most recognized universities in the world were released because their classes were small. Entire educational majors and departments were eliminated. Across the university, about one-third of the employees were gone.

Liberty had a counseling center with more than a dozen professional counselors who provided free guidance to students and the public. They were all cut. Teachers and workers who had been charter members of Thomas Road Baptist Church were cut, and so were some church deacons who worked at the university.

A. L. Williams told Jerry to leave town on Friday, before the cuts were announced, and not come back until Tuesday. Williams didn't want people to appeal to Jerry's heart of compassion. Jerry might have put some back on the payroll. Jerry did leave town, but flew back in on Sunday morning to preach and left during the closing prayer so that no one could get to him.

Suddenly, the university displayed a strength it had not seen before. There were several strong, effective teachers who had large classes (300 to 350 students). These classes were money-makers, so those faculty members were retained, while many Ph.D.s with smaller seminar classes were laid off because of those courses' narrow appeal.

The indebtedness was a dark cloud, but the loyalty of workers shone brightly. One morning, Jerry announced in chapel that the finances were so bad that we didn't have money to buy toilet paper. The statement was a hyperbole, but the next day dozens of faculty members arrived on campus with a briefcase in one hand and a bag of toilet tissue in the other. We would not let the school collapse. There was a deep commitment and loyalty that got Liberty through those difficult days.

In addition to laying off personnel, the CPAs cut majors, classes and programs that were not cost-efficient. The university lost 20 percent of its students, going from a high of 5,000 to approximately 4,000.

When finances started to level out, and income began covering expenses, we thought Liberty was through the rough waters. But many of our creditors complained to the accrediting agency, SACS. In turn, SACS informed Liberty that it could lose its accreditation if the financial issues were not solved. Jerry Falwell told the faculty, "If we lose accreditation, we lose everything."

A Fasting Miracle

One Sunday morning, I walked into the back room early to see Jerry Falwell in make-up, getting ready for Sunday morning television. I was struck by how thin he was. Jerry had always been overweight, and he had tried every new diet that came down the road, but whatever he was doing now *really worked*. So, I sarcastically asked, "What new dumb diet are you on now?" I was not slamming him; that's the way friends talk sometimes.

"I'm not on a 'dumb' diet," Jerry said, looking up seriously from the sermon notes he was reviewing. "I'm 25 days into a 40-day fast."

He reminded me that Liberty University was in terrible financial trouble, and we could lose accreditation if we didn't solve our financial crisis. He added, "If we don't have accreditation, students won't come." Then he went on to explain that he was on a 40-day fast, praying for $52 million. The university had already eliminated approximately $50 million in debt by selling off our assets (buildings, property, and so on) and through hard-nosed negotiation with those to whom Liberty owed money, but there was still a great financial need.

Jerry had planned to keep his fast a secret, but I pointed out that everyone could see the evidence of it. So, he decided to announce his 40-day fast from the pulpit. While he was speaking, I was walking through the Sunday morning crowd, shaking hands with various individuals. First, it was Mrs. Gladys Rudder, a longtime faithful church member, who said to me, "Now Jerry's messed it up; he's told everybody he's on a fast."

Then Mrs. Betty Hamlett said, "A fast should be secret, because Jesus said, 'When ye fast, be not, as the hypocrites . . . that they may appear unto men to fast' " (Matt. 6:16, *KJV*). She continued to quote the Scripture: "When thou fastest . . . [do it] in secret" (vv. 17-18, *KJV*).

About three or four rows farther on, another lady said the same thing. So, I slipped onto the platform to tell Jerry what I had been hearing. He introduced me, and I explained to the Sunday morning congregation that some fasts were to be private, especially when there was a private need. But other fasts were public, such as when Ezra called a public fast by more than 4,000 people who were on their way back to Jerusalem from Babylon. The congregation seemed to accept my explanation—and Jerry's fast.

"Don't seek my pocketbook. Seek my heart," God kept telling Jerry during that fast. He finished the 40-day fast without receiving any answers beyond that instruction. So, he immediately began doing everything SACS was demanding of the university for re-affirmation. First, he dropped his family members from board membership at the university. Second, he eliminated dual service by deacons from the church who were also on the board of directors of the university. Third, 12 individuals had been given honorary titles of Vice President; all of those titles and positions were dropped. Jerry did many other things Liberty had to do—and God saw the integrity of his heart. Twenty-five days after the conclusion of his first fast, as Jerry was praying one morning, he felt God was saying, "Now you can ask me for money."

So, Jerry Falwell went on a second 40-day fast—an undertaking perhaps unheard of in Christian history. Jerry said to me on several occasions, "The first 40 days were easy. The second 40 days were torturous, almost impossible."[20]

After the second 40-day fast ended, God began to work mightily. One day I got a demanding phone call from Jerry. He said, "Get down here to my office immediately! I want you to see a miracle."

When I entered his office, he explained that a courier would be arriving shortly from A. L. Williams with a check that was unbelievable. Within 10 minutes, a gentleman walked into the office with a small letter satchel, unzipped it, and handed Jerry a check. Jerry held the check up triumphantly—yet delicately—by the two upper edges, announcing, "It reads $27 million. That's more money in one place than any one of us will ever see in our lifetime."

"Let me hold it," I requested.

"No," he laughed. "The next person to touch this will be the bank teller when I deposit it."

Later, when I told the story about the check, some people doubted me—thinking that only a wire or bank letter could be used to transfer this amount of money. But a Xerox copy of the check is available for all to see the mighty miracle God did.

But a $27 million check was not the only thing A. L. Williams did. He transferred much of the indebtedness of Liberty University to his various companies. (In our darkest days, our debtors had eliminated the interest on our loans or reduced it to a very low rate. Williams felt it better to assume a debt at no interest than to use good money to pay off old debts.) SACS was satisfied, and Liberty's accreditation was re-affirmed.

Finding Prayer Partners

In 1991, C. Peter Wagner published a book called *Prayer Shield*—I thought it was an outstanding book with a poor title.[21] The book told how pastors could develop a team of prayer partners to support their ministries, but the idea of a *prayer shield*—protection over ministry—was only one byproduct of prayer support.

I had been meeting with a group of prayer warriors early every Sunday morning to pray for the Pastor's Bible Class. I brought a Xerox copy of Wagner's book with sections highlighted in yellow to read to my prayer partners, explaining the contribution that they could make to a pastor's ministry. After reading, I asked one of the most difficult questions I ever posed to an audience (this was a group of about 10 people). The question seemed egotistical and self-centered, yet it had eternal implications. I asked, "Will you make my ministry your prayer ministry?" Then I added, "Don't respond this morning, but I want you to pray about taking on this responsibility; then talk with me privately."

The very next week, Buddy Bryant became my prayer partner and has stayed in that role for more than 20 years. I attribute much of any accomplishments I've achieved to Buddy Bryant—and later to Charlie Padgett, who also became a valued prayer partner.[22]

Buddy Bryant is a logger who employs six people cutting timber out in the bush. He told me, "I get up at four o'clock every morning to pray for you until I leave for work a little after five." Then he went on to explain, "While the other loggers play rock and roll music through their earphones, I only wear ear plugs to block out the whine of the chainsaw, but all the while I'm praying for you."

My success each week is determined by my early Sunday morning meeting with my prayer partners, where we share requests and pray for one another.

Another Sunday morning prayer experience began more than 20 years ago. The Sunday after I took over the Pastor's Bible Class, Jerry decided to begin broadcasting it live over WLBU, the television station owned by the ministry. He said, "Phone me around 7:00 Sunday morning; let's go over details about the program."

When we finished talking, I said, "Let me pray."

The following Sunday, we talked again to coordinate the program, and then we did the same the week after that. Each time, I prayed. Out of those few weeks grew a habit that continued for 20 years. I'd phone Jerry each Sunday around 7:00 A.M. to ask, "What's the biggest prayer request for this week?"

That wasn't the only time we prayed together. Each Wednesday night at prayer meeting, we sat next to each other on the platform. When prayer time came, Jerry would instruct the audience, "Divide into groups of two or three to pray together." He told those who didn't like to pray in public, "Pray privately."

Then Jerry and I knelt to pray. He always prayed first. As I now look back on his prayers, I wish I had recorded them for others to hear. His deep voice resonated confidence—like he knew God was going to answer just because he asked for something.

And his prayers were intimate! Jerry talked to God as though he were on a first-name basis with Him. I became confident in all I did for God just by hearing him pray.

When Elmer and I would pray at night, he would often overwhelm me with some gigantic request for God, such as ideas for a book he was writing that would change the face of evangelism, or a scheduled meeting with Billy Graham, or the need to pray for Jerry Falwell to raise $5 million to finish seven dorms. But then Elmer also prayed about minutia—little things most people don't pray about, such as finding lost gardening tools, or getting a parking place near the door of a store so he could save time, or thinking of an illustration to use in an article he was writing. Praying with Elmer is an adventure; I never know what will come out of his mouth—or rather, out of his heart. —Ruth Towns

Think about it! I have had opportunities to kneel and pray with towering giants whose accomplishments for God have been titanic: Jerry Falwell, Bill Bright, Billy Graham, Yonggi Cho, John R. Rice, Dallas Billington, Beauchamp Vick, Jack Hayford, and others.

Ten Innovative Churches

In 1991, I presented the Baby Boomer seminar at a hotel near the airport in Burbank, California. Bill Greig Jr., president of Gospel Light/Regal Books at the time, said to me, "You've got to write this into a book for Regal Books."

I was flattered but answered, "People won't read a theoretical book telling them why churches ought to change." But I couldn't get the idea out of my head. A couple of days later, I phoned Bill to say, "Instead of a theoretical book about the influence of baby boomers, let me write a book that describes boomers' influences on several churches. Let me write a book that paints portraits of 10 churches; then people can see the changes I am talking about."

The book would be like an art gallery, where people could study in depth the changes that would happen in American churches—before they happened. It would describe 10 churches that had successfully changed and were making a great impact for God. We went ahead with the project, and the book was called *10 of Today's Most Innovative Churches* (with the subtitle, "What They're Doing, How They're Doing It and How You Can Apply Their Ideas in Your Church").[23]

These 10 churches were very different from one another—different denominations, different methodology, and from different sections of the country—and they were impacting their communities in different ways. But they were all boomer churches: They had especially targeted the generation born between 1946 and 1964.[24]

The Baby Boomer seminar played out in the early '90s. I had gone to most major metropolitan areas of the country, and attendance had far exceeded any expectation. But when we tried to conduct a second seminar in each city, attendance was so pathetic that we dropped the Baby Boomer seminar.

It wasn't just the Baby Boomer seminar that declined; it seemed that the popularity of the church growth movement was declining. There were voices that spoke of having healthy churches. Some pastors criticized anyone who emphasized numbers, saying such things as, "I'd rather have a healthy biblical church than a growing big church." Perhaps they had tried to grow and couldn't—so they criticized the thing they couldn't do, or they turned to other areas of emphasis in church ministry.

The megachurch came under fire, being criticized for the egos of pastors and the big budgets devoted to advertisement. People complained that individuals were lost in a big crowd without having their needs met. Questions were asked: "How can a church better minister to average believers with all their needs?" The conclusion: *Bigger was not better*.

My Venture into Fasting

On my regular visits to Gospel Light in Ventura, California, I suggested lists of books that they should seek to publish—books that would be on the cutting edge of Christianity. On one such visit, I gave them a list of seven books, and in the middle was the simple word "fasting." The focus group at Gospel Light latched onto that idea and decided to publish a book about fasting, suggesting names of famous authors who could write this book, such as Bill Bright, Jack Hayford, Cindy Jacobs, and so on. But each of the people they suggested was tied up in other writing projects. So, finally I sheepishly lifted my hand and said, "I can write your book."

Bill Greig III said, "I think we can probably sell 10,000 or 12,000 copies of a book on fasting." He didn't expect it to be a big seller, but added, "It's an important topic and we should do it anyway."

"What do you know about fasting?" someone asked me. "You're a Baptist preacher."

The assumption was that only Pentecostals fasted, and Baptists were not interested. But I answered, "I've been teaching a class on fasting every August to incoming student leadership at Liberty." Then I told them that Jerry Falwell had called the entire Liberty University community to fast on many occasions. So they acquiesced and told me to go ahead and write the book.

When I got home, I began making notes on paper, but I couldn't come up with any ideas of what to write about fasting. At that point, Ruth said to me, "Since the book is on fasting, don't you think you ought to fast about it?"

"Yes," was all I could say.

The following Monday—the usual day I fast—I prayed and researched the topic. At sundown, I ended the fast, and then Ruth and I went out to eat at a local restaurant. She was interested in what I was going to write, asking, "What did God say to you about fasting?"

My answer was simple: "I don't have anything." I went on to say that I had studied all day, and the only thing I had was "a sermon on fasting with nine points."

Stunned, I stopped at the phrase "nine points." Those words didn't slowly drift out of my mouth. It was as if the Holy Spirit was giving me those words. I abruptly slapped my hand on the table. "I'm going to write a book with nine chapters." Each chapter in the book would cover one of the nine points of my sermon. In the introduction of the book, I mentioned that no one had written a significant book on fasting in the last 100 years. I bemoaned the fact that the church was weak and anemic, because it had not fasted. I had no idea that this fasting book would become the new standard by which later books on fasting would be judged.[25]

I worked on the book for about three months, fasting each Monday as I wrote a chapter each week. Then each Sunday, I taught a lesson in the Pastor's Bible class based on the chapter I had just written. The class members helped to focus the book because of their feedback.

Again, Ruth and I went out to eat. I began to tell her the chapter titles and she replied, "These chapter titles sound more like a textbook for school than something laypeople would read." So she suggested, "Why don't you fast and pray for God to give you exciting chapter titles that will make the book reader-friendly?"

I worked on the titles for the next week, and nothing came. Again, on Monday night I broke my fast as Ruth and I went out to eat. I told her, "I didn't come up with any titles that were exciting."

Then she told me that the choir at Thomas Road Baptist Church had agreed to a "Daniel Fast"—eating only vegetables. The money they saved by not purchasing meat and desserts would be given to a foreign mission project.

"That's it," I said to Ruth, again slapping the table. Then, grabbing a napkin, I began to write the titles for my nine chapters:

1. The Disciple's Fast to free oneself from addiction
2. The Ezra Fast to solve problems
3. The Samuel Fast for revival and evangelism
4. The Elijah Fast to overcome unwanted habits
5. The Widow's Fast to provide basic necessities and needs
6. The Saint Paul Fast for insight or for guidance in difficult decisions
7. The Daniel Fast for health and physical healing
8. The John the Baptist Fast for one's outward testimony
9. The Esther Fast for spiritual warfare against satanic or demonic evil[26]

My First 40-Day Fast

In the 1990s—shortly after Jerry Falwell finished his two 40-day fasts—God spoke to my heart about fasting for 40 days. Even though I said yes to the idea, I couldn't make myself begin. In my mind, a 40-day fast was too great—and what if I failed? I had written a book on fasting, and if I failed, the credibility of the book would be destroyed.

Bill Bright, president of Campus Crusade for Christ, was holding annual fasting and prayer conferences across America. He had asked me to be on the advisory board for these conferences. Each conference lasted for three days, and people fasted and prayed the whole time. It was not a conference of sermons, but a prayer meeting conference. I had no trouble with a 3-day fast, or a 10-day fast—but 40 days was another issue.

God addressed my hesitancy in an unexpected way. During one of these conferences, I was sitting at a table with Bill Bright and Pat Robertson—president of Regent College in Virginia Beach, Virginia, and television host of *The 700 Club*. As we were praying, Pat Robertson told God, "Lord, this idea of a 40-day fast is new to me, and I'm scared to do it." Robertson went on to commit himself to doing it, and he asked God to help him. His honesty and integrity touched my heart. I looked up to him as a spiritual giant. He voiced my prayer when he admitted being afraid to fast for 40 days.

As soon as he finished, I prayed, "Lord, I am like Pat Robertson. I am afraid to do this, but if he and Bill Bright can both fast for 40 days, I can do it." I committed myself to begin when Bill Bright and Pat Robertson began; they fasted for 40 days beginning with Lent in February and ending on Good Friday of that year.

Each day, I arose early to meet God in devotions; then, after coffee for breakfast, I went back to my office for prayer.

During the lunch hour each day, I closed my office door and spent approximately one hour in prayer. When I returned home in the evenings, I again substituted the time of the evening meal for prayer.

I was surprised at how easy the 40-day fast was. Day after day, I went from prayer time to prayer time, and only a few times did I get hungry. Once during the 40 days, I visited my mother in Savannah, Georgia, and took her out to a waterfront restaurant for a seafood meal. She ordered Savannah red rice—a meal she had cooked during my boyhood—made with rice, red tomatoes and scrambled eggs. As I watched her enjoy each forkful, I found myself envious of her pleasure in eating.

I had never noticed how completely a pizza could fill a television screen until I was fasting. Also, advertisements for Red Lobster seafood were bigger than the television screen. Each time I found myself attracted to food, I prayed for the purposes of my fast.

During my 40-day fast, I reread 14 books on the spiritual life that had made a deep impression on me when I was a young Christian:

Power Through Prayer by E. M. Bounds
Your God Is Too Small by J. B. Phillips
Spiritual Maturity by J. Oswald Sanders
God's Way of Holiness by Horatius Bonar
Spiritual Secret of Hudson Taylor by Dr. and Mrs. Howard Taylor
Abide in Christ by Andrew Murray
The Saving Life of Christ by Ian Thomas
Bone of His Bone by F. J. Huegel
The Pursuit of God by A. W. Tozer
The Kneeling Christian by An Unknown Christian
Prayer: Asking and Receiving by John R. Rice

Crowded to Christ by L. E. Maxwell
The Christian's Secret of a Happy Life by Hannah Whitall Smith
The Pilgrim's Progress by John Bunyan

During my 40-day fast, I was scheduled to speak at a leadership banquet of the Nazarene Theological Seminary and Nazarene Publishing House in Kansas City, Missouri. They served an elaborate feast of barbecued chicken, barbecued ribs and barbecued steak. When the waitress came to my table, I told her, "I'll just have a cup of coffee with cream." That's the answer I've always given in a restaurant during a fast.

Most servers understand that you might be sick, or figure there is some other reason you are not eating. I've found that if I don't make a big deal of it, neither does anyone else. However, I explained to the people at my table, "You eat what you planned to eat, and do not feel guilty about my not eating." I find that my guests are usually more concerned about my not eating than I am.

That evening, I spoke to the Nazarenes on the 10 Most Innovative Churches. Before the meal, I prayed for God to open up a door for me to speak at 14 statewide Nazarene conventions because of that night's sermon. God answered that prayer, and within the next two years, I spoke on Sunday School and/or fasting at 15 Nazarene state conventions.

Ruth had two different reactions to my fast. At the beginning, because I took her out to eat and only ordered coffee, she was irritated that I was not enjoying food with her. However, toward the end of the 40-day fast, she acquiesced—wanting the fellowship with God that I had. Later, she confessed that she had wished she were fasting with me.

Praying the Lord's Prayer

In 1996, Ruth and I took a ministry trip to Moscow and Saint Petersburg, Russia. On a Sunday morning, we were crossing the White Sea on a riverboat when it occurred to me that there was no church service planned. Going to the captain, I asked if we could use the boat's dining room for a church service, and he agreed. Over half the group was from the Russian Orthodox Church, and the others were from the United

States. I knew that almost none would have a Bible with them, so I preached on something most everyone knew: the Lord's Prayer.

The sermon ended with all praying the Lord's Prayer together in different languages. Then I asked the people to commit themselves to praying the Lord's Prayer every day for the next 30 days. Almost every hand went up in agreement. After the sermon, Bill Greig Jr. said, "Elmer, you've got to write a book for Regal Books on the Lord's Prayer."

Immediately after Sunday lunch, I began writing the book—and within three months delivered a manuscript to Regal Books. It became one of those steady sellers that sold more than 100,000 copies. Later, when I served on the Foreign Missions Committee of the Billy Graham Organization and was planning the Amsterdam 2000 Conference, I said to Billy, "Billy, you ought to give this book on the Lord's Prayer away as a premium to all of those who listen to you on radio and television and read your newspaper."

"Why?" was his simple question to me. I told him that Roman Catholics, Orthodox, and many high church people pray the Lord's Prayer on a regular basis, although many of them are not saved.

"If they pray properly the Lord's Prayer, they will get saved."

Billy Graham's organization distributed more than 250,000 copies of *Praying the Lord's Prayer for Spiritual Breakthrough.*[27]

12

A New Century

(2000–2012)

Many people were expecting some type of catastrophe when the year 2000 was ushered in. Twelve hours before Y2K dawned upon Lynchburg, Virginia, I sat in my reclining chair in front of the television set, using my Dish satellite to tune into New Zealand coverage so I could watch the new century—and a new millennium—dawn upon the world. I had not hoarded food—as some did, expecting a catastrophe with Y2K—but I didn't know what to expect. I was curious to see what God would do.

The new millennium arrived in New Zealand just as any other day, and within a few minutes, televisions switched to Sydney, Australia. Nothing unusual happened there, either—other than throngs of people welcoming in a new era. Then, I watched the new millennium dawning upon Tokyo, Singapore and Mumbai. After a few hours in front of the television set, I arose, knowing that God was in control of the universe and that He had made me a part of a new millennium. So, I asked a question: What does this new millennium hold for Elmer Towns?

I was 68 years old and had lived longer than most of the men in the Towns family, as well as most of those in the McFaddin family. I prayed, "Lord, may I accomplish more in the next 10 years than I have in all the previous decades."

A Son's Death

The new decade found me busier than ever, teaching my Sunday School class at Thomas Road Baptist Church, as well as teaching large classes at Liberty in New Testament Survey and Systematic Theology. On January 27, 2002, I had flown to St. Louis, Missouri, with a view of preaching at one of the largest Southern Baptist churches in the state: First Baptist Church in Arnold, Missouri.

As I was waiting by the carousel to retrieve my suitcase, a delegation of four well-dressed couples walked up to me and introduced themselves. They were Pastor Brad East and his wife, as well as three other staff members and their wives. I was still in a good mood, so I cracked, "I bet you dressed up to meet me so we could go out to a fancy restaurant and have a good meal . . ."

"No ," Pastor East interrupted me. He went on, "I don't know how to break this to you, but your son, Sam, was killed in an automobile accident this morning."

It's never easy to tell anyone that a loved family member has died, and it's especially hard when it is a tragic, unexpected blow. Just the previous evening, Ruth and I had had dinner with Sam and our grandchildren, Brad (age 2) and Collyn (age 3). When he left, I didn't give him my special affirmation of "good boy." Now I think of a thousand things I wish I had told him.

I don't remember anything I said after Pastor East told me Sam was dead, nor do I recall how I reacted. The first thing I remember is getting back on the same plane to return to Virginia. The business manager of the church had quickly turned around my ticket so I could go home. The group stayed with me until I boarded the plane. I had been upgraded to first class; I didn't realize at first that it was a providential upgrade.

The cabin attendant had been told that I had lost a loved one, and she came back to say a few words of consolation. A very distinguished African-American lady sitting next to me heard what the flight attendant said. She asked me, "May I give you a book to read? It's a gift-book I got from the Billy Graham Evangelistic Association."

I don't remember responding to the lady as she dug in her purse. She handed me a copy of *Praying the 23rd Psalm*, the book I had written for people in grief.[1] I was so much in grief I didn't even tell her the coincidence. Thanking her, I turned to a familiar passage, and read, "Yea, though I walk through the valley of the shadow of death, I will fear no evil; for You are with me" (Ps. 23:4).

Here I was, being comforted—not by a stranger or someone I admired— but with the words I had written to comfort others. I read, "To the unsaved, death is real. But if you walk with the Shepherd, death is only a shadow. Since shadows are created when something obscures the light, your death will obscure the light only for a moment. You will walk into that dark shadow, momentarily losing perspective of what you see in this light. But the instant you lose sight of earthly things, the shadow of death melts in the light of the other side. You walk through a doorway with the Shepherd into the other side."[2]

The next three days are a blur in my memory. Ruth went to Whitten's Funeral Home to view the body; I didn't. I wanted to remember Sam with his laughing, infectious smile and twinkling eyes. I wanted to remember him in life, not as a corpse on a table. Many ministers preach the sermon when burying their loved ones, but I couldn't do it. Jerry Falwell preached Sam's sermon, and I kept thinking as I looked at the casket, *He's not there; he's with Jesus.*

Comfort is expressed in many ways. We find comfortable clothes, a comfortable chair, a comfortable way of doing things. But we seldom prepare to extend comfort to someone who has experienced a death in the family—or to receive comfort when we experience a loss ourselves. When our son, Sam, died suddenly in an automobile accident, I was not prepared for such a tragedy.

People quoted Bible verses and poems to me. I wasn't ready for their beautiful cards or their expressions of love and concern. Flowers and food were appreciated. Some comments were hard to hear, like: "Oh, I understand."

NO, YOU DON'T; not unless you had a son die! I wanted to answer, but I couldn't be nice, so I said nothing. We were shocked, stunned and in a daze, going through the necessary motions.

Men and women express grief differently. I almost ignored Elmer while I stumbled through my own emotions. He found more work to keep himself busy. (Keeping busy is characteristic for Elmer.)

Don't believe people who say, "Oh, you'll be okay; you'll get over it." Never!

True comfort is knowing that Sam is with his heavenly Father, and that one day we'll worship our Savior together. —Ruth Towns

Ruth and I rode in the funeral car following the hearse to the cemetery. I turned to say, "I thought you and Sam would be sitting in a funeral car, following my hearse on the way to bury me."

"I did too," Ruth answered, "but I believe God has left you alive for a purpose. You are to accomplish something with your life for the kingdom of God, and I dedicate myself to making it happen."

After that, I saw more care and concern for me physically from Ruth. She did more to save me time so I could spend time studying, teaching, or otherwise doing the will of God. The ministry God had begun in my life, she committed herself to amplify.

The Shock of Cancer

Three years later, I found myself working as hard as ever, but getting more tired, so that I needed to take a nap in the middle of the day—usually an hour, if I had time. I led a group of Liberty students on a tour following the steps of Paul through Greece and Ephesus. We also visited the Isle of Patmos, where the apostle John wrote the book of Revelation. Every time we rode by bus from one spot to another, I fell sound asleep on the bus. In the evening, I went to bed early, and in the morning, I woke up tired.

In the summer of 2005, I had a complete physical, including a colonoscopy, by Dr. Catalano. It was my fifth exam in the last 25 years by Dr. Catalano. As I was getting dressed, he walked into the room to tell Ruth and me, "You've got a malignant cyst in your colon that has to come out immediately." He went on to explain that the cyst was the size of a walnut. The word malignant didn't scare me, because I didn't quite understand its full meaning. Dr. Catalano was more than a physician—he was a friend—so he insisted that I take care of it immediately. I asked which surgeon he would see if he had my problem. He told me Dr. Kittrell. "Then I want him," I said.

Taking out his cell phone, Dr. Catalano personally called Dr. Kittrell. "This has to come out immediately," Catalano spoke into the cell phone. Then he added, "I don't want to wait three or four weeks. What about this Friday afternoon?" Catalano told us that most surgeons leave some free time in the schedule on Friday afternoon. Dr. Kittrell agreed to operate in four days.

Riding home, Ruth asked me how I felt about having cancer.

I reacted negatively to the word "cancer," snapping, "*I don't have cancer*. Catalano said I only had a malignant cyst."

"Malignant means cancer," Ruth carefully explained.

I was in denial; I couldn't believe I had cancer. I thought only sinful lifestyles led to cancer—I had never smoked and had always taken good care of my body, so I couldn't have this dreaded disease. Not me! The next day Dr. Kittrell examined me, and when I asked, he said, "You have cancer."

I recognized the truth of what he said, but still couldn't accept its meaning. Millions of people in America had cancer, and so did I. I insisted that Ruth not tell Polly or Debbie—or anyone else. Obviously, I prayed much by myself, and Ruth and I prayed together.

The night following my meeting with Dr. Kittrell, I was preaching at a prayer meeting at Thomas Road Baptist Church. Requests were read for two or three people who had cancer and were in the hospital. I became greatly convicted by God that I was *not* going to be healed if I didn't tell everyone in the church that I had cancer and ask the congregation to pray for my healing. Sitting in the pulpit chair, I was faced with a leap of faith. Would I remain silent and suffer alone, or would I tell everyone in the church that I had cancer? The surgery was two days away.

When it was time for me to preach, I announced, "You must pray for me; I am having surgery on Friday afternoon for cancer." Then I invited the group to pray with me as I bowed my head and asked in faith for healing.

Immediately after the service, I caught Steve and Shirley Jones—two of my prayer partners from my Sunday morning prayer meeting. Knowing that God used their prayer ministry greatly, I wanted them to pray for me. Steve was a recovering alcoholic who had been saved and delivered from drinking at Elim Home, a ministry of Thomas Road Baptist Church. There in the church parking lot, we prayed for my healing.

On Friday afternoon, Dr. Kittrell talked to Ruth and me before I was wheeled into surgery. He explained, "This will probably take around an hour and 15 minutes. I'll make a small incision in your stomach, pull out the colon, cut off a small section, and sew it back together."

Rather than an hour and 15 minutes, the surgery took three hours. Ruth was beside herself with worry. When she couldn't take it any longer, she started toward the surgical unit door that said "No Admittance." She was going to find out what had happened to me. But Dr. Kittrell pushed on the door first and told her, "We got it all." It had turned out the cancerous cyst was not the size of a walnut; it was the size of a grapefruit.

Later, in his office, Dr. Kittrell told us, "When I looked inside to see the cyst, I broke out laughing." When the nurse asked him why he laughed, he said, "I haven't seen a cyst like that since a picture in medical school." He explained that it was a fast-growing cancerous cyst that was like a rotten grapefruit—it was very dangerous because it was encapsulating poison inside a hard outer shell. He went on to assure us, "When I lifted the 'grapefruit' out of your body, I knew that I had it all because this is not a cancer that spreads; rather, it grows until it explodes."

When I tell people I had 14 inches of colon removed, I like to tell them, "Now, I'm a semi-colon."

Even though Dr. Kittrell said he got it all, I went through chemotherapy for the next nine months, just to be safe. The pill technically was a poison, designed to crawl along the edge of the skin of my body, attacking and killing any cancerous cells it found along the way. As a result, I itched terribly. The temptation was to scratch and scratch. But I learned to pray each time I itched, thanking God for life and a new opportunity to live for Him.

The Towns-Alumni Auditorium

Behind the School of Religion building, there is a perfect natural amphitheater—a small hill running down to a creek. On several occasions when Jerry Falwell and I were driving around campus, I'd have him drive into the lower level parking lot so I could show him how the amphitheater would be a perfect classroom to seat 1,000: "All it needs is a roof, walls and floor."

Jerry always agreed, but finally told me his son, Jerry Jr., said we couldn't do it because of the expressway setback. I had an answer: "There's a movie theater next to the campus that got a variance to construct over the expressway setback line."

"But you've got to raise the money," Jerry told me.

For 10 years, I had taught a doctorate class to pastors. I always joked with them that someday I'd ask each of them for a $1,000 donation to build a state-of-the-art electronic classroom. So I dictated a letter to approximately 500 pastors—including some personal friends—asking for a gift of $1,000 from them personally or from their churches. Liberty's alumni department coordinated the effort. My students responded admirably. Finally, I was told by Ron Godwin, Jerry's executive assistant, "You can stop raising money. We've got enough to finish it." That's the only time I ever heard that anyone or anything at Liberty had enough money.

Fourteen pastors donated $10,000; John Maxwell gave $50,000; and Greg and Dottie Clendenin donated $200,000. (Greg and Dottie were original students, and Greg was the first catcher on our baseball team.) Because the amphitheater was my idea, and I had worked hard to raise the money from alumni, Jerry named the new classroom the Towns-Alumni Auditorium. When the project was dedicated, he named the entire building the Elmer Towns Religion Hall.

I've given a speech to pastors' wives many times that reflects my attitude toward ministry. "First," I tell them, "God can use you in ministry, even if you're not musically talented. I've hung on to that hope for years. Second, I didn't marry Elmer to be his associate pastor or associate teacher. I don't even feel God has called me to full-time ministry. I believe God called me to be a wife and homemaker. That's all I've ever wanted to be, and I've tried to be the best at that calling as I can be." —Ruth Towns

I should feel positively elated that a building at Liberty University is named for me, and that Winnipeg Bible College has a building called the Elmer Towns Dorm. But I find that these honors come with a heavy weight of expectation. I feel a convicting pressure to live for God and not mess up at the end of my life. I have preached about the drunkenness of elderly Noah, the skepticism of an aged Solomon, and the fleshly sin of an old David. I'm determined not to ease up or drift into retirement to savor the fruits of my labor. The Elmer Towns Religion Hall is a heavy burden. I tell my friends, "Don't let anyone name something significant for you in life; wait until you die, because then it won't matter."

Great Is Thy Faithfulness

Right before the last chapel/convocation of the school year, on Wednesday, May 9, 2007, Jerry Falwell and I were the last persons to leave the green room. We had prayed, and all the other leaders had gone to sit on the platform. Jerry and I were alone as we walked through the tunnel to the Vines Center. He stopped still, waited a few seconds, and then asked, "Elmer, why did you sell your lake house?" (We each had second homes across a small peninsula from each other at Smith Mountain Lake.)

I answered, "The house was a pain in the neck." I explained that a robber had broken a window for entry during the winter, and the pipes froze and broke, causing extensive water damage. In addition, there was always maintenance.

Jerry and I had the same conversation the following Sunday. Everyone had left the green room to go to the church platform at Thomas Road Baptist Church. Again, we walked alone to the back curtains—and again he paused, waited a few seconds, and asked, "Elmer, why did you sell your lake home?"

I gave him the same answer—then said goodbye, as I was heading to California, where I had a board meeting for Gospel Light. I was puzzled by his repeated question. After Jerry's death, I looked back on this moment and realized he must have had a sudden pain, seizure or shortness of breath. He wanted to be physically strong when he walked out before a big audience.

Two days later on Tuesday, May 15, I was chairing the board meeting for Gospel Light Worldwide in California when my cell phone rang. I looked down and saw that it was Renee Grooms, my administrative assistant, calling from her office. Usually I wouldn't have answered the phone in a board meeting, but something made me take that call, even though I was in the middle of a business meeting.

"Hello?"

"Jerry's dead . . ." Her panic-stricken voice keep repeating, "Jerry's dead."

The board members saw shock in my face. I was paralyzed with grief; I couldn't even cry. After I shared what I knew, I left to drive 70 miles to the Los Angeles Airport. Renee was trying to arrange a flight home for me. I prayed in puzzlement all the way to the airport. I still had not wept.

As I rode the tram from the car rental station to the terminal, Renee phoned to instruct me to go quickly to Delta. She had purchased an emergency ticket for me.

"STOP!" I yelled, seeing that the tram was just passing Delta.

I walked around people in line to get to the ticket agent. She was holding my ticket, and then she walked me to the front of security, telling them to give me priority. When I got through security, the agent yelled out, "Run!"

As soon as I stepped onto the plane, the door closed. It was the last flight that would get me to Lynchburg that evening. All the way home, I thanked God for all the good things Jerry had done. But I still didn't shed tears, even though I was deeply grieved.

When I got to Virginia, I phoned Ruth to get an update. I told her, "I don't know why, but I've got to go straight to the church." *Maybe they've already got his body lying in state*, I thought.

The church building was locked down. A panic-motivated public had begun stealing things to have keepsakes about Jerry. Security personnel expressed condolences, and then they let me enter. The auditorium was blackened, but one spotlight shone down on the pulpit. The body was not there. I walked behind the pulpit—the place where Jerry was best remembered—and thought, *The messenger is dead; he won't preach again . . .*

Then I couldn't control myself. I cried openly, and loudly. I wept for several minutes. Then I realized someone was standing in the darkness over to my left. It was an eerie feeling; I couldn't see anyone, but I knew a person was hidden in the shadows. I yelled out, "Who's there?"

"Gary Lowe," a voice came back.

Gary had been the organist at the church for years, and he was also a musical instrument salesman. He walked slowly to the stage. It was empty except for the pulpit (a new organ had been installed that day) and a lone folding chair. Nothing else; the stage was lonely.

"The folding chair was for Dr. Falwell." Gary explained that after he finished installing the organ that morning, he was supposed to have given Jerry a private concert—the first recital—that evening.

"Would you take Jerry's place?"

"No, I can't take his place; no one can do that." Gary was the first to hear the explanation I would give to many over the next few days. I quickly added, "But I would be honored to hear the first concert."

"What would you like to hear?" Gary asked.

"Play the first hymn sung in the first chapel of Liberty 36 years ago: 'Great Is Thy Faithfulness.' " Then Gary began softly—just as our life begins softly, just as Liberty University had begun unobtrusively:

"Great is Thy faithfulness," O God my Father,
There is no shadow of turning with Thee;
Thou changest not, Thy compassions, they fail not
As Thou hast been Thou forever wilt be.[3]

As Gary played the next verse, he reached to pull out all the stops. His fingers glided confidently over the new keyboard; his feet danced over the pedals. The organ—as though it had been awakened and come to life—roared with thunderous worship. The sound shook the rafters with vibration, and the whole sanctuary came alive to God's benediction to Jerry's life.

Pardon for sin and a peace that endureth,
Thy own dear presence to cheer and to guide;
Strength for today and bright hope for tomorrow,
Blessings all mine, with ten thousand beside![4]

EPILOGUE

I've walked with God's giants; I have learned from them and been motivated by them. I've interviewed giants, told their stories, and held them up as examples for others to follow. I've never intended to be a giant, or thought of myself that way. I'm not a giant—though I do want to be a giant-maker.

I've never seen myself as a great example. True, God has worked through me to accomplish His will, but my life has been a demonstration not of my own greatness, but of God's power and grace. When people look at me, I pray that they see Jesus—not me.

I'm a man of average abilities. I don't consider myself to have a great pulpit presence, nor is my teaching deep or philosophical. What I have accomplished is God working through me. At the beginning of my ministry I started praying before presenting a message, "Lord, forgive all my sins—including those ignorant ones—by the blood of Christ." Then I'd pray, "Lord, fill me with Your Holy Spirit and anoint me to serve You." I still pray that as an elderly man. That's my prayer for this book.

On several occasions, I've had second thoughts about finishing these memoirs. I don't want to embarrass anyone with the illustrations. I don't want anyone to misinterpret my motives for including the things that are here. I've left out many events, people and failures that could have been included. Perhaps I've included things that only inflame self-pride. But these omissions and inclusions represent the things I felt were important about my life—things I felt you should know.

I'm an average person. My spelling is average, my grammar is average, and my vocabulary is average. My grades were never superlative. I'm just a clay pot who personifies the verse "We have this treasure in earthen vessels" (2 Cor. 4:7). I know that God called me. Why? "For you see your calling, brethren, that not many wise according to the flesh, not many mighty, not many noble, *are called.* But God has chosen the foolish things of the world to put to shame the wise, and God has chosen the weak things of the world to put to shame the things which are mighty" (1 Cor. 1:26-27).

May God use the words and illustrations I have shared in this book to bring glory to Himself and help others follow Him closely.

You should know I am an ordinary man who has had an incredible journey. I am not an incredible man, but I serve an incredible God. I don't have great faith in God; I have faith in a great God—and that makes faith easy.

- First-year enrollment: 154; 2011–2012 enrollment: 13,168 residential and 84,653 online (the total of 97,821 students makes Liberty the world's largest Christian university and America's largest private not-for-profit university).
- First-year budget: $152,000; current budget: more than $806 million.
- First-year faculty: 1 full-time (Elmer Towns), 14 part-time; current faculty: 2,351 members including residential, part-time residential and adjunct online professors.
- First graduation (1973): 14 graduates; projected for 2012: more than 12,500 graduates.
- Total number of students trained at Liberty University and Liberty Home Bible Institute: more than 300,000.
- Liberty Baptist Theological Seminary has 11,288 students enrolled for the 2011–2012 school year (821 residential students in Lynchburg, Virginia, and 10,467 online students). This is probably the largest seminary in the world.
- Liberty was probably the first theological seminary to offer accredited online education. There were some previous correspondence seminaries, but their academic standards were usually questionable, and they were neither recognized nor accredited. Liberty and Liberty Baptist Theological Seminary Online grew because it was grounded in an accredited residential program with fully qualified academic professors.
- The University's students represent 80 countries of the world and 48 denominations. The seminary offers classes in English, Korean and Spanish.
- Seminary students are registered in the following programs: Ph.D. (57); D.Min. (339); Th.M. (157); M.Div. (4,124); M.A.R. (2,174); Master of Religious Education (368) and Professional Master of Arts (4,069).

When I speak of the accomplishments of Liberty, I'm not taking credit for its success, nor for its greatness. The vision and faith of Jerry Falwell drove Liberty to success, and the University's influence will be his legacy. Many other faculty and executives who also contributed to Liberty's greatness include: Pierre Guillermin, who was president of Liberty University from 1975 to 1995, and was the one most responsible for its accreditation; J. Gordon Henry, an academic dean who led to academic excellence; Ed Dobson and Vernon Brewer, who led students to maturity; Roscoe Brewer, who contributed foreign mission vision; Gordon Luff, who gave passion for youth ministry; Harold Willmington and Ed Hindson, who contributed dedication to Bible knowledge; and James Stevens, my associate dean in the School of Religion and seminary for 28 years, who solved an inestimable number of problems behind the scenes. These and many I didn't name—but could have—are responsible for greatness and excellence in things I couldn't do and didn't do. I thank God for them all.

Perhaps the Greatest Miracle: One Billion Dollars

Twenty years ago, in 1992, Liberty was $104 million in debt and facing the threat of bankruptcy. Because of Jerry Falwell's faith, he fasted 40 days to save Liberty. Then, 25 days later, he began his second 40-day fast. This was an incredible step of faith, and it resulted in the greatest miracle in the history of Liberty when all the bills were paid and Liberty was debt free.

I told Jerry, "You could have died in that second 40-day fast." He responded, "I would gladly die to see Liberty thrive."

God in heaven must have seen Jerry's heart better than all of us. The Bible promises God can do "exceedingly abundantly above all that we ask of Him" (Eph. 3:20). God blessed Liberty—I think based on Jerry's sacrificial prayer—in the next 20 years so that by 2012 Liberty's net assets are worth $1.2 billion and has one of the highest bond ratings by secular investment corporations (AA+). To God be the glory!

ENDNOTES

Chapter 3: The Columbia Bible College Years

1. Elmer L. Towns, *Stories About My First Church* (Ventura, CA: Regal Books, 1997). This book is available at www.elmertowns.com. Go to Resources on the tool bar to read the entire book for free.

Chapter 4: The Northwestern Years

1. Elmer L. Towns, *Teaching Teens* (Grand Rapids, MI: Baker Book House, 1965) and *Successful Biblical Youth Work* (Nashville, TN: Impact Books, 1973, revised edition). *Successful Biblical Youth Work* was the first book published by Regal and became a textbook for seminaries, Christian colleges and Bible colleges.
2. This statement became the founding philosophy of the youth department of Liberty University, which became a leader in youth work in the United States. At one time, 25 percent of the mega-churches in the Southern Baptist Convention had a youth leader from Liberty University. However, a statement alone would never make a department famous or influential. The vast influence of the department is credited to Gordon Luff, the founding chair, and Dave Adams, who succeeded him. Both men lived out this philosophy as youth pastors of Thomas Road Baptist Church, where their students achieved great success.

Chapter 5: The Dallas Theological Seminary Years

1. Dr. Hyles would move to Hammond, Indiana, and build the largest Sunday School in the world, with more than 20,000 in attendance. See Elmer L. Towns, *The World's Largest Sunday School* (Nashville, TN: Thomas Nelson, 1974).
2. I graduated from Southern Methodist University on August 27, 1958.

Chapter 6: The Midwest Bible College Years

1. Elmer L. Towns, *Teaching Teens* (Winnipeg, Canada: Winnipeg Bible College Press, 1963).
2. Harold L. Willmington, *Willmington's Guide to the Bible* (Carol Stream, IL: Tyndale House Publishers, 1981).
3. See Lois E. Lebar, *Education That Is Christian* (Wheaton, IL: Victor Books, 1995); and *Children in the Bible School: The HOW of Christian Education* (Old Tappan, NJ: Fleming Revell Publishing Company, 1952); and Mary E. Lebar, *Children Can Worship Meaningfully at Church and Home* (Wheaton, IL: Victor Books, 1976).

Chapter 7: The Canadian Years

1. The Province of Manitoba didn't accredit colleges, but the government gave approval to recognize Winnipeg Bible College's degrees, and WBC course credits were transferable to other governmentally approved colleges and universities.
2. Winnipeg Bible College became accredited with the Accrediting Association of Bible Colleges in 1973; it was the first Bible college in Western Canada to receive accreditation.
3. Elmer Towns, *Teaching Teens* (Winnipeg, Canada: Winnipeg Bible College Press, 1963); Elmer Towns and R. Wesley Affleck, *The Deity of the Saviour* (Winnipeg, MB Canada: Winnipeg Bible College Press, 1965).
4. This article laid the foundation for the organizational structure of Liberty University, and I believe it was one key to Liberty's success.

Chapter 8: The Trinity Evangelical Divinity School Years

1. "Sunday School . . . Now!" Sunday School Now Resources. http://www.sundayschoolnow.net/worker_training_as_goes_sunday_school.htm (accessed April 2011).

2. Elmer L. Towns, *10 Sunday Schools That Dared to Change* (Ventura, CA: Regal Books, 1993), p. 22.
3. Elmer L. Towns, *The Ten Largest Sunday Schools and What Makes Them Grow* (Grand Rapids, MI: Baker Book House, 1969).
4. Jerry Falwell and Elmer L. Towns, *Capturing a Town for* Christ (Old Tappan, NJ: Fleming Revell Publishing Company, 1973).
5. Gene Raskin, "Those Were the Days, My Friend," performed by Mary Hopkin, Apple Records, 1968. http://www.lyricsmode.com/lyrics/m/mary_hopkin/those_were_the_days_my_friend.html (accessed May 2011).
6. For more information about Jerry Falwell, see "Founder," Liberty University website, http://www.liberty.edu/aboutliberty/index.cfm?PID=6921.

Chapter 9: The Early Liberty University Years

1. The pejorative term "hillbilly" is a put-down used by those prejudiced for cosmopolitan ways. That night, I used this term to suggest that we should teach classical music and drama, not just Southern Gospel. I used the term to suggest that the new college would position itself to serve all of evangelical Christianity, not just the narrow section served by Baptist Bible College.
2. Liberty University had two previous names in the early years. First it was called Lynchburg Baptist College, and then Liberty Baptist College, but in this book it will be called by its present name, Liberty University, because that identification is in the minds of most people.
3. Jerry Falwell and Elmer L. Towns, *Church Aflame* (Nashville, TN: Impact Books, 1971).
4. See Elmer L. Towns, *Friend Day* (Lynchburg, VA: Church Growth Institute, 1984) for more information about this major evangelistic event.
5. These lectures later became the basis of *The Ten Greatest Revivals Ever*, which I co-wrote with Douglas Porter (Ann Arbor, MI: Servant Publications, 2000).

Chapter 10: A Desert Experience in the Interim Years

1. Elmer L. Towns, *Is the Day of the Denomination Dead?* (Nashville, TN: Thomas Nelson Publishing, 1973).
2. American Missionary Fellowship, *Wikipedia.* http://en.wikipedia.org/wiki/American_Missionary_ Fellowship (accessed October 2011).
3. These events became the basis for the Church Growth Institute in Lynchburg, Virginia, and for the seminar *154 Steps to Revitalize Your Sunday School and Keep Your Church Growing.*

Chapter 11: Great Ministry at Liberty

1. Liberty University is not anti-Calvinistic. Liberty trains all evangelicals who want its education. But that doesn't mean Liberty is pro-Calvinistic. It's non-Calvinistic. The term Calvinism is used to describe what many advocates of Calvinism call TULIP, i.e., the five points of Calvinism: Total Depravity, Unconditional Election, Limited Atonement, Irresistible Grace, and Perseverance of the Saints.
2. Jay E. Adams, *Competent to Counsel* (Nutley, NJ: Presbyterian and Reformed Publishing Company, 1970), 70.
3. Elmer L. Towns, John N. Vaughan and David J. Seifert, *The Complete Book of Church Growth* (Carol Stream, IL: Tyndale House, 1982). When the manuscript was halfway completed, I discovered Dave Seifert had researched several other areas of growth in churches, i.e., Church Growth and growth in cell churches.
4. Larry Gilbert, *The Team Ministry Spiritual Gifts Inventory* (Lynchburg, VA: Church Growth Institute). The inventory can be taken online at http://www.churchgrowth.org/cgi-cg/gifts.cgi?intro=1.
5. Elmer L. Towns, *Friend Day* (Resource Packet) (Lynchburg, VA: Church Growth Institute, 1984). Although my name appears as the author of *Friend Day*, Larry Gilbert produced the artwork and drawings from his background as owner of a sign-painting company. Also, his lay ministry in local churches helped to apply the principles of Friend Day to the thinking of lay workers.

Later, the *Friend Day Resource Packet w/CDs* (version 2011a)—an update of the original *Friend Day*—was released with new applications of evangelism for churches.

6. Friend Day was first implemented by Pastor Wendell Zimmerman, Kansas City (MO) Baptist Temple, and from there its success spread to other Baptist Bible Fellowship churches. I organized the event into workable principles and shared them with churches all over America.
7. Elmer L. Towns, *154 Steps to Revitalize Your Sunday School and Keep Your Church Growing* (Colorado Springs, CO: Scripture Press/Chariot Victor Publishing, 1988).
8. Elmer L. Towns, *How to Go to Two Services* (Resource Packet) (Lynchburg, VA: Church Growth Institute, 1989).
9. Elmer L. Towns, *How to Reach the Baby Boomer* (Resource Packet) (Lynchburg, VA: Church Growth Institute, 1990).
10. Elmer L. Towns and Larry Gilbert, *Second Friend Day* (Resource Packet) (Lynchburg, VA: Church Growth Institute, 1989); Elmer L. Towns, *Friend Day Tune-Up Kit* (Resource Packet) (Lynchburg, VA: Church Growth Institute, 1999).
11. The church was averaging approximately 70,000 in attendance at the time and had 10,000 small groups.
12. The original name was LUSLLL, but over time was changed to Liberty Online, because it became known as online education.
13. Liberty University School of Lifelong Learning is now named Liberty University Online. For more information, visit http://www.libertyonlinedegrees.com/index.php/programs/.
14. Stephen Richard (Sam) Towns, *Elmer L. Towns: A Biographical and Chronological Presentation of His Writings* (Doctor of Ministry Thesis, Fuller Theological Seminary, 1988); available at http://www.elmertowns.com/bio/Dr._Sam_Towns_Dis–locked.PDF.
15. In 2005 I was restored to the position of vice president, and in 2009 I once again became dean of Liberty Baptist Theological Seminary, as well as being dean of the School of Religion.
16. Douglas Porter, comp., "Appendix 5: An Annotated Bibliography about Revival" in Elmer L. Towns and Neil T. Anderson, *Rivers of Revival* (Ventura, CA: Regal Books, 1997); Elmer L. Towns and Douglas Porter, *Churches That Multiply* (Kansas City, MO: Beacon Hill Press, 2002); Ibid., *Revival and Church Growth Work Text* (Ft. Worth, TX: Harcourt College Publishers, 2000); Ibid., *Ask Me to Pray for You Resource Packet* (Lynchburg, VA: Church Growth Institute, 2003); Ibid., *The Ten Greatest Revivals* (Ann Arbor, MI: Servant Publications, 2000).
17. Elmer L. Towns, *The Names of Jesus* (Colorado Springs, CO: Accent Publications, 1987).
18. Elmer L. Towns, *My Father's Names* (Ventura, CA: Regal Books, 1991).
19. Elmer L. Towns, *The Names of the Holy Spirit* (Ventura, CA: Regal Books, 1994).
20. Elmer L. Towns and Jerry Falwell, *Fasting Can Change Your Life* (Ventura, CA: Regal Books, 1998), pp. 15-21.
21. C. Peter Wagner, *Prayer Shield* (Ventura, CA: Regal Books, 1992).
22. Other prayer partners over the years: Olive Ackerman, Margie Balta, Katie Bowles, Harry and Janet Coric, Randy Dodge, Mike and Pat Dykty, Ruth Harrison, Paul Johnson, Shirley and Steve Jones, Tip and Laurie Killingsworth, Donald May, Esther Morrison, Linda Norris, Gladys Rudder, Pat Sheehan, Fay Wilson, John Wright and Charles Yancey.
23. Elmer L. Towns, *10 of Today's Most Innovative Churches* (Ventura, CA: Regal Books, 1991).
24. The 10 churches/pastors profiled were: (1) Pastor John Maxwell, Skyline Wesleyan Church, San Diego, California—emphasized and applied aggressive pastoral leadership to the entire church family; (2) Pastor Bill Hybels, Willow Creek Community Church, South Barrington, Illinois—emphasized seeker evangelism with a view of adapting contemporary evangelism, music and preaching to the worship service to reach seekers with salvation; (3) Pastor Jack Hayford, The Church On The Way, Van Nuys, California—emphasized praise worship music, rather than the traditional Sunday morning liturgical service or traditional evangelistic preaching; (4) Pastor Dale Galloway, New Hope Community Church, Portland, Oregon—saturated his city with small home cell groups to reach the lost (while Sunday morning was important, Dale said, "We don't

have small groups; we are small groups."); (5) Pastor Randy Pope, Perimeter Church, greater Atlanta, Georgia—planned to build an extended geographical parish church in 100 locations around the perimeter of Atlanta, each church reaching both into the city and out to the suburbs, but through one infrastructure, one pastor, one purpose and one organization; (6) Pastors Homer Lindsay Jr. and Jerry Vines, First Baptist Church, downtown Jacksonville, Florida—the two were equal pastors of one large congregation, perhaps the first notable church led by a pastoral team; (7) Pastor Ray Cotton, Central Community Church, Wichita, Kansas—brought innovation to the traditional liturgical worship service, where people could touch God as they worshiped, and have God touch them; (8) Pastor Ed Young, Second Baptist Church, Houston, Texas—built on strong adult classes among other methods of outreach; (9) Pastor Mike McIntosh, Horizon Christian Fellowship, San Diego, California—built a church of young people, following the Calvary Chapel model; and (10) Pastor Paul Walker, Mt. Peron Church of God, greater Atlanta, Georgia—built one church in multiple locations.

25. This book has sold more than 400,000 copies and has remained on Regal's bestseller list for years.
26. Elmer Towns, *Fasting for Spiritual Breakthrough* (Ventura, CA: Regal Books, 1996).
27. Ibid.

Chapter 12: A New Century

1. Elmer L. Towns, *Praying the 23rd Psalm* (Ventura, CA: Regal Books, 2001).
2. Ibid., p. 84.
3. Thomas Obediah Chisholm (1866-1960), "Great Is Thy Faithfulness" (Carol Stream, IL: Hope Publishing, 1923). Available from hymnal.net at http://www.hymnal.net/hymn.php/h/19.
4. Elmer L. Towns, *Praying the Lord's Prayer for Spiritual Breakthrough* (Ventura, CA: Regal Books, 1997).

CURRICULUM VITAE FOR

DR. ELMER LEON TOWNS

www.elmertowns.com
web address: elmertowns@liberty.edu

Noted Overall Accomplishments

- Teacher, writer, university administrator, bestselling author, Gold Medallion winner
- Authority in Sunday School, church growth, spirituality and fasting
- Co-founder of Liberty University, Lynchburg, Virginia, 1971
- Co-founder of Baptist University of America, Decatur, Georgia, 1974

Academic Positions

- Resident faculty: Dallas Bible College, Midwest Bible College, Winnipeg Bible College and Theological Seminary (name changed to Providence), Trinity Evangelical Divinity School, Liberty University, Liberty Baptist Theological Seminary, Baptist University of America
- Adjunct or visiting faculty at 38 colleges and seminaries (taught for credit)
- Lectured or spoke at more than 85 colleges and seminaries

Education

- Bachelor of Arts, Northwestern College, Minneapolis, Minnesota, 1954
- Master of Arts, Southern Methodist University, Dallas, Texas, 1958
- Master of Theology, Dallas Theological Seminary, Dallas, Texas, 1958
- Master of Religious Education, Garrett Theological Seminary, Evanston, Illinois, 1970
- Doctor of Ministry, Fuller Theological Seminary, Pasadena, California, 1983

Positions

- Pastor, Westminster Presbyterian Church, Savannah, Georgia, 1952-1953
- Youth pastor, New Brighton (Minnesota) Community Church, 1953-1954
- Pastor, Faith Bible Church, Dallas, Texas, 1956-1958
- Instructor, Dallas Bible College, Dallas, Texas, 1957-1958
- Secretary, St. Louis Sunday School Association, 1959-1960

- Advisory Council, Accrediting Association of Bible Colleges, Fort Wayne, Indiana, 1959-1961
- Executive Secretary, Research Commission, National Sunday School Association, 1961
- President, Winnipeg Bible College, Winnipeg, Manitoba, 1961-1965
- Lead Winnipeg Bible College to accreditation by AABC (the Accrediting Association of Bible Colleges), 1963
- Lead Winnipeg Bible College to provincial recognition to award secular degrees and begin a theological seminary, 1964
- President, Canadian Conference of Christian Educators, 1963-1964
- Board member, Scripture Press Foundation, 1965-1967
- Board member, Evangelical Teacher Training Association (ETTA), 1968-1971
- Executive Vice President and Co-founder, Liberty Baptist College, Lynchburg, Virginia, 1971-1973
- Teacher, Liberty University, Lynchburg, Virginia, 1971-present
- Executive Vice President and Co-founder, Baptist University of America, Decatur, Georgia, 1974-1977
- Founder, Sunday School Museum and Hall of Fame, Savannah, Georgia, 1974-1981
- President, Sunday School Research Institute, Savannah, Georgia, 1973-1984
- Board member, International Christian Education Association, Detroit, Michigan, 1977-1987
- Editor-in-Chief, Jerry Falwell Ministries, Lynchburg, Virginia, 1977-1980
- Enshrined in Savannah (Georgia) Hall of Fame, 1978
- Teacher, Liberty Baptist Theological Seminary, Lynchburg, Virginia, 1978-present
- Board member, Liberty Baptist Missions, 1978-1984
- Dean, Liberty Baptist Theological Seminary, Lynchburg, Virginia, 1979-1992, 2009-present
- Dean, School of Religion, Liberty University, Lynchburg, Virginia, 1980-present
- Founding board, Transnational Association of Christian Schools (TRACS)—the U.S. Department of Education recognized this accrediting agency for colleges, seminaries and high schools
- Parade Marshal, Bicentennial Sunday School in Savannah, Georgia, 1980
- Executive Director, Liberty Baptist Fellowship for Church Planting, 1981-1992 (planted 93 churches)
- Lead Liberty Baptist Theological Seminary to associate membership accreditation in Association of Theological Schools (ATS) and accreditation by Southern Association of Colleges and Schools (SACS), 1986

- Co-founder/contributor, Church Growth Institute, Forest, Virginia, 1984-2000
- Directed reaffirmation for Southern Association of Schools and Colleges (SACS) for the School of Religion, Liberty University, 1985, 1996
- Teacher, Pastor's Bible Class, Thomas Road Baptist Church, 26 years (1986-present)
- Board member, Gospel Light Publications (Sunday School), 1992-Present
- Organizing committee member on Fasting and Prayer (Bill Bright—Campus Crusade for Christ), 1992-2000
- Member, planning committee and speaker for Billy Graham Conference on Evangelism, Amsterdam, 1992-2000
- President, American Society of Church Growth, 1995
- Consultant in the formation of Beeson Divinity School (campus of Samford University), Birmingham, Alabama, 1997
- Dean, Global Pastors Network, Chair, Bible Knowledge; Campus Crusade, Orlando, Florida, 2003-2006
- President, Gospel Light Worldwide (Foreign Missions Literature), 2004-2010

General Editor and/or Writer of Encyclopedias

- *Sunday School Teachers and Guidebook*, Creation House, 1974
- *Sunday School Encyclopedia*, Tyndale House Publishing, 1992
- *Practical Encyclopedia of Evangelism and Church Growth*, Regal Books, 1995

Editorial Positions

- *Missionary Crusader*, Lubbock, Texas, 1955-1958
- *The Witness*, Winnipeg, Manitoba, Canada, 1961-1965
- *Evangelical Christian*, Toronto, Canada, 1965-1967
- *Bible Expositor and Illuminator,* Cleveland, Ohio, 1967-1971
- *Christian Life Magazine*, Wheaton, Illinois, 1967-1982
- *Faith Aflame,* Lynchburg, Virginia, 1978-1979
- *Journal Champion, Liberty Journal*, Editor-in-Chief, Lynchburg, Virginia, 1978-1980
- *King James Sunday School Curriculum,* Editor, Scripture Press, Wheaton, Illinois, Kindergarten to Adult, 1979-1984
- *National Liberty Journal* (Church Growth), Lynchburg, Virginia, 1980-1999
- *Christianity Today Magazine,* Advisory Editor, Carol Stream, Illinois, 1980-2011
- *Fundamentalist Journal,* Lynchburg, Virginia, 1982-1989

Contributor to Encyclopedias

- *Dictionary of Christianity in America,* Daniel G. Reid, ed., "Baptist Mid-Missions," "Dallas Franklin Billington," "Francis Scott Key (1780-18943)," "Richard

Volley Clearwaters (1900-1998)," "Stephen Paxson (1837-1881)," "Fundamentalist Baptist Fellowship," 1990

- *Twentieth-Century Dictionary of Christian Biography,* J. D. Douglas, ed., 1995
- *Dictionary of Premillennial Theology,* Mal Couch, ed., "The Course of this Present Age," "Literal Interpretation of Prophecy," "Post-Tribulational View of Prophecy," 1996
- *New Twentieth-Century Encyclopedia of Religious Knowledge*
- *The Southern Baptist Encyclopedia,* with Ergun Caner and Emir Caner, eds.
- *The Popular Encyclopedia of Bible Prophecy*, with Tim LaHaye and Ed Hindson, eds., 2004
- *The Popular Encyclopedia of Apologetics*, with Ed Hindson and Ergun Caner, eds., 2008

Contributor to Reference Bibles

- *Bi-Centennial Sunday School Bible,* editor, Regal, 1975
- *Illustrated Bible Stories for Children,* with Lane Easterly, J. F. Allen, Bernice Richter, Thomas Nelson, 1975
- *Liberty Annotated Reference Bible*, Thomas Nelson
- *Liberty Bible Commentary*, "Deuteronomy"
- *Prophecy Study Bible*, Tim LaHaye, "Dispensationalism," "Hell," "The Judgments," "The Kingdom Parables," "The Partial Rapture," "The Post Tribulation," 2000
- *Prayer Journey Bible* (*King James Version*, 2011)

Noted Doctoral Research on Elmer Towns

- *Elmer L. Towns, A Biographical and Chronological Presentation of His Writings 1963–1985*, submitted to Fuller Theological Seminary by Stephen S. Towns, 1986.
- *An Analysis of the FRIEND DAY PROGRAM,* written by Elmer Towns and published by Church Growth Institute, Lynchburg, Virginia, submitted to Liberty Baptist Theological Seminary by Rick L. Rasberry, 1995.
- *A Chronological Presentation of the Writings of Elmer L. Towns from 1986-1999*, submitted to Liberty Baptist Theological Seminary by David Allan Brown, 1999.
- *A Chronological Presentation of the Writings of Elmer L. Towns from 1980-2005,* submitted to Liberty Baptist Theological Seminary by Gabriel Benjamin Etzel, 2005.
- *Theological Paradigm for Higher Education: The Educational Leadership of Elmer L. Towns,* submitted to Southeastern Baptist Theological Seminary by David Edgell, 2012. This project presents the model of Christian higher education of Elmer Towns and seeks to understand how his leadership

has significantly impacted Liberty University as its co-founder and to identify a theological paradigm for higher education. It examines Elmer Towns's background in higher education and presents a church based model for Christian higher education that was applied at Liberty University. The project examines a theological paradigm for higher education that is grounded in Towns's view of systematic theology and sociological research. The project also examines his educational leadership at the school in the areas of supervision, curriculum, student life and external affairs. The research method is qualitative and uses a mixture of research methods including examination of documents, interviews with faculty and administration, and insights gained from observations.

Honorary Doctors Degrees

- Doctor of Divinity, Baptist Bible College, Springfield, Missouri, 1971
- Doctor Litterarum, California Graduate School of Theology, Anaheim, California, 1972
- Doctor of Divinity, Evangelical Theological Seminary, Washington, DC, 2000
- Doctor of Divinity, Providence Theological Seminary, Otterburne, Manitoba, Canada, 2004
- Doctor of Letters, Louisiana Baptist University, 2007
- Doctor of Divinity, Tennessee Temple Theological Seminary, 2008

Honors/Awards

- Professor of the Year, Liberty University Student Government, Lynchburg, Virginia, 1990
- Donald A. McGavran Award, American Society for Church Growth, Fuller Theological Seminary, Pasadena, California, 1994
- Distinguished Professor, Systematic Theology, Board of Trustees, Liberty University, Lynchburg, Virginia, 1999
- Preached in all 50 of the United States
- Preached in all 10 provinces of Canada
- Bronze Telly Award for "Through the Decades," presented by Cable Television Industry, 2009

Books by Elmer Towns Translated into Foreign Languages

- 127 titles
- 34 different languages
- Span of more than 28 years
- Most titles—37 in Korean

- Bestselling foreign language book—*The Names of the Father* (i.e., *Nama, Nama, Alla*), in Arabic

Books Listed on Bestselling List

- *10 Largest Sunday Schools and What Makes Them Grow*, Baker Book House, 1969
- *Church Aflame*, with Jerry Falwell, Impact Books, 1971
- *America's Fastest Growing Churches*, Impact Books, 1972
- *Capturing a Town for Christ*, with Jerry Falwell, Fleming H. Revell/Baker Book House, 1973
- *Successful Sunday School Teachers and Guidebook*, Creation House, 1974
- *10 of Today's Innovative Churches*, Regal, 1990
- *Fasting for Spiritual Breakthrough*, Regal, 1996
- *Bible Answers to Almost All Your Questions*, Thomas Nelson, Inc., 2003

Adjunct or Visiting Professor/ and or Lecturer (Taught Courses for Credit)

- Asbury College, Wilmore, Kentucky
- Asbury Theological Seminary, Louisville, Kentucky
- Asbury Theological Seminary, Wilmore, Kentucky, 1999, 2001, 2003
- Azusa Pacific University, Azusa, California, 1997
- Baptist Bible College West, Anaheim, California, 1998, 1999
- Baptist Missionary Association Theological Seminary, Jacksonville, Texas
- Birmingham Theological Seminary (campus of Briarwood Presbyterian Church), Birmingham, Alabama, 1997, 1998
- California Graduate School of Theology, Glendale, California, 1973-1981
- Canadian Bible College, Regina, Saskatchewan, Canada
- Dallas Theological Seminary Extension, Philadelphia, Pennsylvania, 1999
- Dallas Theological Seminary, Dallas, Texas, 1999
- Denver Baptist Theological Seminary, Denver, Colorado
- Evangel Theological Seminary, Harrisonburg, Virginia, 2001, 2003
- Grace Theological Seminary, Winona Lake, Indiana, 1987
- Gulf Coast Bible College, Houston, Texas
- Horizon Bible Institute (on campus of Horizon Christian Fellowship), San Diego, California, 1997
- Hyles-Anderson College, Hammond, Indiana
- Indiana Wesleyan University, Marion, Indiana
- Luther Rice Seminary, Jacksonville, Florida
- Mid America Christian University, Oklahoma City, Oklahoma
- Midwestern Baptist Theological Seminary, Kansas City, Missouri, 2006
- Midwestern Bible College, St. Louis, Missouri, 1952-61

- Northwestern Baptist Theological Seminary, Vancouver, British Columbia, Canada, 1990
- Northwestern School of Ministry, Kirkland, Washington, 1997
- Pacific Coast Baptist Bible College, San Dimas, California
- Saints Bible Institute, Italy
- Shasta Bible College, Redding, California
- Southern Baptist Theological Seminary, Louisville, Kentucky, 1993
- Southwestern School of Ministry, Oklahoma City, Oklahoma
- Tennessee Temple Theological Seminary, Chattanooga, Tennessee, 1992
- The John Wesley College, Owosso, Michigan
- Trinity Evangelical Divinity School, Deerfield, Illinois, 1965-1971; 1985
- Wellspring School of Theology, Cincinnati, Ohio, 2002
- Winebrenner Theological Seminary, Findlay, Ohio, 2003
- Winona Lake School of Theology (summer school), Winona Lake, Indiana, 1966-1968
- Word of Life Bible Institute, Schroon Lake, New York, 1983-1994

Guest Lectureship and Special Speaker at Colleges

- Altoona Bible Institute, Manitoba, Canada
- Anderson University, Anderson, Indiana
- Assembly of God Theological Society, Springfield, Missouri
- Atlantic Christian University, Monkton, New Brunswick, Canada
- Baptist Bible College and Theological Seminary, Seoul, Korea
- Baptist Bible College, Springfield, Missouri
- Beeson Divinity School, Birmingham, Alabama
- Berean Baptist College, Calgary, Alberta, Canada
- Bethany Nazarene University, Bethany, Oklahoma
- Bethel Theological Seminary, St. Paul, Minnesota
- Biola University and Talbot Theological Seminary, La Mirada, California
- Bob Jones College, Seoul, Korea
- Briercrest Bible Institute, Caronport, Saskatchewan, Canada
- Broadfording Christian College, Hagerstown, Maryland
- Bryan College, Dayton, Tennessee
- California Baptist College, Sacramento, California
- Capital Bible Seminary, Annandale, Virginia
- Carolina Bible Institute & Seminary, Pine Level, North Carolina
- Central Baptist College, Conway, Arkansas
- Central Baptist Theological Seminary, Minneapolis, Minnesota
- Central Baptist Theological Seminary, Toronto, Ontario, Canada
- Central Bible College, Springfield, Missouri

- Chongshin University, Seoul, Korea
- Circleville Bible College, Circleville, Ohio
- Colorado Christian College, Denver, Colorado
- Columbia Bible College, Columbia, South Carolina
- Covenant College, Chattanooga, Tennessee
- Covenant Theological Seminary, St. Louis, Missouri
- Crown College, Crown Point, Indiana
- Davis College, Johnson City, New York
- Eastern Nazarene College, Quincy, Massachusetts
- Eastern Wesleyan College, Allentown, Pennsylvania
- Faith Way Bible College, Greater Detroit, Michigan
- Florida Bible College, Fort Lauderdale, Florida
- Free Will Baptist Bible College, Nashville, Tennessee
- Fudan University, Shanghai, China
- Fuller Theological Seminary, Pasadena, California
- George Fox College, Newburn, Oregon
- Georgia Baptist College, Wynette County, Georgia
- Indiana Baptist College, Indianapolis, Indiana
- John Wesley College, High Point, North Carolina
- John Wesley College, Owasso, Michigan
- Korean Baptist Theological Seminary, Seoul, Korea
- Korean Theological Seminary, Koshin University in Pusan, Korea
- Liberty Baptist College, "The History of Wesleyanism," delivered in Bristol and London, England
- Liberty University, Lynchburg, Virginia, "Journeys of the Apostle Paul," Athens, Greece
- Massillon Bible College, Massillon, Ohio
- Messiah College, Grantham, Pennsylvania
- Miami Christian University, Miami, Florida
- Mid America Nazarene University, Olathe, Kansas
- Midwestern Baptist College, Pontiac, Michigan
- Mountain View Bible College, Didsbury, Alberta, Canada
- Nazarene Bible College, Colorado Springs, Colorado
- Nazarene Theological Seminary, Kansas City, Kansas
- New Orleans Baptist Theological Seminary, New Orleans, Louisiana
- North Central University, Minneapolis, Minnesota
- Northeastern Bible College, Essex Falls, New Jersey
- Northwest Nazarene University, Nampa, Idaho
- Olivet Nazarene University, Bourbonnais, Illinois
- Ontario Bible College, London, Ontario, Canada

- Oxford University, St. Regis College, Oxford, England
- Pacific Coast Baptist Bible College, National City, California
- Practical Bible College, Johnson City, New York
- Prairie Bible Institute, Three Hills, Alberta, Canada
- Providence College and Seminary, Otterburne, Manitoba, Canada
- Reformed Theological Seminary, Jackson, Mississippi
- Southeastern Baptist College (Baptist Missionary Association), Laurel, Mississippi
- Southeastern Baptist Theological Seminary, Wake Forest, North Carolina
- Southeastern College, Lakeland, Florida
- Southern Nazarene University, Bethany, Oklahoma
- Southwestern Baptist Theological Seminary, Fort Worth, Texas
- Southwestern University, Waxahachie, Texas
- Spurgeon Baptist Bible College, Mulberry, Florida
- Steinbeck Bible Institute, Steinbeck, Manitoba, Canada
- The Jerry Falwell College, Trivandrum, India
- The United Wesleyan College, Allentown, Pennsylvania
- Trevecca Nazarene University, Nashville, Tennessee
- Trinity Baptist College, Jacksonville, Florida
- University of Florida, Gainesville, Florida
- Vanguard University, Costa Mesa, California
- Virginia Theological Seminary, Lynchburg, Virginia
- Wesley Biblical Seminary, Jackson, Mississippi
- Western Baptist College, Salem, Oregon
- Western Evangelical Seminary, Greater Portland, Oregon

Resource Packets

- *The Campaign of the Twelve*, 1972. Randleman, North Carolina: Sunday School Outreach.
- *The Founders of Sunday School*, 1980. Randleman, North Carolina: Sunday School Outreach.
- *FRANtastic Days*, 1984. Lynchburg, Virginia: Church Growth Institute.
- *Friend Day*, 1984. Lynchburg, Virginia: Church Growth Institute.
- *Tithing Is Christian*, 1984. Lynchburg, Virginia: Church Growth Institute.
- *FRANgelism*, 1985. Lynchburg, Virginia: Church Growth Institute.
- *Becoming a Leader*, 1986. Lynchburg, Virginia: Church Growth Institute.
- *Christian Living*, 1986. Lynchburg, Virginia: Church Growth Institute.
- *My Father's Names*, 1986. Lynchburg, Virginia: Church Growth Institute.
- *Outreach 12*, 1986. Lynchburg, Virginia: Church Growth Institute.

- *Second Friend Day*, 1986. Lynchburg, Virginia: Church Growth Institute.
- *Tithing Is Christian*, 1986. Lynchburg, Virginia: Church Growth Institute.
- *154 Steps to Revitalize Your Sunday School and Keep Your Church Growing*, 1987. Lynchburg, Virginia: Church Growth Institute.
- *Team Leadership*, 1988. Lynchburg, Virginia: Church Growth Institute.
- *How to Go to Two Services*, 1989. Lynchburg, Virginia: Church Growth Institute.
- *How to Reach Your Friends for Christ*, 1989. Lynchburg, Virginia: Church Growth Institute.
- *Towns on Teacher Training*, 1989. Lynchburg, Virginia: Church Growth Institute.
- *How to Reach the Baby Boomer*, 1990. Lynchburg, Virginia: Church Growth Institute.
- *Spiritual Factors of Church Growth*, 1990. Lynchburg, Virginia: Church Growth Institute.
- *The Names of Jesus*, 1990. Lynchburg, Virginia: Church Growth Institute.
- *Foundational Doctrines of the Faith*, 1992. Lynchburg, Virginia: Church Growth Institute.
- *Our Family Giving to God's Family*, 1992. Lynchburg, Virginia: Church Growth Institute.
- *Getting a Church Started*, 1993. Lynchburg, Virginia: Church Growth Institute.
- *Sunday School Enrollment*, 1993. Lynchburg, Virginia: Church Growth Institute.
- *Towns on Church Growth*, 1993. Lynchburg, Virginia: Church Growth Institute.
- *Habits of the Heart*, 1994. Lynchburg, Virginia: Church Growth Institute.
- *Our Family Giving to God's Family*, 1994. Lynchburg, Virginia: Church Growth Institute.
- *Sunday School Survival Kit*, 1994. Lynchburg, Virginia: Church Growth Institute.
- *Vision Day*, 1994. Lynchburg, Virginia: Church Growth Institute.
- *What Is Right*, 1995. Lynchburg, Virginia: Church Growth Institute.
- *When God Is Silent*, 1995. Lynchburg, Virginia: Church Growth Institute.
- *Fasting for Spiritual Breakthrough*, 1996. Lynchburg, Virginia: Church Growth Institute.
- *What the Bible Is All About*, 1996. Ventura, CA: Gospel Light.
- *From Victory to Victory*, 1997. Lynchburg, Virginia: Church Growth Institute.
- *Ask Me to Pray for You*, 2003. Lynchburg, Virginia: Church Growth Institute.

Audiovisual Resources

- *The Master Teacher* (DVD), 1973. Gainesville, Florida: Genesis.
- *Cassette Campus* (cassettes), 1974. Winona Lake, Indiana: Ken Anderson.

- *154 Steps to Revitalize Your Sunday School and Keep Your Church Growing* (DVD), 1976. Lynchburg, Virginia: Church Leadership Institute.
- *Murder of a Gentle People* (DVD), 1978. Lynchburg, Virginia: The Old Time Gospel Hour.
- *The Laws of Successful Biblical Sunday School Growth* (cassettes), 1982. Lynchburg, Virginia: Church Leadership Institute.
- *The Names of Jesus* (cassettes), 1982. Lynchburg, Virginia: Church Leadership Institute.
- *154 Steps to Revitalize Your Sunday School and Keep Your Church Growing* (cassettes), 1983. Lynchburg, Virginia: Church Leadership Institute.
- *Say It Faith* (cassettes), 1983. Lynchburg, Virginia: Church Leadership Institute.
- *Towns on Teacher Training* (DVD), 1987. Lynchburg, Virginia: Church Growth Institute.
- *A Briefing Seminar on the Future of the Sunday School and Church Growth* (DVD), 1988. Lynchburg, Virginia: Church Growth Institute.
- *How to Put Your Sunday School on the Cutting Edge* (DVD), 1990. Lynchburg, Virginia: Church Growth Institute.
- *The Names of the Holy Spirit* (DVD), 1995. Ventura, California: Regal.
- *What Every Sunday School Teacher Should Know* (DVD), 1995. Ventura, California: Regal.
- *How to Study and Teach the Bible* (DVD), 1996. Ventura, California: Gospel Light.
- *Praying the Lord's Prayer for Spiritual Breakthrough* (DVD), 1997. Ventura, California: Gospel Light.
- *Taking the Sunday School into the Twenty-first Century* (DVD), 1997. Ventura, California: Gospel Light.
- *Leading Your Sunday School into the Twenty-first Century* (DVD), 1998. Ventura, California: Gospel Light.

Tracts by Elmer L. Towns

- *The Laws of Sunday School Growth*, 1959. St. Louis, Missouri: Berean Missions.
- *I Love Sunday School*, 1973. Savannah, Georgia: Sunday School Research Institute.
- *I Believe in Tithing*, 1976. King of Prussia, Pennsylvania: Neibauer Press.
- *Why Tithe?* 1976. King of Prussia, Pennsylvania: Neibauer Press.

Unpublished Works

- *An Analysis of the Implications of Teaching Morals in the Public Schools*. Unpublished Master's thesis, Southern Methodist University, 1958.

- *The New Testament Doctrine of the Heart.* Unpublished Master's thesis, Dallas Theological Seminary, 1958.
- *An Analysis of the Gift of Faith in Church Growth.* Unpublished Doctoral project, Fuller Theological Seminary, 1983.

Conclusion

Recognized by the North American Association of Professors of Christian Education (NAPCE) as one of the leading Christian Educators of the twentieth century (see Christian Educators: Timothy Paul Jones and Mark Senter; available http://www2.talbot.edu/ce20/educators/view.cfm?n=elmer_towns#author-info [accessed September 2011]). The following summarizes their observation of Elmer Towns: "Other Christian educators have criticized Elmer Towns for having had a narrower influence, due to his fundamentalist orientation, than he might otherwise have had (see, e.g., S. Towns, 1985, pp. 106-07). There is, however, another possibility that is equally worthy of consideration: Perhaps it is precisely because of his unswerving fundamentalist orientation that Towns' contributions have been so vital. Fundamentalist and conservative-evangelical congregations trusted Towns due to a shared theological orientation; therefore, Towns was able to penetrate these churches with insights from the social sciences and the church-growth movement–insights that might otherwise have been rejected or ignored. If this analysis is correct, it is possible that Towns' primary contribution is not to be found on the campus of Liberty University or even in the thousands of pages that his reflections and research have filled. It is, rather, to be found in the collective concurrence of a myriad of church leaders that it is possible to recognize the cultural relativity of methodologies and the usefulness of the social sciences without compromising even the most conservative strands of Christian theology."

LIST OF RESOURCES BY

ELMER L. TOWNS

Books

8 Laws of Leadership, The
10 Greatest Revivals Ever, The (with Douglas Porter)
10 Largest Churches
10 Largest Sunday Schools and What Makes Them Grow, The
10 of Today's Innovative Churches
10 Questions Every Christian Must Answer (with Alex McFarland and Warren Cole Smith)
10 Sunday Schools that Dared to Change
11 Innovations in the Local Church (with Ed Stetzer and Warren Bird)
154 Steps to Revitalize Your Sunday School and Keep Your Church Growing
365 Ways to Know God
America's Fastest Growing Churches
Apostles' Creed
Becoming a Leader (with Jerry Falwell)
Beginner's Guide to Fasting, The
Beginner's Guide to Reading the Bible, A
Bible Answers for Almost All Your Questions
Biblical Grandparents
Biblical Meditation for Spiritual Breakthrough
Biblical Studies for Fasting
Biblical Studies for Fasting for Personal and Group Study
Bibliography of Youth Work
Bright Future of Sunday School, The
Campaign of the Twelve
Capturing a Town for Christ (with Jerry Falwell)
Capturing the Power of Vision
Christ BC: An 8-to-13-Week Study for Adults
Christ-Centered Youth Work
Christian Hall of Fame, The
Christian Journalism (with Marie Chapman)
Christmas Traditions (with Stan Toler, Linda Toler and Ruth Towns)
Church Aflame (with Jerry Falwell)
Church Growth: State of the Art (with C. Peter Wagner and Winn Arn)
Churches that Multiply (with Douglas Porter)
*Complete Book of Church Growth, The (*with John Vaughan and David Seifert)
Concise Bible Doctrines
Core Christianity
Daniel Fast for Spiritual Breakthrough, The
Deity of the Savior, The
Developing a Giving Church
Encountering God for Spiritual Breakthrough
Essence of the New Testament (with the faculty of Liberty University)
Evangelize Through Christian Education
Evangelize Through Christian Education Leader's Guide
Everychurch Guide to Church Growth, The (with Thom S. Rainer and C. Peter Wagner)
Fasting Can Change Your Life (with Jerry Falwell)
Fasting for Financial Breakthrough
Fasting for Spiritual Breakthrough
Fasting for Spiritual Breakthrough Leader's Guide
Fasting for Spiritual Breakthrough Study Guide
Fasting to Know God
Foundational Doctrines of the Faith
Founders of Sunday School: 200 Years (1780–1980)
Fresh Start in Life Now that You Are a Christian, A
Friend Day: A Day Your Friend Could Remember for Eternity
Friend Day Tune-up Kit
From Victory to Victory
Future of Sunday School and Church Growth, The (with video)
Getting a Church Started in the Face of Insurmountable Odds
Getting a Church Started Student Manual
God Bless You
God Encounters
God Is Able
God Laughs (with Charles Billingsley)
God Laughs Study Guide
Good Book on Leadership, The (with John Borek and Danny Lovett)
Gospel of John: Believe and Live, The (with Ed Hindson and Mal Couch)
Great Soul-Winning Churches
Greatest Book in the Bible, The

Habits of the Heart
Have the Public Schools "Had It"?
History Makers of the Old Testament
History of Religious Educators, A
How Can You Produce Church Growth?
How God Answers Prayer
How to Clean Up Your Town for Christ (with Jerry Falwell)
How to Create and Present High Impact Bible Studies
How to Grow a Successful Sunday School
How to Pray When You Don't Know What to Say
How to Pray for Your Job (with David Earley)
How to Reach the Baby Boomer
How to Reach Your Friends for Christ
How to Recruit Sunday School Teachers
How to Study and Teach the Bible
Into the Future (with Warren Bird)
Is the Day of the Denomination Dead?
John: The Greatest Book in the Bible
Joined Together (with Ruth Towns)
Journey Through the New Testament, A
Journey Through the Old Testament, A
Knowing God Through Fasting
Laws of Successful Biblical Sunday School Growth
Leaders on Leadership (with George Barna, Jack Hayford, Gene Getz, et al.)
Leading with Vision: Book 1 [Beeson Pastoral Series] (with John Maxwell, Maxie Dunnam and Dr. Gale Galloway)
Malachi: Hope at the End of an Age (with Ron Phillips)
Masters of the Faith
Ministering to the Young Single Adult
My Angel Named Herman
My Father's Names
My Father's Names Group Study Guide
Names of Jesus, The
Names of Jesus Group Study Guide, The
Names of the Holy Spirit, The
Names of the Holy Spirit Group Study Guide, The
Names of the Holy Spirit Leader's Guide, The
Our Family Giving to God's Family
Outreach 12
Perimeters of Light (with Ed Stetzer)
Practical Encyclopedia of Evangelism and Church Growth, A
Prayer Journey Bible (KJV)
Prayer Journey Bible (PEB)
Prayer Partners
Praying for Your Children (with David Earley)
Praying for Your Job (with David Earley)
Praying for Your Second Chance: Numbers—Deuteronomy
Praying Genesis
Praying Paul's Letters
Praying the 23rd Psalm
Praying the Book of Acts of the Apostles and the General Epistles
Praying the Book of Job
Praying the Book of Revelation
Praying the Gospels
Praying the Heart of David: First and Second Samuel and First Chronicles
Praying the Lord's Prayer for Spiritual Breakthrough
Praying the New Testament
Praying the Proverbs, Song of Solomon, Ecclesiastes
Praying the Psalms
Praying When God Speaks: Isaiah, Habakkuk, Hosea, Joel, Micah, Amos, Nahum, Jonah and Zephaniah
Praying When You're Caught in the Middle: Jeremiah, Lamentations and Ezekiel
Praying with the Conquerors: Joshua, Judges and Ruth
Praying with the Kings: 1 and 2 Kings and 2 Chronicles
Praying Your Way Back to God: Daniel, Esther, Ezra, Haggai, Malachi, Nehemiah, Obadiah and Zechariah
Praying Your Way Out of Bondage: Exodus–Leviticus
Profitable Preparation for Teaching
Putting an End to Worship Wars
Rivers of Revival (with Neil Anderson)
Say-It-Faith: Building the Sunday School by Faith (with David L. Keith)
Second Friend Day
Seeing the Invisible
Single Adult and the Church, The
Son, The
Stepping Out on Faith (with Jerry Falwell)
Stories About My First Church
Stories on the Front Porch
Story of the History of Worship (with Vernon Whaley)
Successful Biblical Youth Work
Successful Christian Life, The
Successful Church Libraries (with Cyril J. Barber)
Successful Lesson Preparation
Successful Ministry to the Retarded
Successful Sunday School and Teacher's Guidebook, The
Successful Teaching Ideas (with Marie Chapman and Roberta L. Groff)
Teaching Teens
Team Ministry: A Guide to Spiritual Gifts and Lay Involvement (with Larry Gilbert)
Team Teaching with Success
Theology for Today
Tithing Is Christian
Towns' Sunday School Encyclopedia
Towns on Church Growth
Towns Sunday School Survey
Triune God, The
Triune God Leader's Guide, The
Understanding the Christian Life

Understanding the Deeper Life
Walking with Giants
What Christianity Is All About
What Every Pastor Should Know About Sunday School
What Every Sunday School Teacher Should Know About Sunday School
What Is Right: Biblical Principles for Decision-Making (with Timothy J. Pierce)
What the Faith Is All About
What the Faith Is All About Leader's Guide
What the New Testament Is All About
What the Old Testament Is All About
What's Right with the Church
When God Is Silent (with Cindy Spear and Timothy J. Pierce)
Winning the Winnable: Friendship Evangelism
Women Gifted for Ministry (with Ruth Towns)
World's Largest Sunday School
Worship Encounters
Year-Round Book of Sermon Ideas Stories and Quotes, The
Year-Round Church Event Book, The
Your Ministry of Evangelism

Resource Packets

12 Disciples Sunday School Campaign
154 Steps to Revitalize Your Sunday School and Keep Your Church Growing
Ask Me to Pray for You (with Douglas Porter)
Becoming a Leader
Equipping Disciples
F.R.A.N.gelism
F.R.A.N.tastic Days
Getting a Church Started
God Is Able
History of Religious Educators, A
How to Go to Two Services
How to Reach the Baby Boomer
My Friendship Connection (with Vernon Brady)
Our Family Giving to God's Family
Outreach 12
Say-It-Faith
Second Friend Day
Spiritual Factors of Church Growth
Successful Christian Life, The
Sunday School Enrollment
Sunday School Survival Kit: How to Turn Around Your Sunday School, The
Teaching to Influence Lives (with Stan Toler)
Tithing Is Christian
Towns on Teacher Training
Vision Day: Capturing the Power of Vision

Worktexts for Use in Classrooms

Biblical Foundations for Church Planting
Biblical Models for Leadership
Biblical Models for Leadership (online edition)
Biblical Studies for Fasting Workbook
Book of Acts: Semester IV, The
Church Growth I
Ecclesiology/Eschatology
Evangelism and Church Growth
Evangelism and the Christian Life (CHMN 101)
Gospel of John, The
Journey Through the New Testament, A
Journey Through the New Testament: A Listening Guide, A (with David Brown)
Journey Through the New Testament, A (with David Brown)
Journey Through the Old Testament, A (with David Brown)
New Testament Survey (BIBL 110)
New Testament Survey, The (with David Brown)
New Testament
Old Testament Survey (BIBL 105)
Revival and Church Growth (with Douglas Porter)
Soteriology
Spiritual Foundations of Church Growth
Spiritual Foundations of Church Growth Lecture Text
Survey of Christian Doctrine
Theology 201
Theology 201 Listening Guide
Theology 202
Theology Survey I
Theology Survey I (THEO 201) (with Gabriel Etzel)
Theology Survey II
Twenty-first Century Tools and Techniques
Twenty-first Century Tools and Techniques (Korean edition)
Twenty-first Century Tools and Techniques for the Revitalization of the Church
What the New Testament Is all About (with David Brown)

ALSO BY
ELMER L. TOWNS

The Daniel Fast for Spiritual Breakthrough
ISBN 08307.54733
ISBN 978.08307.54731

Fasting for Financial Breakthrough
ISBN 08307.29631
ISBN 978.08307.29630

Fasting for Spiritual Breakthrough
ISBN 08307.18397
ISBN 978.08307.18399

How to Pray When You Don't Know What to Say
ISBN 08307.41879
ISBN 978.08307.41878

What Every Sunday School Teacher Should Know
ISBN 08307.28740
ISBN 978.08307.28749

What's Right with the Church
ISBN 08307.51343
ISBN 978.08307.51341

Available at Bookstores Everywhere!

Go to **www.regalbooks.com** to learn more about your favorite Regal books and authors. Visit us online today!

www.regalbooks.com